IDIOT'S
GUIDES.
AS EASY AS IT GETS!

Mindfulness

by Domyo Sater Burk

ALPHA
A member of Penguin Group (USA) Inc.

ALPHA BOOKS

Published by Penguin Group (USA) Inc.

Penguin Group (USA) Inc., 375 Hudson Street, New York, New York 10014, USA • Penguin Group (Canada), 90 Eglinton Avenue East, Suite 700, Toronto, Ontario M4P 2Y3, Canada (a division of Pearson Penguin Canada Inc.) • Penguin Books Ltd., 80 Strand, London WC2R 0RL, England • Penguin Ireland, 25 St. Stephen's Green, Dublin 2, Ireland (a division of Penguin Books Ltd.) • Penguin Group (Australia), 250 Camberwell Road, Camberwell, Victoria 3124, Australia (a division of Pearson Australia Group Pty. Ltd.) • Penguin Books India Pvt. Ltd., 11 Community Centre, Panchsheel Park, New Delhi—110 017, India • Penguin Group (NZ), 67 Apollo Drive, Rosedale, North Shore, Auckland 1311, New Zealand (a division of Pearson New Zealand Ltd.) • Penguin Books (South Africa) (Pty.) Ltd., 24 Sturdee Avenue, Rosebank, Johannesburg 2196, South Africa • Penguin Books Ltd., Registered Offices: 80 Strand, London WC2R 0RL, England

International Standard Book Number: 978-1-61564-618-0

Library of Congress Catalog Card Number: 2014935266

16 15   8 7 6 5 4 3 2

Interpretation of the printing code: The rightmost number of the first series of numbers is the year of the book's printing; the rightmost number of the second series of numbers is the number of the book's printing. For example, a printing code of 14-1 shows that the first printing occurred in 2014.

Printed in the United States of America

Note: This publication contains the opinions and ideas of its author. It is intended to provide helpful and informative material on the subject matter covered. It is sold with the understanding that the author and publisher are not engaged in rendering professional services in the book. If the reader requires personal assistance or advice, a competent professional should be consulted. The author and publisher specifically disclaim any responsibility for any liability, loss, or risk, personal or otherwise, which is incurred as a consequence, directly or indirectly, of the use and application of any of the contents of this book.

Most Alpha books are available at special quantity discounts for bulk purchases for sales promotions, premiums, fund-raising, or educational use. Special books, or book excerpts, can also be created to fit specific needs. For details, write: Special Markets, Alpha Books, 375 Hudson Street, New York, NY 10014.

Publisher: *Mike Sanders*
Executive Managing Editor: *Billy Fields*
Executive Acquisitions Editor: *Lori Cates Hand*
Development Editor: *John Etchison*
Production Editor: *Jana M. Stefanciosa*

Cover Designer: *Laura Merriman*
Book Designer: *William Thomas*
Indexer: *Tonya Heard*
Layout: *Ayanna Lacey*
Proofreader: *Sara Smith*

Contents

Appendixes

Introduction

Over the last 25 years, the practice of mindfulness has been shown to be very beneficial to all kinds of people, for all kinds of reasons. It's really quite amazing. Mindfulness has been shown to improve cardiovascular health, increase rates of healing, decrease reported pain levels, and improve immune response. There is evidence it can decrease anxiety and stress, provide a way to cope with depression, increase levels of satisfaction with relationships and work situations, and help people change problematic behaviors. It has been effective with populations that other methods have not reliably been able to benefit, including at-risk youth, prison inmates, and people suffering from certain kinds of intense and complicated mental illnesses.

Is mindfulness a fad? Is it a quick, easy answer to things we'll later discover has a serious downside? Ten or twenty years from now, are we going to look back and laugh, saying, "Remember when mindfulness was all the rage?"

I don't think so. Mindfulness isn't a special technique you add to your life; it's about learning to use your body and mind more effectively. It's a simple process of cultivating receptive awareness of your present experience, no matter what it is. To do this, you have to learn to let go of your stimulus-independent thinking, such as ruminating on the past, planning, analyzing, evaluating, judging, fantasizing, and daydreaming.

What's remarkable is that such a simple practice makes such a big difference. Science will undoubtedly be able to explain why this is the case someday, but in the meantime we have to rely on our subjective experience of mindfulness to understand it. Essentially, it seems that human intelligence, while very advantageous in many ways, also causes you problems.

You come to rely too heavily on the abstract world that only exists in your own mind. You spend more time thinking about things that aren't actually going on around you than you do paying attention to your present experience. You perceive things through the filter of your ideas and judgments, and fail to notice cause-and-effect relationships because you're so preoccupied with your thoughts. You believe your feelings, concepts, judgments, and emotions reflect reality, and therefore you're compelled to defend or act on them.

Simply and repeatedly turning your attention back to the present moment counteracts the effects of spending so much time stuck in your head. It isn't easy to make mindfulness a stronger habit than dwelling on stimulus-independent thinking, but each time you become aware of your actual experience here and now, it helps you gain perspective on your life. For a moment, you notice what's in your own mind versus what's actually going on. This moment opens up many possibilities for different ways of thinking and behaving.

The greatest thing about mindfulness is that it's very simple to do, and anyone can do it. The necessary tools are accessible to anyone, they cost nothing, and they have no negative side effects! It may sound too good to be true, so I'll let you know what the catch is: mindfulness takes work. This book will tell you what that work entails so you can make mindfulness a part of your life, no matter what kind of life you lead.

What You Will Learn in This Book

This book is divided into five parts, which will walk you through the various aspects of mindfulness and how to work on them.

Part 1, What You Need to Know About Mindfulness, explains what mindfulness is and why it's such a big deal. I cover some of the benefits of mindfulness practice and our current understanding of how mindfulness works. Of particular interest is why humans aren't naturally mindful, and why cultivating awareness of the present has such a profound effect. In this part I also introduce mindfulness as a practice, including its 3 aspects (aspiration, awareness, and attitude) and 12 principles you can use to guide you efforts.

Part 2, Cultivating Mindful Awareness, tells you how to work on the "awareness" aspect of mindfulness, which involves shifting your attention away from stimulus-independent thinking toward a particular object. The chapters in this part walk you through the traditional Buddhist objects of mindfulness: body and physical sensations; feelings of like, dislike, or neutrality; mind states; and psychophysical factors like desire, lethargy, curiosity, and joy. This part also includes a chapter on the role of meditation in cultivating awareness, and instructions for how to do it.

Part 3, Developing a Receptive Attitude, explains how mindfulness depends in part on your attitude. Even if you're able to pay attention to the things going on around you, you may not be receptive to certain aspects of your experience. The chapters in this part discuss how to let go of judgment and cultivate more acceptance, curiosity, energy, courage, and joy. I also cover the importance of becoming more comfortable with silence and stillness. The great thing is, mindfulness helps you work on your attitude, and a receptive attitude supports your mindfulness, so it's a positive feedback loop.

Part 4, Working Toward Greater Happiness, addresses the third aspect of mindfulness: the "aspiration" to greater happiness for self and others. It describes how to apply mindfulness to different areas of your life to understand them better and investigate new ways of thinking, feeling, and acting. The chapters cover the role of compassion in making changes, learning to deal with strong negative emotions, decreasing stress levels while still getting things done, cultivating a more positive view of your life regardless of whether you've achieved your goals, and getting free of self-concern and narratives about who you are.

Part 5, A Mindful Life, tells you how to work mindfulness into your everyday life, and how to develop a strong, stable mindfulness "practice" if you want to live a more mindful life long term. This part also covers the value of mindful ethics and how to work with your own ethical standards to increase your mindfulness and happiness. Finally, I discuss how a mindful life can increase your sense of intimacy with others, help you understand interdependence, and help you find meaning and purpose.

At the end of the book, you'll find a glossary; a list of resources including articles, books, and websites; a list of 12 mindfulness principles; and a compilation of all of the mindful exercises found throughout the book.

Extras

Throughout the chapters of the book, you'll find four types of additional information, set apart with a title and special type, to help you understand the information in the chapter, give you food for thought, or offer a suggestion for an exercise you can do:

 DEFINITION

In these sidebars you'll find definitions or clarifications of any specialized terms, or terms that are being used in a way you might not expect.

 KEEP IN MIND

Here you'll find additional pieces of information, references, or reflections that complement the material you're reading in the main text.

 TAKE CARE

When there's something being discussed that may be easily misunderstood, or there's a common trap I'd love for you to be able to avoid, you'll find one of these sidebars.

 MINDFUL EXERCISE

Each chapter contains one or two mindful exercises for you to try. They're related to the topic being discussed in the chapter, and can help you put mindfulness into practice as you read through the book. For your convenience, all of the mindful exercises can also be found in Appendix D, and you can do them in any order you like.

And There's More

We've included online audio recordings of guided meditations to help you expand on the mindfulness exercises found throughout this book. Go to idiotsguides.com/mindfulness to experience these meditations spoken to you by the author.

Acknowledgments

My first thanks must be extended to my husband, John. His companionship, honest feedback, patience, and generous support make all of my work possible. Gratitude must also go to my parents, who generously supported and encouraged my education and writing from the beginning.

Any time I'm writing or teaching about mindfulness or Buddhism, I have to acknowledge the invaluable guidance and support of my Zen ordination and transmission teacher, Gyokuko Carlson Roshi, and my other Zen teacher, Kyogen Carlson Roshi. May what I offer benefit others in at least a few of the ways my teachers have benefitted me.

Thanks also to the Bright Way Zen sangha, who continue in their unwavering support of my writing, even though it means I spend less time prepping for talks and taking care of our community. Bright Way Zen students are a source of deep inspiration and learning for me. Special thanks to Bright Way Zen member Lorna Simons, who *once again* volunteered her time to edit everything I wrote (and thereby increased my sense of well-being).

Trademarks

All terms mentioned in this book that are known to be or are suspected of being trademarks or service marks have been appropriately capitalized. Alpha Books and Penguin Group (USA) Inc. cannot attest to the accuracy of this information. Use of a term in this book should not be regarded as affecting the validity of any trademark or service mark.

What You Need to Know About Mindfulness

The first part of this book will answer your basic questions about mindfulness: what exactly is meant by mindfulness, anyway? If it's just about paying attention to your life, what's so special about it? Why aren't people naturally mindful? How does mindfulness work, and how do you start cultivating it?

I give you a brief history of the development of mindfulness from its Buddhist roots to its modern application. In case you aren't already enthused about practicing it, I describe some of the many benefits of mindfulness. A long list of such benefits has been objectively proven by extensive scientific research, such as improved cardiovascular health and an increased tolerance for pain. Others I describe reflect the subjective experience of practitioners, including feeling less stressed and having a greater appreciation for your daily life.

Finally, I introduce a way to approach mindfulness practice that includes 3 aspects and 12 principles. You can use this introduction to start working on mindfulness right away, and the rest of the book will go into more detail about each of the ideas that are presented in this part.

Introducing Mindfulness

Mindfulness is consciously maintaining awareness of your present experience with a receptive attitude, in order to relieve stress and work toward the greatest happiness for yourself and others. Mindfulness helps you relieve stress because it allows you to perceive things more clearly. You get more in touch with the truth of your life, and of life in general, and consequently make more beneficial choices.

In this chapter I introduce mindfulness as a concept and practice, and give you a sense of how it has developed over 2,000 years from a Buddhist practice to a widely used technique in professional therapeutic settings. I'll also discuss why mindfulness has become so popular, and why you might want to practice it.

In This Chapter

- What mindfulness is
- How mindfulness arose in Buddhism
- Recent development of the concept of mindfulness
- Why mindfulness has caught on
- What mindfulness can do for you

The Big Deal

Mindfulness may sound pretty simple and straightforward—I mean, who doesn't know how to be aware? Actually, most of us don't know how to be mindful at will, or don't make it a priority to do so. You're likely to lack mindfulness exactly when you need it most—when things are painful, difficult, stressful, or not how you would like them to be.

The amazing thing is that mindfulness can make a huge difference in your life. It has always been central to the practice of Buddhism and other spiritual practices, but only in the 1980s and 1990s did mindfulness became a subject of great interest to doctors, psychologists, and others involved in relieving people's suffering. Since then, a growing body of research has proven the effectiveness of mindfulness-based interventions on a variety of human complaints, including stress, chronic pain, and depression.

Mindfulness is now being taught in all kinds of settings, including hospitals, mental health treatment programs, schools, psychotherapists' offices, the military, and corporations. Generally speaking, when people cultivate mindfulness, they experience important benefits. This chapter presents some of those benefits, and a brief history of how mindfulness has come to be understood, used, and accepted in the West.

What Is Mindfulness?

While mindfulness is fairly simple to do, it is actually quite difficult to define. Researchers, psychologists, mindfulness teachers, and Buddhists continue to debate exactly what mindfulness entails. A particular teacher may suggest acceptance is essential, while a researcher insists that mindfulness involves "bare attention" without any kind of added emotional engagement. A Buddhist may insist that ethics have a role, while a psychotherapist helps patients suffering from posttraumatic stress by employing only basic awareness practices. It is probably not surprising that a subjective mental experience like mindfulness eludes a definition everyone agrees on.

State, Trait, or Practice?

Part of the problem in defining mindfulness is that it can refer to a state of mind, a trait, or a practice you engage in over time. A mindful state of mind is something that may occur for only a few moments as you rest in the awareness of holding a mug of coffee—you feel the warmth on your hands, notice the rich smell, and anticipate the taste. Mindfulness as a trait is a feature of your personality or a habit you can try to work on. How often are you aware of your present experience, as opposed to thinking about the past, the future, or somewhere else? Mindfulness as a practice is a way to cultivate mindfulness as a trait, as well as being a way of approaching your life with the intention to notice what's going on around you, to reduce stress, and to increase happiness.

KEEP IN MIND

If you find it hard to get your mind around exactly what mindfulness is by reading, remember that it is an experience. It can be difficult to define, but after trying it yourself, it will become clearer what the term refers to.

Mindfulness is a state, a trait, *and* a practice, and it will be discussed in different ways at different times, even in this book. If a discussion of mindfulness ever seems a little confusing, it may help to consider what kind of mindfulness is being referred to.

Mindful Versus Mindless

It may be tricky to define mindfulness using words, but you can easily recognize its opposite—mindlessness—in your experience. The classic example is arriving somewhere in your car and realizing you don't remember much of anything about the drive there. Chances are, you spent the commute thinking about all kinds of things other than your current experience. You maintained just enough awareness of driving to avoid accidents and get where you were going, but most other aspects of your experience were ignored.

Neither mindlessness nor mindfulness is ever an all-or-nothing mental state. In the example mentioned above where you were driving rather mindlessly, you still may have been nominally aware of your posture, the music playing on the radio, and the heaviness of the traffic. Even if you were making an effort to be mindful, there would have been an infinite number of things in your immediate environment competing for your attention. It is impossible to be aware of everything, so fortunately this is not what mindfulness is. Instead, what you try to do is maintain a relative *receptivity* to your present experience. Thoughts may go through your mind, but you're more likely to notice the color of the sky, the car that wants to merge in front of you, and the tension you're carrying in your shoulders.

Buddhist Roots

Mindfulness was identified as a distinct mental process by Buddhists over 2,500 years ago. The exact meaning of the term changed somewhat over time as different schools of Buddhism developed in different areas of the world. Since the adoption of the concept of mindfulness by mental and physical health professionals in the mid-1980s, the term often refers to many more aspects of mental and emotional training than the Buddhist use of the word, which is more specialized.

Freedom from Stress

The ancient Buddhist way of approaching mindfulness assumes from the outset that you want to reduce stress and increase happiness for yourself and for others. The very first teaching of Siddhartha Gautama (who was referred to as the "Buddha," or awakened one) was that life is stressful. The Buddhist term for this stress is *dukkha*, which is often translated as suffering but can refer to any lack of ease or happiness—from vague existential dissatisfaction to acute suffering. The reason for this stress, according to Buddhism, is that everything (including you) is constantly changing and ungraspable, and you want it to be otherwise. That desire for things to be other than they are leads to resistance and tension, among other things.

 **DEFINITION**

Dukkha is a Buddhist term that refers to the pervasive and sometimes subtle stress of living. It can be translated as stress, dissatisfaction, unease, or suffering. It results from your resistance to life being impermanent, out of your control, and ultimately impossible to grasp.

The good news, according to the Buddhists, is you can free yourself from stress by giving up your resistance to how things are. That doesn't mean you become passive and stop trying to change anything; it just means you go about doing whatever you need to do without carrying an extra sense that *things shouldn't be this way*. Basically, like it or not, things *are* this way, so there's no use making yourself miserable wishing it were otherwise.

Mindfulness and the Eightfold Path

But *how* do you go about giving up your resistance to how things are? Buddhism acknowledges that this is not easy by laying out a rich system of teachings and practices to help you do it. One aspect of this system is appropriate (or correct) mindfulness, which is one of the steps on the Buddhist "Noble Eightfold Path." The other seven steps, or components, are appropriate understanding, appropriate intention, appropriate speech, appropriate action, appropriate livelihood, appropriate effort, and appropriate concentration.

Mindfulness in Buddhist terminology is a translation of the ancient Pali word *sati*, which can also be taken to mean remembering or presence of mind. It refers specifically to remembering to return your attention to your direct experience when it has wandered and then keeping yourself from forgetting to pay attention again. When you're mindful, your consciousness is present and you're able to notice what is going on. In Buddhism, mindfulness is distinguished from concentration, which is your ability to focus on a particular object or subject without getting distracted. Although these two mental factors are differentiated, they rarely operate independently. Concentration provides the power behind your effort, while mindfulness provides a perspective on what's going on.

Modern Expansion of Meaning

Modern secular uses of the term *mindfulness,* including those in this book, tend to fold other aspects of the Buddhist Eightfold Path into the concept of mindfulness. Secular mindfulness is generally conceived as including some ability to pay attention (concentration), and the development of useful insight into habits of mind and body (understanding). It also tends to assume that you're seeking to reduce stress or pain (intention), and you're willing to work at it (effort). The appropriate behavioral aspects of the Eightfold Path (speech, action, and livelihood) have usually been left out of secular mindfulness training and research, but some psychotherapists and scientists are beginning to question even this exclusion.

Mindfulness-Based Stress Reduction

The expansion of the meaning of the term *mindfulness* is due in large part to Jon Kabat-Zinn, the creator of Mindfulness-Based Stress Reduction (MBSR). Kabat-Zinn is a Buddhist practitioner and molecular biologist who investigated the beneficial effects of mindfulness on the stress levels and symptom management of various kinds of patients in a medical setting. In 1979 he began to offer a standardized eight-week course in mindfulness which has now been used throughout the world and made the subject of much research. Kabat-Zinn has explained his intention in creating MBSR was to make the valuable techniques and resources of the *dharma,* or Buddhist teachings and practice, available and accessible to a much wider audience—including those who would never be interested in studying Buddhism or participating at a Zen temple.

 **DEFINITION**

> **Dharma** can be understood at two different levels. It can refer to the teachings of Buddhism, but it also refers to what is true and helpful in a larger sense. From the Buddhist point of view, if it teaches you to better understand your life and to reduce stress in a lasting way, it's dharma.

The influence of Kabat-Zinn and MBSR on the modern secular use of the term *mindfulness* is difficult to overestimate. The standardized MBSR course allowed researchers to repeatedly test participants from many different populations before and after the program, under a variety of conditions, and provide evidence of its effectiveness. This legitimized the use of mindfulness-based applications in professional settings. MBSR subsequently inspired the development of a number of other mindfulness-based interventions, including Dialectical Behavioral Therapy (DBT) and Mindfulness-Based Cognitive Therapy (MBCT). The interest in mindfulness-based applications has skyrocketed; since the early 2000s, the number of research papers referencing *mindfulness* in their abstract has increased exponentially every year.

Mindfulness as an Umbrella Term

Because he wanted all kinds of people to be open to it, and needed it to be taken seriously in the medical and scientific community, Kabat-Zinn was very careful about not associating MBSR too much with Buddhism. In fact, it was initially called the "Stress Reduction and Relaxation Program." Only later was the program renamed "mindfulness-based" in order to differentiate it from other approaches to stress reduction that were being developed.

Kabat-Zinn explains that he and his colleagues used the word *mindfulness* "intentionally as an umbrella term to describe our work and to link it explicitly with what I have always considered to be a universal dharma that is co-extensive, if not identical, with the teachings of the Buddha, the Buddhadharma. By 'umbrella term' I mean that it is used in certain contexts as a placeholder for the entire dharma, that it is meant to carry multiple meanings and traditions simultaneously, not in the service of finessing and confounding real differences, but as a potentially skillful means for bringing the streams of alive, embodied dharma understanding and of clinical medicine together."

There continues to be much debate among professionals who use or study mindfulness-based applications regarding the exact meaning of *mindfulness* and what it does or does not include. However, it is safe to say the use of the term in secular contexts is evolving away from its technical Buddhist meaning. Mindfulness outside of Buddhist contexts is probably better thought of as a growing and developing practice or discipline in and of itself—springing from Buddhist roots, but a new and independent organism.

TAKE CARE

If you're inclined to try to decide which is more legitimate, secular mindfulness or mindfulness as practiced in a Buddhist context, you might end up wasting time and energy. While it is interesting to compare the two, each offers a similar way to reduce stress and increase happiness. For some people, the rich Buddhist tradition gives mindfulness context, community, and aliveness. For others, mindfulness seems most relevant and real when approached in scientifically-based, secular way, free of religious or cultural trappings. If you're in doubt about which way is best for you, try them both!

The Benefits of Mindfulness

There are two ways to discuss the benefits of mindfulness: subjective and objective. The subjective evidence of its benefits are the effects reported by people who practice it, and by those who use mindfulness-based approaches in working with others. The objective evidence is the result of research studies published in peer-reviewed journals.

Subjective Experience

The first thing that will probably happen when you try to be more mindful is that you start noticing more of what's going on in your life. Some of what you notice will be unpleasant or uncomfortable. (This is probably why you weren't giving it your full attention.) However, much of it will be neutral or pleasant stuff you were just missing because you were caught up in a train of thought. This is a lovely benefit of mindfulness because it helps you appreciate your life more.

Another subjective benefit of mindfulness is the reduction in stress that occurs when you open your awareness to the present moment. I will explain further how and why this works in the next chapter, but in summary it is simply this: no matter what is going on in your "here and now," it presents only a tiny fraction of the opportunities for stress that arise from things that are elsewhere (anywhere in the world) and in the future (infinite possibilities). Time spent mindful of the present moment gives your body and mind the chance to rest and recharge before taking up more abstract challenges once again.

One of the most important benefits of mindfulness is a process psychologists call *decentering*. Basically, your thoughts and emotions are part of your present experience, so you learn to pay attention to them in the same way you pay attention to a sensation of warmth or the sound of someone's voice. In the process, you observe your thoughts and feelings arising, changing, and passing away—and consequently become less identified with them. "I *am* angry" becomes "I am *feeling* some anger right now." Even a slight increase in the sense of space between you and your thoughts and emotions makes them less likely to overwhelm and control you.

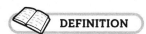 **DEFINITION**

Decentering is the process of becoming less identified with your thoughts and emotions. Rather than perceiving your internal experience as being synonymous with and inseparable from who you are, you develop a sense of awareness that is no longer centered on that internal experience; it becomes part of your overall experience and therefore you have some choice in how to respond to it.

As you start to cultivate receptivity and openness to your present experience, you also begin to see things more clearly. You notice chains of cause and effect: when you think about some particular thing you start to feel angry; when you start to feel angry you tend to dwell even more on that particular thing; when you spend a bunch of time dwelling in this anger, you get in an overall irritable, bad mood. This may sound simple, and you may assume you already know these kinds of things about yourself. However, there's a big difference between knowing in an intellectual sense and intimately knowing because you have carefully witnessed a pattern unfold again and again.

Once you start to see things in your life more clearly, you also see new possibilities open up in terms of how you might think, speak, and act. Because you're paying closer attention, you sometimes have the chance to explore these new possibilities instead of being immediately caught up in the force of habit. This process can lead to lasting, positive change.

Objective Evidence

It's impossible to report briefly on all the results of the hundreds, if not thousands, of research studies on the effects of mindfulness. I summarize some of the findings here, but if you're interested in reading more, many of the scientific articles are now available to the public online. Most studies involve administering some kind of survey to subjects before and after they experience mindfulness-based training or intervention. Others measure physical conditions or reactions of subjects before, during, or after mindfulness meditation sessions. Still others use functional magnetic resonance imaging (fMRI) to measure brain activity during various kinds of mindfulness exercises or meditation.

Research has repeatedly provided evidence that mindfulness training can reduce stress, facilitate healing processes, help manage physical pain, and provide valuable tools for relieving anxiety and depression—among many other things. Significant effects have been found after just a few mindfulness training sessions, and researchers usually find the strength of effects increases the longer and more intensively someone has been practicing mindfulness meditation. Scientists admit they have not yet identified precisely what is occurring in subjects when they meditate or practice mindfulness, but here are some of the things they have found:

- Decreased anxiety and improved mood when facing a wide variety of conditions, including cancer, generalized anxiety disorder, and depression (Hofmann et al. 2010)

- Reduction in perceived stress and rumination, or thinking repeatedly and obsessively about a particular topic (Shapiro et al. 2008)

- Increase in self-compassion, reduction in symptoms of stress and mood disturbance, and increase in perspective-taking (Birnie et al. 2010)

- Higher level of satisfaction in a romantic relationship, lower emotional stress responses, positive pre- and post-conflict changes in perception of the relationship (Barnes et al. 2007)

- Reduced frequency of panic attacks (Miller et al. 1995)

In addition to emotional or psychological benefits, there is evidence that mindfulness has physical and behavioral effects, including the following:

- Better cardiovascular health, as well as improved scores on measures of general well-being, affect, and social well-being (Prazak et al. 2012)

- Increased rates of healing for psoriasis patients (Kabat-Zinn et al. 1998)

- Decrease in the reported intensity of pain for chronic pain patients (Reiner et al. 2013)

- Improved attention and a decrease in stress-related hormones and increased immunoreactivity in response to a stressful task (Tang et al. 2007)

- Decrease in emotional eating habits associated with psychological distress (Pidgeon et al. 2013)

Even if any single study has limitations, the cumulative evidence of many studies suggests mindfulness can be extremely beneficial for many kinds of people, and for many kinds of reasons. This explains why the technique has become widely accepted in professional and medical settings. People are no longer willing to leave meditation and mindfulness to the Buddhists—it's time to find ways for everyone to benefit.

Natural Yet Difficult

In a sense, there is nothing special at all about mindfulness. It is a natural human experience that is accessible to anyone—not just to Buddhists, "spiritual" people, or those with formal training in mindfulness or meditation. In fact, in some ways young children are naturally mindful because they are so open-minded and curious. Because so many things are new to them, they pay close attention to what is going on. They are relatively free of the burden of memories, and of abstract concerns about the future, so they tend to be in the present. They perceive things directly rather than through the filter of their conditioning, expectations, or fears, which is why children often make astute observations that have not occurred to the adults around them.

 MINDFUL EXERCISE

Get started right away! As you read this book right now, what is your posture? Are you seated or standing? Don't change your posture—not yet. Just become aware of it. Is your body aligned, or are you slouching in some way? Are there any areas where your body is tense where it doesn't need to be? Don't judge, just notice. How often throughout the day do you become aware of your posture like this? If you spend most of the day unaware, you can carry around lots of tension without ever realizing it.

As people grow up and function as adults in society, they generally become less and less mindful. When they try to be mindful it can be very difficult because of their well-formed habit of spending their time planning, analyzing, ruminating, and worrying instead of paying attention to the present moment. *In theory* it is possible for you to be perfectly mindful, but *in practice* it can be very challenging.

Simply remembering to be present takes work as you go about your usual activities. Being receptive to your present experience takes additional effort as you habitually judge everything that happens in terms of how it relates to you: is this pleasant, unpleasant, or neutral (and therefore uninteresting)? Is this something you've experienced before, and therefore you have ready-made concepts to apply to it? Is this something you find threatening to your sense of self? Your judgments and preconceptions are filters that prevent you from directly experiencing your life and perceiving it clearly.

Mindfulness presents something of a paradox: it is about being more attentive to your life just as it is, letting go of comparing it to the past or future, but on the other hand it can transform your life. There are many things that are difficult, if not impossible, to change about yourself and the world around you. Mindfulness is not a miraculous approach that will make everything go your way. However, simply by relating to your experience differently you can transform dissatisfaction into contentment, stress into acceptance, and the mundane into the precious.

The process of becoming more mindful takes time and energy, but it can pay off no matter where you're starting on your journey. If you're suffering from acute anxiety or pervasive depression, mindfulness practice can decrease your symptoms and give you a new sense of hope and freedom. If you're feeling generally dissatisfied or stressed and it is starting to take a toll on your happiness or health, mindfulness can help you get back in touch with what really matters to you. If you're simply curious about whether mindfulness can increase your sense of intimacy and connection with other people and with your life in general, you will probably find that it can. Ultimately, it is about learning how to function optimally as a human being.

The Least You Need to Know

- Essentially, mindfulness has three components: maintaining awareness of your present experience, cultivating a receptive attitude toward it, and trying to see clearly the causes of stress in your life.
- In Buddhism, mindfulness is just one of eight aspects of the Noble Eightfold Path. The modern concept of mindfulness includes many of those other aspects (such as understanding, concentration, effort, and intention).
- If you ever feel confused about *exactly* what mindfulness is, don't worry—even Buddhist scholars, professional mindfulness teachers, and researchers still argue about it.

- There is overwhelming evidence of the benefits of mindfulness—both from subjective reports of those who practice it and objective data from hundreds of research studies.

- Mindfulness is a fundamentally human experience that is accessible to anyone at any time. It can also be very challenging because you've built up strong habits of *not* being mindful.

CHAPTER

2

How Mindfulness Works

Mindfulness seems like a simple thing—why don't we already
do it? Why does deliberately maintaining awareness of your
present experience seem to make such a difference? In this
chapter I explain how mindfulness affects your brain and your
life, in case you like to understand what you're doing before
you do it. I also talk about why most of us default to mindlessness rather than mindfulness, because knowing this can be
helpful in your mindfulness practice.

Basically, paying attention to your present experience and
learning to be truly receptive to it gets you "out of your head"
and back in touch with reality. It turns out reality—no matter
what is going on—is easier to deal with than all of the things
you might be imagining about it. And yet you're wired to
survive. This means you automatically start worrying about
yourself when your mind isn't otherwise occupied. The good
news is that mindfulness training can change the way your
mind works. In fact, it can even change your brain!

In This Chapter

- Why mindfulness has to be learned
- How mindfulness changes your mind and brain
- Dealing more positively with stress
- Breaking free of mental habits
- Getting more perspective on your life

Why Aren't You Naturally Mindful?

Human beings have extremely complex and powerful minds, but this can get us into trouble. You are able to anticipate and worry about an almost infinite number of things, which potentially leads to a great deal of stress. You also have a very expansive and complicated sense of self, which probably inspires you to take a lot of things personally and results in emotional agitation.

It's Stressful to Be Human

The structure and function of every cell in your body are aimed at your survival and reproduction. You have complex responses to all of your experiences, including your thoughts and feelings. Many of these physical, chemical, and emotional responses are orchestrated by your autonomic nervous system before you're even conscious of having a response.

 TAKE CARE

It isn't fruitful to try to get rid of any aspects of being human, including stress responses, abstract thinking, or negative thoughts and emotions. Even if you could get rid of them, this kind of effort just causes more stress! Instead, mindfulness gives you greater awareness of, and objectivity about, your experiences. This gives you more freedom to respond in different ways. It changes your relationship to your stress responses, thoughts, and emotions—it doesn't make them go away.

When your body and/or mind perceives a potential threat, hormones cascade through you in a stress response. This prepares you physically to fight, flee, or freeze depending on what looks like your best option for survival. This system evolved in human beings when they were faced with literal life-or-death situations on a daily basis, and it obviously served us well for millennia. A stress response in an animal with a simpler mind happens in reaction to something in its environment, and subsides when the threat passes. Until the animal encounters another potential threat, it can go about its business with relative calm.

In modern life, however, the stress response has some serious negative side effects. You can recall past traumas and anticipate an almost infinite number of possible future ones. You are aware of threats outside your immediate environment, and you understand how certain things can be a threat without immediately appearing that way. As Robert Sapolsky writes in *Why Zebras Don't Get Ulcers,* your body reacts in the same way to your anticipation of a stressor as it does to your direct experience of one. Additionally, he explains, "If you *repeatedly turn on* the stress-response, or if you *cannot turn off* the stress-response at the end of a stressful event, the stress-response can eventually become damaging." This leads to lowered immunity, high blood pressure, muscular tension, and all kinds of physical and emotional problems.

Your Complex Sense of Self

There's another reason why you don't naturally tend to dwell peacefully in the present moment: you are not only concerned with your physical well-being, you also have a complex sense of self and are therefore preoccupied with your welfare in a much broader sense.

There are a whole list of things you probably consider essential to who you are, including your relationships, work, skills, home, freedom, opportunities, opinions, and preferences. Human beings develop an elaborate sense of identity that can make possessions, relationships, conditions, and attributes seem as vital to them as their physical survival. A classic example of this is people who compromise their health and safety in order to maintain a particular physical appearance, or in order to compete in a job that gives them status and power.

Your complex sense of self means you have a lot more to worry about than an animal does. For example, there are probably no direct threats to your survival before you leave for work in the morning. However, what would be a relatively peaceful morning to a very simple creature could be quite stressful for you. Perhaps you wake up with the worry that you may be losing your job soon because of layoffs. Then your teenage daughter gives you some attitude and you worry about whether she is going to have the discipline to finish high school, and you face a challenge to your idea of yourself as a good parent. The dog seems sick and you wonder when you're going to find the time to take him to the vet, and how you're going to afford to pay for it. Your knee is bothering you again and you worry it might be getting more serious. And you haven't even left the house yet!

Your Mind's Default Mode

Researchers have recently made a very interesting discovery: when you're not otherwise occupied, you're usually engaged in very active self-referential thinking. It's like your mind takes advantage of any down time by analyzing, planning, and evaluating all the stuff in your life so you can be better prepared for it. This thinking is what researchers call "stimulus-independent thought" because it is all in your head—it generally has little or nothing to do with what is going on around you at the moment.

This stimulus-independent, self-referential processing is called the brain's *default mode*. It was discovered when scientists began using functional magnetic resonance imaging (fMRI) to measure and map the activity in people's brains while they were engaged in certain activities. They compared their measurements with baseline readings taken when people were doing nothing but just sitting still—and soon discovered people's brains were quite active even when they were supposedly doing nothing.

 **DEFINITION**

> Your brain's **default mode** is a highly active mental state that occurs when it is not otherwise occupied—such as when you're engaged in a very simple activity, or not doing anything at all. In default mode your mind is busy with self-referential processing, including evaluating past events, anticipating future ones, imagining the outcomes of various plans of action, and guessing how other people might be feeling about you.

The default mode is actually quite amazing. Consider what you're capable of thinking about while you're doing something that doesn't require much brain power, like cleaning your house. While vacuuming, you can think about a friend of yours who you haven't seen in years, who lives far away. You can replay your last conversation with her, and recall the words of anger that were exchanged. You can then imagine alternative scenarios and rehearse different responses you might have given, along with the likely results. You can contemplate what your friend is doing at that moment, and make various plans for how you might reach out to her in the future. Again, you can imagine how the different plans might play out, role-playing as you try to picture things from her perspective.

The ability to engage in elaborate stimulus-independent thinking has many benefits, but it can become problematic. When this is your default mode, your mind never gets a rest. It rarely tunes into what is going on in your immediate experience—around you, or within you. Not only do you miss out on many direct experiences, your stimulus-independent thinking can lose touch with reality. Patterns of thought can become dysfunctional, anxiety-producing, or depressing, and you may not know how to break out of them. You can lose perspective and begin to perceive your thoughts as being reality, instead of just your thoughts about it.

The Mindful Mind

Mindfulness training can help you change the way you deal with stress, how you think about yourself, and how you use your mind. Your brain has evolved to take care of you, but that doesn't mean it is always engaged in the activity most beneficial to you in the long term. The power of awareness, coupled with intentionality, can guide your mind toward better habits.

The essence of Buddhism, which has been teaching and developing mindfulness for over 2,000 years, can be phrased like this: life can be tough, but your experience of it depends largely on how you use your mind. Change your mind, change your experience; change your experience, change your reactions; change your reactions, change your behaviors. Once you change your behaviors, you might even change the circumstances of your life and things will be a little less difficult. Still, the most important part is your mind.

Healthier Responses to Stressors

There is an ancient Buddhist teaching that lists eight different kinds of stressors human beings face: birth, old age, illness, death, not getting what you want, getting what you don't want, separation from what is beloved, and the experience of constant change. (You can't hold on to or rely on anything forever.) According to Buddhism, there is no way to escape these stressors if you're a human being. The question, then, is how you can face them in the best way you can. This is what mindfulness aims to help you do.

Tolerance for Discomfort

Mindfulness asks you to turn toward your experiences instead of away from them. This runs counter to cultural common sense, which suggests you try to avoid unpleasant feelings and sensations at all costs—through distraction, medication, intoxication, or getting as far away from the source of the unpleasantness as possible. Alternatively, it is acceptable to try to end unpleasantness by striving to change your circumstances.

When you allow yourself to experience your uncomfortable responses to a stressor through mindfulness, you stop trying to avoid the unpleasantness or change things, at least for the moment. The idea is that your best course of action in the circumstances will become clear only if you actually pay attention to what is going on. It is difficult to do this when you're trying to either flee or fight. Instead, you take the risk of spending a little time directly experiencing your stress.

What you discover when you do this is that even stressors and your responses are subject to change. Even in the midst of physical pain, grief, or confusion, there are moments when the unpleasantness is lighter. Often, things pass away completely after a while. In short, tolerating discomfort for a while pretty much never kills you. Over time you become better able to tolerate discomfort, whether it is physical, psychological, or emotional. Consequently you become less reactive to it, and have some time to contemplate alternatives to avoidance or resistance.

Perspective on Your Reactions

When you pay mindful attention in stressful situations, an interesting thing happens: you start observing your own reactions to stressors with some objectivity. They begin to appear more like *aspects* of your entire experience, rather than seeming like they *are* your entire experience.

When your reactions go unexamined, you're likely to believe they are fundamentally true, or real, and you have no choice in the matter. For example, let's say your boss unfairly reprimands you in front of your co-workers. Almost instantaneously, anger and an associated story arise in you. "She is wrong," you think. "This is unfair, and she is inconsiderate. Now people think I'm stupid." Potentially, this reactive story can take on a life of its own. You can hold on to an idea about your boss, about why this situation occurred, and about other people's reactions. Once you identify yourself as angry, it may be difficult to let go of the anger. You need to justify and feed it.

KEEP IN MIND

You probably take it for granted that there are many things children need to develop with the guidance of wise adults, including self-discipline, moral behavior, generosity, and how to conduct themselves authentically but harmoniously within their culture. The ability to use your mind in a healthy and effective way—as opposed to being used by it—can be thought of as another aspect of being human that benefits from education and training.

Observed with some mindfulness, the example described above can be viewed somewhat differently. In addition to observing your boss, co-workers, and the unfolding situation, you observe your own reactions. "Hmmm," a part of you thinks. "I am experiencing quite a lot of anger. I am thinking my boss is wrong and inconsiderate. I am worried that now people think I'm stupid."

There may not be anything you can do about your immediate reactions, but you have a choice about how you *react to your reactions*. When you see them as part of a complex series of causes and effects, you can accept that you're thinking and feeling the way you are. Then you can consider other possibilities. Perhaps your boss has just experienced a major family trauma, and was misinformed by a co-worker about your actions. Maybe your co-workers were too busy with their own work to even notice your interaction with your boss, much less judge you for it. And maybe, just maybe, later in the day you just don't feel angry anymore. Anger arose, anger passed away. If you view it more objectively, rather than believing it has to be true, you may be able to just let it go.

Greater Objectivity About Self

Mindfulness can also help you relate in a healthier way to your sense of self. Your stress responses to perceived threats are dramatically increased when your sense of self includes all the things you identify with, like your reputation, material wealth, relationships, job, or even health. When you shed the light of awareness on yourself, you start to appreciate how resistance to change with respect to these self-related things can cause more pain than the change itself.

Noticing Impermanence

You are most likely to notice that you think of something as being part of you when it seems to be coming to an end or changing. This probably feels uncomfortable, if not downright traumatic. Too much change to who you think you are reminds you of how little control you have over what happens to you and those you care about, and makes you wonder what you can rely on. It can make you question who you are and can be quite disorienting.

The classic example of an experience of self-related impermanence is losing a job, particularly one you were passionate about or were proud of. For most people, an incredible amount of self-identity is tied up in their jobs. Losing one can bring up feelings of worthlessness, confusion, and despair. The job was evidence you were capable, useful, and valued. Without it, confidence can be shaken in many other areas of life. The future you were counting on has just been altered, perhaps radically.

 MINDFUL EXERCISE

> Make a list of all of the things you feel help define who you are. Be honest! Don't censor your list because you know something is impermanent or because you think it's superficial. Your gender, height, nationality, family-of-origin story, physical attractiveness, musical tastes, ability to cook, etc., are all valid characteristics to identify. Consider how long this list could get, and how almost everything on it is subject to change—if not literally, then in terms of how you think about it. Instead of letting this make you feel insecure, however, see if it can help you feel grateful for these things that compose your unique life.

When you can approach self-related impermanence with mindfulness, change and loss may still be difficult, but they are also opportunities to learn more about the nature of self. When you have attentively watched part of your sense of self shift dramatically, you become aware that just about everything else you rely on to define you can also shift. This may be scary to think about, but it can also encourage you to clarify what really matters to you. It can inspire you to search for deeper things on which you can rely, rather than trying to hold on to more transient things like material possessions, status, or roles.

A Dynamic Sense of Self

Maintaining awareness of your experience over time—not just when things are particularly interesting or pleasant, but at all kinds of times—gives you a different sense of self. Somehow, despite changing circumstances and mind states, there you are: a vital, dynamic awareness. This awareness does not depend on the details of your life, or on the current constellation of relationships with people and things that constitute your conventional self. This awareness is space through which the content of your life moves—so if your sense of self is based in this awareness, it doesn't feel so threatening when the content changes.

It's a little like you begin to see your awareness as a blank movie screen, and your life as the movie that is being shown on it. Your "self" as you usually define it is just one character in the movie, and that character has an interesting story to live out. Limitations and foibles are just part of what make the character unique. Changes and challenges are part of an unfolding drama that will lead to development, maturity, and insight. Even the character's dark times of confusion, stagnation, or angst are viewed against the larger perspective of the movie: as being natural, adding to the drama, and contributing to the character's ultimate realizations or decisions.

Such objectivity with respect to your sense of self doesn't result in feeling distant from your life, or in emotional withdrawal. Quite the contrary. Self-concern tends to limit your ability to perceive things clearly, and distorts your relationship to everything you experience because it is all evaluated in terms of how it benefits, threatens, or is irrelevant to your "self." A more spacious, dynamic sense of self actually opens you up more, emotionally and psychologically.

Choice Instead of Default

What about the default mode—the self-referential, stimulus-independent thinking your mind does when it isn't busy with something else? Mindfulness training, in large part, involves willingly foregoing this default mode in favor of paying attention to your present experience. Fortunately, this does not result in you being unprepared to deal with life because you haven't thought about it enough in your spare time. In fact, most mindfulness practitioners report that they are able to respond to life more effectively and make better decisions, despite the fact that they spend less time in default mode.

 KEEP IN MIND

Mindfulness meditation has been shown via functional magnetic resonance imaging (fMRI) to decrease activity in the default mode network. There is also evidence that long-term meditation practice changes the connections between the default mode network and the rest of the brain. Scientists aren't quite sure yet what these changed connections mean, but they may reflect the ability of experienced meditators to maintain some awareness of their present experience even when they are engaged in self-referential thinking.

Getting Unstuck from Your Head

If you really pay attention to what your mind is doing in default mode, you'll realize much of it is of very limited usefulness. This is why the subjective experience of default mode is generally called "mind wandering." You often replay the same stories over and over. You fantasize about things you could have said or done in the past that would have led to more gratifying results. You mull over arguments you'd like to make to certain people but probably never will. You imagine going places and doing things you're unlikely to ever go or do. Through it all, you mind holds on to a vague conviction that the subject matter is very compelling, but the subjects are generally compelling not because they are significant or productive, but because they are about *you*.

This is not to say that everything you think about when your mind wanders is *selfish*, just that it's basically self-referential. This is natural, of course—who else do you know better? It's also not pathological, but even if you're thinking about helping others, you're thinking about *you* helping others.

Self-referential thinking is a very limited way of dealing with your life. It has its place, but too much of it can lead to compulsive rumination and worry. Rumination is about the past and worry is about the future, but both involve repeatedly calling to mind the symptoms or causes of your distress. You try to explain these causes or think about how to change them, but after a while, because most of this processing is just happening in your mind, your thinking gets stuck in a rut. You dwell on the same things over and over, without a fresh perspective, a break, or new input from your life.

Mindfulness helps you get unstuck from your head in two ways. First, as you train in mindfulness you practice letting go of trains of thought and returning your attention to something that is happening in the present. After a while you get better at doing this, and this skill serves you well when you're stuck in a particularly compelling cycle of rumination or worry. Second, as you pay more attention to your mental processes themselves, you're more likely to notice that a particular pattern of thinking leads to negative results like anxiety, depression, anger, or obsession. When you see this clearly, at least part of you is going to get interested in getting free from that pattern of thought.

Becoming Free from the Tyranny of Your Mind

You may resist the idea of mindfulness training because it seems to be about "controlling" your mind. Rather than relaxing into default mode, you exert effort to remain aware of what's going on around you. Rather than letting your mind wander over the things that keep it amused, you try to pay attention to the present moment—which may not seem interesting. Rather than indulging in worry and rumination, you try to let go of repetitive trains of thought. This may seem like hard work, and it can be.

However, there's another way to look at mindfulness training: it frees you from the tyranny of your mind. As discussed earlier in the section on "Your Complex Sense of Self," there is a way you can experience a deeper sense of self that is not completely identified with the contents or impulses of your mind. When you're able to tune into this spacious awareness, you begin to recognize that your mind tends to pull you out of it by convincing you that what you're thinking is fundamentally true and deeply important. Your default patterns of mind take over.

Our default modes of thinking can sometimes lead to serious problems. For example, overactivity in the default mode network has been associated with depression. Researchers have also found the default network's connectivity to certain other brain regions is increased in depressed subjects. This suggests a physical basis for the observation that when you're depressed, it is easy for your attention to be pulled inward into self-referential thinking and away from tasks or perceptions of your external environment.

 TAKE CARE

When you first begin trying to be more mindful, it can be rather nerve-racking. You may notice your mind is very active with all kinds of things you would rather it didn't dwell on, or you may notice annoying habits and tendencies you have that you would like to fix. Through it all, it may feel like there is a burdensome sense of self-consciousness that has been added to your life. Be patient! This is a natural stage as you start turning your attention to your own mental processes. After a while, mindfulness starts to feel easier and more natural.

There is also evidence that the more your mind wanders, the less happy you are (Killingsworth and Gilbert 2010), so it's a good idea to make some conscious choices about how you want your mind to operate. Mindfulness training involves spending less time letting the mind follow habitual patterns, so the actual experience of a mindful moment can be a relief if you're struggling with depression, anxiety, or trauma. In addition, practicing mindfulness over time helps you get better at letting go of default modes of thinking. You end up being able to do it more quickly, more often, and with less effort. Your mind may still wander or fall into habits, but you're never that far from the present moment. Just by recognizing what's going on in your mind, you can bring yourself back.

Mindfulness and Insight

The most transformational aspect of mindfulness is the way it helps you perceive things more clearly. You might think you need to consciously keep in mind your knowledge, opinions, and intentions when you interact with the world in order to navigate your life effectively. This is not the case. In fact, your preconceived ideas about the things and people you encounter act like filters, coloring the way you perceive the world. To some extent these filters are unavoidable—you can never be completely objective—but you can become much more aware of when they are operating. You can also learn to view them as one part of your whole experience, rather than letting them dictate the nature of it.

Developing Greater Receptivity

Let's say you're facing a challenge. Your daughter has been struggling academically and would benefit from going to a more expensive school. You can't afford the school without making some major lifestyle changes, or perhaps even getting a new, more stressful job. You worry about how these changes might affect you and your daughter. They might make things worse despite a new school. You probably try to answer or resolve your issue by thinking things over in your mind. You may search for more information, or get feedback from people you trust.

All of these typical ways of searching for answers and resolution are valuable, but they require you to do two things from the outset: decide what the question is, and decide where and how you might find an answer. Sometimes you can successfully deal with things this way, but the more complex the issue you're facing, the more likely it is you will fail to obtain a truly satisfactory result.

Practicing mindfulness in the midst of a challenge makes you more receptive to ways your issue might be reframed, and to completely novel sources of insight into it. When you temporarily set aside your conscious thinking on a subject, your mind has a chance to process it in a different way. Answers can arise in surprising places and suggest a deeper question than you anticipated.

To continue with our example, in a quiet moment while drinking your morning coffee, you might connect with a felt sense of the value of just being physically present in your daughter's life. This gives you confidence you will be able to be there for her, as best you can, even in the midst of lifestyle and job stress. Suddenly the challenge of paying for a new school seems less daunting. When you explain such insight in words it usually doesn't seem very profound, but it can be powerful because it is *experienced*. Mindfulness opens you up to these kinds of insights.

Getting the Self Out of the Way

In your default mode of thinking, your self is generally front and center. As you encounter each situation or person, you're asking yourself questions like, "Do I like this? Is this unpleasant or threatening? Is this boring and not worth my time and attention? What does this person think of me? Do I need anything from them? Am I at a disadvantage in this situation? Am I capable here, or am I liable to make a mistake and look like a fool? Does this person have expectations of me I want to fulfill?"

All of these self-centered thoughts affect the way we perceive things and interact with life. It's like looking at the world through a tube, restricting our field of vision. This limitation is especially obvious when you deal with close family members: the more preoccupied you are with your relationship to someone, the less clearly and objectively you perceive them and their actions. Choices someone makes that don't even affect you directly can be upsetting because of what it might imply about how the person thinks about or relates to you.

Fortunately, you don't have to feel guilty about your natural self-centeredness, or try valiantly to fight your selfishness. Simply by practicing mindfulness you can get self out of the way for a moment and get a fresh perspective. When you turn your attention to your present experience, you have to give up your thoughts about past and future. You have to loosen your grip on your beliefs about how things are in order to see, hear, smell, taste, and touch. You might notice the texture of the skin on your aging mother's hands and for a moment perceive the loneliness that drives her to be judgmental sometimes. It is possible to perceive such things directly, without the reference point of self.

The Least You Need to Know

- Humans evolved a stress response and a tendency to spend their spare time doing self-referential processing. These things are helpful for survival when facing daily life-or-death challenges, but in modern life they lead to a number of mental and physical problems.
- Mindfulness involves deliberately foregoing your default mode of self-referential mind wandering. It also asks you to observe your own mental processes as part of your whole experience.
- You may not have much choice about your initial reactions to things, but mindfulness can give you more choice about how you *react to your reactions*.
- By paying closer attention to the moment-by-moment unfolding of your life, you can start to gain some objectivity about your sense of self. Then it's possible to take change in stride and stop taking things quite so personally.
- Mindfulness can lead to insight into your life by widening your field of perception and by helping you experience things more directly, without the filter of self-concern.

Practicing Mindfulness

In this chapter I present the essence of how to practice mindfulness. The remainder of the book gives you detailed instructions about how to cultivate the various aspects of mindfulness, and discusses how to apply it in your life—but if you want to study a single chapter and then get started, this is the one to read.

Mindfulness is a whole body-and-mind experience, somewhat like long-distance running. There's no simple answer to the question, "How do you do long-distance running?" Running includes an intention to get somewhere on foot relatively quickly, a particular way of moving the body, a relationship to pacing and breathing, a process of increasing your endurance over time, and a mental attitude that keeps you going through physical and mental discomfort—among other things. Mindfulness is similar in that it involves motivation, purpose, training, techniques, and attitude. Mindfulness is also similar to running in that you have to *do* it in order to really understand it!

In This Chapter

- A concise definition of mindfulness
- The three important aspects of mindful practice
- A list of useful principles
- How to work toward greater happiness
- Seeing things more clearly
- The right attitude for mindfulness

The Three Components of Mindfulness

In this book I use a definition of mindfulness that is informed by modern secular usage of the term as well as by Buddhism: *consciously maintaining awareness of your present experience with a receptive attitude, in order to perceive things more clearly and consequently increase happiness for self and other.*

This definition of mindfulness has three components:

1. An *aspiration* to reduce stress and increase happiness.

2. *Awareness* of your present experience.

3. A receptive *attitude.*

A significant portion of this book is devoted to each of these three components. Part 2 gives instructions for how to cultivate the ability to maintain awareness of the present. Part 3 tells you how to cultivate a receptive and accepting attitude in order to see your life more clearly. Part 4 walks you through using mindfulness to increase happiness in different areas of your life.

Summary of the Mindful Process

So, you begin with aspiration. While *aspiration* may sound a little grand, what it really amounts to is some kind of positive motivation. If you had no motivation, you wouldn't even have picked up this book! It arises from a recognition that you would like to experience something different within your life. Perhaps you're experiencing lots of stress and want to achieve some inner peace. Perhaps you're feeling anguish and suffering and are looking for a way to find some joy and ease. Perhaps you feel pretty good but would like to be able to be more intimate with your life, or more compassionate, patient, or appreciative. In any case, all of these motivations essentially amount to some kind of aspiration to reduce stress and increase happiness for yourself and/or others.

Next, you turn your attention to what is happening around and within you. This is "attention training" and can be challenging because of deeply ingrained mental habits like daydreaming and worry. Fortunately, there are all kinds of exercises you can do to increase the amount of time you spend aware of the present. In general, the more present you can be, the happier you will feel.

 KEEP IN MIND

The three-component definition of mindfulness used in this book applies equally well to a state (a description of your actions in a moment of mindfulness), a trait (your attempt to become a mindful person who is more likely to be doing this at any given moment), and a practice (your ongoing effort to develop and strengthen all three of these components).

Once you have some sustained awareness of what's going on in the moment, you work on your attitude toward your experience. Things like judgment and fear can prevent you from perceiving clearly, so you try to cultivate receptivity through openness and acceptance. Finally, you pay particular attention whenever you feel stress, whether it is triggered by external events or your own thoughts and feelings. If you perceive clearly enough, you can better understand the nature of the stress, and how and why it arises. Then you can investigate alternative ways of thinking and behaving that relieve some of the stress and lead to greater happiness.

Why Intention Matters

Sometimes people use the term *mindfulness* to refer only to attention training, or to cultivating an accepting awareness. In certain circumstances these more limited definitions may be useful. For example, if you're only interested in attention training, it can be used to increase your skill at certain tasks. In addition, simply paying attention to the present moment instead of worrying can reduce stress, at least temporarily! If you're primarily interested in becoming more accepting of your life, developing the third component of mindfulness can be very helpful.

Whatever your underlying intention, it frames your entire approach to mindfulness. It will determine the depth of your motivation, the obstacles you're likely to face, and the things that it will be most fruitful for you to pay attention to.

After all, what is mindfulness *for*? Paying attention to the present moment without an agenda can make you a better gambler or sharpshooter, but chances are you will have to ignore some of the deep truths of your life while you engage in an activity that generates significant negative consequences. Returning your attention to your breath may keep you from exploding with anger when your spouse nags you, or your boss requires you to work overtime for no extra pay, but simply maintaining some equanimity in such situations—while a good thing—may not be a sufficient response in the long run. Mindfulness as presented in this book is practiced within the context of your intention to reduce stress and increase happiness for self and other in the long term.

Twelve Principles of Mindfulness

The following are 12 principles to keep in mind when practicing mindfulness. The first four principles have to do with mindful aspiration, the second four are about awareness, and the last four address attitude.

1. You, and all other beings, just want to be happy.

2. The greatest happiness is that which applies in the longest term and at the largest scale—which includes the happiness of others.

3. Change occurs naturally when you see clearly what leads to greater happiness.

4. You can only take care of your life and the lives of others by clearly seeing what does and doesn't lead toward greater happiness.

5. To see clearly, you have to drop below the level of ordinary thinking and experience things directly.

6. When your mind wanders, your perspective shrinks and your ability to see clearly is compromised.

7. You can change your mind's default mode by repeatedly turning your attention to something that is happening in the present.

8. Attention is deliberately focusing your mind, but it can lead to a more continuous, natural, receptive awareness.

9. The first step to learning something new is admitting you don't know.

10. You are unlikely to see something clearly as long as you fear or reject it.

11. Comfort with inner and outer stillness and silence is comfort with reality.

12. Mindfulness is its own reward.

This may seem like a lot to take in at once, but don't worry. I explain each of these principles and their relationship to the three components of mindfulness. (The 12 principles can also be found in Appendix C.) This list is meant to introduce you to the important things to understand about mindfulness in a straightforward and condensed way. If you don't like lists, just read the explanations and let the ideas wash over you.

The Four Principles of Aspiration

It isn't necessary that you fully understand, accept, or believe any of the 12 principles. In fact, it is essential that you question them and test them out for yourself! That said, it works well if you adopt them as working theories as you set about mindfulness practice. They can help motivate you, guide your efforts, and point you toward aspects of your experience it is valuable for you to understand in a deeper way.

The first four principles explain why mindfulness leads to greater happiness. It is not unreasonable to resist the practice of mindfulness because it runs counter to typical "common sense," which tells you the way to greater happiness involves grasping after what you want and pushing away what you don't want. Hopefully, the principles will convince you that mindfulness just might work. Then, when you prove the truth of these principles for yourself, they can be a source of deep aspiration and energy.

One: We All Just Want to Be Happy

The first principle is that *you, and all other beings, just want to be happy*. Happiness is really just a more complex, evolved experience of the pain-versus-pleasure reflexes of very simple animals. While an amoeba flinches away from something that causes it pain and moves toward food, as human beings we require something more. Happiness is a complex state that includes physical, emotional, and psychological ease and comfort, and yet in some ways your orientation toward it remains as basic as that of an amoeba toward sustenance. You're hardwired to recognize it and move toward it.

 MINDFUL EXERCISE

Get into a comfortable physical position and close your eyes. Imagine you're in a setting in which you feel completely happy and at ease. Are you sitting next to a campfire in the wilderness? Are you at home on a Friday evening with your cat on your lap? Are you at a concert listening to deeply moving music? What is present or absent in your body and mind? Is there a sense of fullness in your chest? Is your breathing deeper? Do you have a sense that, for now, nothing needs to be done? Explore the nature of the deepest kind of happiness you can call to mind.

However, the idea that all of us just want to be happy begs the question, "Then why do people so often do things that actually *decrease* their happiness, or the happiness of others?" The basic answer is this: when you do something that compromises your happiness in one sense, it's only because you're trying to increase your happiness in another sense.

Typically, you act to increase short-term happiness at the expense of long-term happiness, and act to increase obvious happiness at the expense of more subtle forms of happiness. You're also inclined to increase your own happiness at the expense of the happiness of others, despite observing that generosity and compassion are two of the most reliable sources of long-term, personal satisfaction.

Here's a classic example of choosing short-term over long-term happiness: you're feeling anxious, depressed, or sad, and seek some relief. You turn to something that reliably makes you feel better, or at least distracts you from your sorrows. Perhaps you go shopping, or indulge in a rich meal or alcohol. Perhaps you engage in a dangerous or illegal activity because of the pleasure or excitement it brings. Later, with a hangover, depleted bank account, broken diet, or traffic ticket, you wonder why you keep doing this to yourself. Well, it's because you want to be happy.

Two: Greater and Lesser Happiness

This brings us to the second principle: *the greatest happiness is that which applies in the longest term and at the largest scale—which includes the happiness of others.* Just as you naturally recognize happiness, you can recognize greater and lesser happiness. The happiness of eating an ice cream cone is less than the happiness of meeting a dear friend for lunch. The happiness of the lunch date is less than that of getting the job of your dreams. The happiness of your dream job is less than that of looking back over your life with a sense of satisfaction that you did right by your loved ones and made the most of your opportunities.

At times you probably get quite caught up in seeking lesser happiness, usually at the expense of greater happiness, as discussed in the example in the previous section about seeking short-term relief from emotional discomfort. This is because you lose perspective. The "little" things become all-important, like getting through traffic, keeping your house clean, or winning an argument.

As you strive for these small sources of happiness, part of you is probably aware that you're compromising greater ones—like your physical and mental health, enjoyment of life, or emotional intimacy with your significant others. Something that dramatically shifts your perspective, such as a tragedy or a terminal diagnosis, can make you wonder how you could ever have gotten so wrapped up in all the little concerns of life.

A deep part of you recognizes that any source of happiness that is bounded in space and time is lesser than a source that is unbounded. Material things, or things that begin and end, can provide great pleasure and joy, but don't quite compare to something intangible and boundless, like a sense of integrity or the appreciation of the beauty of nature. The greatest experiences of happiness tend to take your breath away, leave you speechless, or move you to tears.

This deep part of you also recognizes that your happiness is intimately connected with the happiness of others. You can experience this directly when you feel pain or discomfort while witnessing someone else's suffering, or when you feel deeply touched by evidence of people's compassion and generosity toward one another. There is also mounting scientific evidence, such as the discovery of *mirror neurons,* that you're wired to share the experience of others.

 **DEFINITION**

Mirror neurons are cells in your brain that are activated when you witness another being's experience or action. They fire in a similar area of your brain as they would if you were the one having the experience or doing the action.

Three: Moving Toward Greater Happiness

For now, let's set aside the question of *how* you keep a large perspective and recognize the greatest sources of happiness in your life, and subsequently avoid compromising them by getting too caught up in the lesser things. The "how" of mindfulness will be covered by the principles of attention and attitude. First, we need to consider why it's good to become more mindful: *change occurs naturally when you see clearly what leads to greater happiness.*

It may seem unnecessary to spell out this principle, seeing as it follows so obviously from the first two principles. You just want to be happy, there are greater and lesser sources of happiness, so if you recognize a greater happiness you'll be motivated to seek it out. However, even though this is obvious in theory, it isn't obvious in real life. Instead, you probably have the experience of wanting greater happiness, trying hard to change, and yet being unable to do so.

The pivotal aspect of this principle is *seeing clearly*. This is not an easy, simple thing to do. It's not just about intellectually understanding something is harmful or beneficial, or that one source of happiness is greater than another. This is direct, personal, unbiased, complete "seeing," or comprehension, of all essential aspects of a situation.

Basically, if you keep choosing to compromise the greater happiness of self and other, it's because you aren't yet seeing clearly enough. If you could *really* see—wholeheartedly experience, intimately feel—how something you do causes suffering or compromises greater happiness, you would want to stop. You wouldn't have to make yourself change. In fact, no one could stop you from changing!

Four: The Importance of Seeing Clearly

Cultivating the ability and willingness to see clearly, or to truly comprehend what is going on in your life, is not just a nice thing to do. It's not just a spiritual feather to add to your cap, or an admirable quality to add to your character. Instead, it's important enough that the fourth principle of mindfulness is: *you can only take care of your life and the lives of others by clearly seeing what does and doesn't lead toward greater happiness.*

Again, this may seem like an obvious thing to state: if you don't know what leads to greater happiness, you won't be as happy, but in practice it is often ignored. Maybe you're happy enough with the sources of happiness you're used to, and you'd rather not bother to compare them to something that might result in greater happiness. Maybe you don't have much faith that you could see clearly even if you tried, or that transformative clear seeing is possible. Maybe you want to stick with your old approach of simply achieving as much happiness as you can through ordinary means, rather than learning something new.

Making a diligent effort to see more clearly takes a leap of faith. For the time being you might have to accept and operate on the assumption that it's possible, *you* can do it, and it's worthwhile. However, chances are you already know, at some level, that this fourth principle is true. Chances are, you really *do* want to take care of your life and the lives of others, and you're aware there is always more to be seen.

The Four Principles of Awareness

Okay, now we get into *how* you see clearly. These principles of awareness apply equally well when you're trying to see more clearly something that is relatively mundane, something of great significance to you, or something universal. You can use these principles when you're trying to figure out the best way to respond to a co-worker, when you're pondering major life decisions, or when you want to better understand the nature of life in general. Mindfulness doesn't give you the answers, it just increases your ability to find them.

Five: Dropping Below Ordinary Thinking

This is one of the most radical principles of mindfulness: *to see clearly, you have to drop below the level of ordinary thinking and experience things directly.* It runs counter to your instinct and to cultural common sense, which tell you to use your intelligence to figure things out. The basic idea here is that your ordinary, discriminatory way of thinking is very useful, but only to a point. After that point it just gets in the way.

Your ordinary way of thinking is all about differentiation—discerning self from other, right from wrong, things you like from things you don't, and things likely to lead to happiness from those likely to lead to misery. This differentiation is essential, as it allows you to tell good food from what's inedible, safety from danger, and culturally appropriate behavior from what would make people avoid you.

However, if you want to engage life in a deeper way and see things more clearly, it is necessary to drop below the evaluations and commentary of the differentiating mind. Your life is much more than a series of definitions, judgments, and categories. It is a full body-mind experience that includes sight, sound, smell, taste, and touch. It includes intuition, intimacy, energy, and spontaneity. Effective and authentic responses to life can—and do—arise in you from a deeper place than your ordinary thinking mind.

It isn't necessary to get rid of thinking; it definitely has its place. You'll just want to set it aside at some point, when it seems to have given you all the useful information it has to give and has started to go in circles. For example, if you're deciding whether to end an intimate relationship, you can ponder all the pros and cons of ending versus continuing it. You can ask for the opinions of others, or read books on relationships in order to get perspective on yours.

TAKE CARE

It can be problematic if you adopt the idea that ordinary thinking is wrong and just obscures some kind of transcendent truth. It's not good to deny what your best discriminatory thinking tells you, and it's not good to set up a duality that pits you against aspects of your own mental processes. It's more helpful to think of there being different levels of truth, or reality. In mindfulness practice you aim to be able to shift easily between different levels of truth depending on what would be most useful.

Ultimately, thinking about what to do is unlikely to give you a satisfying answer. All the things you know about a situation still enter into the equation, but directing your attention the way I describe in Part 2 of this book allows you to attend to your full present experience. Other kinds of factors can make themselves known, some of which your thinking mind may have been dismissing or rejecting. There's no easy way to describe this in words, but practicing mindfulness can help you get to the place where you *just know* the best thing to do.

Six: Letting Go of Mind Wandering

It is probably very rare that you deliberately turn your mind toward a question or problem in your life in order to give it your best mental analysis, setting aside all other thoughts and activities in order to do so. If you consciously think about things this way, it's not a problem. You will be able to tell when the thinking has at least temporarily reached its limits, and it's time to set it aside, collect more information, or pay attention to other things.

Most of the ordinary thinking you do happens in the form of mind wandering, or stimulus-independent thinking. You think briefly about your financial concerns while you're brushing your teeth, then you speculate on the most fun thing to do this weekend while you're making your coffee, and worry about your sore knee while waiting at a stoplight on your way to work. If you start paying attention to your mental processes, you'll see that most of your time is spent entertaining a more or less random series of thoughts. You think about each one only briefly and superficially before leaping to the next.

As discussed in Chapter 2, this is your mind's default mode. When you're not engaged in an activity that requires your full attention, your mind uses the spare bandwidth to process self-referential topics. Because the thoughts are about you and your life in some respect, you probably have a sense that they are important and worthwhile, or at the very least harmless.

KEEP IN MIND

There is some empirical evidence that mind wandering has negative effects. Killingsworth and Gilbert (2010) used an iPhone app to contact people randomly throughout the day with questions about their current activities, mind states, and happiness levels. They obtained over 225,000 samples from about 5,000 people from 83 different countries, ages 18 to 88. They found people were less happy when their minds were wandering, regardless of what activity they were engaged in—even if the task was not considered enjoyable in itself. Happiness was better predicted by what people were thinking than by what they were doing, leading the researchers to conclude, "The ability to think about what is not happening is a cognitive achievement that comes at an emotional cost."

Despite how innocuous mind wandering may seem, the second principle of mindful awareness is this: *when your mind wanders, your perspective shrinks and your ability to see clearly is compromised.* As described in the section above on the first principles of awareness, your ordinary thinking mind is of limited usefulness when it comes to fully engaging your life. If you spend the vast majority of your time either busy with an activity or letting your mind wander, you're basically thinking all the time. That means you'll rarely be taking the opportunity to experience your life directly and see clearly what is going on.

Seven: Changing Your Default Mode

The good thing is, *you can change your mind's default mode by repeatedly turning your attention to something that is happening in the present* (the third principle of awareness). This may seem like an impossible task when you first start paying attention to your mind and notice how often it is spinning around in default mode, jumping from one self-referential topic to another. However, in Chapter 1 I presented the subjective and objective evidence that it is possible to change your mind (and brain, for that matter).

This third principle is the basis for the whole practice of mindfulness, which is a very simple and repetitive effort to cultivate awareness of the present. It takes quite a bit of effort at first to even remember to turn your attention from stimulus-independent thinking to something in the present, like your breath, physical posture, or sensations like sight, sound, smell, taste, or touch. You have to do it over and over, and you might remain aware of the present for only moments at a time.

If you keep at it, eventually you remember to return to the present more often, and you stay present for longer and longer periods of time. You get more comfortable with directly experiencing your life, and with setting aside your ordinary thinking. With diligent practice, being receptively aware of what's going on around and within you becomes your default mode, and stimulus-independent thinking becomes something you engage in deliberately.

Eight: Attention Versus Awareness

The terms *attention* and *awareness* are often used interchangeably, even in this book. At times I may say that in mindfulness you aim to pay attention to your present experience, and at other times you want to cultivate awareness of your present experience. Still, when discussing mindfulness there is an important distinction between attention and awareness, and both are important. This is reflected in the fourth principle of awareness: *Attention is deliberately focusing your mind, but it can lead to a more continuous, natural, receptive awareness.*

Attention is the deliberate focusing of your mind on a particular thing—a sensation, a feeling, a thought, concept, or experience. It requires some effort and energy to focus and then to hold your attention on its object. Working with your attention is the first step in mindfulness practice, and sustained attention is required for you to complete tasks and understand things in everyday life. It is also useful for seeing clearly when you use it to focus on particular things long enough to really understand them.

Awareness is more of a receptive mental state. It still takes some energy and effort to maintain, but this primarily involves not letting your mind wander. Your awareness is always there, waiting to be uncovered under all your mental activity. It is open to whatever arises, and doesn't guess where the next important (or interesting, or entertaining) piece of information is going to come from.

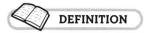 **DEFINITION**

> Attention and awareness both have to do with opening the doors of perception, and both are important in mindfulness, but they are different. **Attention** is the act of focusing your mind on a particular object and then trying to keep it there. **Awareness** is a receptive state of mind that involves a special effort only in that you need to let go of thoughts and prevent your mind from wandering in order to allow it to operate.

It can be difficult to directly work on your awareness because it is much more of a *not doing* than a deliberate activity, but turning your attention to something happening in the present moment is a great first step because it requires you to let go of your stimulus-independent mental activity and gives you something more relevant to do. Once you're able to hold your attention in the present for a while, you can relax a bit and open your awareness to include your wider experience. Eventually, mindful awareness comes to feel more natural, and less special or effortful.

The Four Principles of Attitude

Even if you fully understand why mindfulness is important, and even if you apply yourself to practicing it diligently, you can still run into some obstacles. Not all of these obstacles have to do with the sheer effort it takes to change habits. Some of them have to do with your attitude toward yourself, your life, and the whole process of becoming more mindful.

Mindfulness is about dropping below the level of your discriminatory thinking, directly experiencing your life, and seeing clearly. If you engage it the same way you usually engage activities, chances are you'll use your discriminatory mind to do it, which will just end up getting in the way. Chances are also good there are certain things in your life you'd rather not directly experience, so you'll tend to avoid them—perhaps without even realizing it. Directly working on your attitudes, fears, and resistance can greatly improve your ability to maintain mindful awareness.

Nine: "Don't Know" Mind

Most of the time, as an adult, you probably prefer to feel like you understand all the things you need to understand. Sure, there are things you don't know, but those things aren't directly relevant to you, or you don't really care about them much. Basically, you'd like to believe you're fully equipped to deal competently with your everyday life—and even if you doubt it, you'd probably like others to believe it.

However, as you try to learn to practice mindfulness, it's good to keep in mind the first principle of attitude: *the first step to learning something new is admitting you don't know.* This is especially crucial for something like learning mindfulness, which involves discovering new ways to experience and use your own mind. It's a very personal, directly relevant activity—and it can be disconcerting to let go of ways of operating that you're used to in order to explore the unknown. However, if you find the practice of mindfulness difficult, it may be because you're holding on to preconceived notions about what it might be like, or what it might require.

Getting comfortable with "don't know" mind is very liberating. It opens you up to learning, keeps your mind open and fresh, and prevents you from being limited by your current ways of thinking. It invites you to engage everything in your life with curiosity. What more can you see here? In what ways can you expand or deepen your experience? "Don't know" mind is not an admission of inadequacy or weakness, it is a manifestation of intelligence and a sense of responsibility.

Ten: Courage and Acceptance

There are probably some things in your life you'd rather not directly experience, like disappointment, regret, shame, grief, or the results of trauma. Part of your motivation to let your mind wander or distract yourself is to avoid the unpleasantness of feeling or facing these things. As you pay more attention to your life, it is also possible to discover habits of action, speech, or thought you just never noticed before—and some of these are … well … not so attractive.

If you really want to be more mindful and aware of your life, it's important to keep the next principle in mind: *you are unlikely to see something clearly as long as you fear or reject it.* Remember, seeing clearly means wholeheartedly experiencing and intimately feeling how something you do causes suffering or compromises greater happiness. (See #3 of the "Twelve Principles of Mindfulness" earlier in this chapter.) It's not just a superficial understanding; it's a transformative comprehension.

Seeing clearly requires quite a lot of effort and determination, which means if part of you is resisting the process because of fear or lack of acceptance, the process will be difficult. You can facilitate mindfulness by deliberately working on your courage and acceptance. After practicing for a while, you can sense when fear, rejection, or resistance is arising in you.

Instead of reacting to fear and aversion by trying to avoid or get rid of them, you can turn toward them. It may be uncomfortable, but you allow yourself to experience these things and just try to maintain mindful awareness of the present moment. Often, this lets you gain insight into your fear and aversion, so you can begin taking steps to resolve or let go of them. This will improve the quality of your life, but also help you see more clearly because your mind will be more calm and open.

Eleven: Stillness and Silence

When you're mindful, there is at least a part of you that is still (not grasping after anything, and not pushing anything away) and silent (not engaged in self-referential evaluation or commentary). This can be a disconcerting experience when you aren't used to it, but this brings us to the third principle of attitude: *comfort with inner and outer stillness and silence is comfort with reality.*

 MINDFUL EXERCISE

The next time you're waiting—for the bus, for the doctor, in a line—experiment with not entertaining yourself with anything. Don't listen to music or a podcast, and don't read anything (including the magazines at the checkout stand). Just stand or sit there. Go ahead and look around at your environment. Watch people, and notice things like noise levels, temperature, and your sense of impatience. Observe how strong your urge is to find something to occupy yourself! Anything but just being there. Gently hold the question, "Why do I feel this way?"

Most people are very uncomfortable with stillness and silence. Your mind encourages you to be active and diligent in looking out for yourself and those you care about. It seems natural to continuously work toward things that will bring happiness and safety, avoid those that might bring unhappiness or danger, and think about such activities whenever you aren't actually engaged in them. To sit still and be silent, without anything to distract or entertain you, seems ... Odd? Silly? Boring? A waste of time? Like willingly being vulnerable?

In reality, it is those moments when you're still and silent, inside and outside, that you experience what's going on most fully, directly, clearly, and intimately. Perhaps it is the intensity of this experience that makes people wary of it. In any case, it's rather like there are different levels of reality, and some things are "more real" and others are "less real." There is a certain reality to your thoughts, emotions, and desires, but they are less real than what is unfolding in front of you this very moment. Being in touch with reality is calming, grounding, empowering, and energizing—among other things.

This doesn't mean you can never authentically speak or act, or that you need to spend all your time being still and silent. It is possible to maintain a certain amount of inner stillness and silence even while engaged in activities. It is possible to return to stillness and silence for short periods of time in between speaking and acting. The more comfortable you get with being—at least momentarily—still and silent, the more effective your mindfulness practice will be.

Twelve: The Joy of Presence

From the discussion so far, you might be tempted think that mindfulness, or being fully present for your direct experience of life, is something you do: 1) in order to see clearly; 2) so you know the best ways to deal with your life; and 3) so you can improve your life and be happier. In a way, all of this is true.

However, this brings us to the fourth principle of attitude: *mindfulness is its own reward.* This connects back to the second principle of mindfulness, about greater and lesser happiness. When you're mindful, you're more connected with the reality of your life and with your own vitality. You're able to appreciate *just being alive for its own sake,* which turns out to be the simplest, most reliable, and greatest happiness of all. Experiencing this for yourself can result in an enthusiastic, willing, determined attitude in your efforts to be more mindful.

The Least You Need to Know

- Mindfulness is maintaining *awareness* of your present experience with an open, receptive *attitude,* with the *aspiration* to see clearly and move toward greater happiness.
- All beings just want to be happy, but there are greater and lesser forms of happiness—and you often end up choosing lesser over greater forms without necessarily meaning to.
- When you can see your life more clearly, you more often choose to move toward greater happiness for self and others.

- Seeing clearly is not merely intellectual; it requires letting go of ordinary ways of thinking, mind wandering, close-mindedness, judgment, and fear.
- The good news is that when you *really* understand that a certain course leads toward greater happiness, you will be naturally motivated to take it.

PART 2

Cultivating Mindful Awareness

The first step in mindfulness is learning to pay attention to what's going on in the present moment. This is much more easily said than done! You have strong habits of mind that lead you to thinking about the past, the future, things going on somewhere else, or abstract ideas. Fortunately, people have been working on mindfulness for thousands of years and have come up with lots of techniques and approaches to help you pay more attention to what's going on around you.

In this part of the book I walk you through a series of things you can use as objects for your attention when you're developing your mindful awareness. The list is adapted from an ancient Buddhist one, and includes your body, feelings, states of mind, and various factors such as ill-will or concentration, which can hinder or support your mindfulness. Each chapter introduces the object of attention, how to recognize it, and how to deepen your awareness of it. Finally, I discuss the important role of meditation in mindfulness practice, and how to do it.

Awareness of Your Body

In the ancient Buddhist teaching on mindfulness called the Satipatthana Sutta, the Buddha divides mindfulness practices into four categories. The first of these categories is "observation of the body in the body." Cultivating awareness of the body is considered the first step in mindfulness, and continues to be the most important type of training no matter how long you practice mindfulness.

In this chapter I explain the importance of cultivating body awareness, and how to do it. In brief, techniques for cultivating awareness of the body are many and varied. The classic technique is to follow the sensations of your breathing: in and out, in and out. This gives you something dynamic to pay attention to in the present moment. You can also pay attention to your posture, or concentrate on the sensations of sight, sound, smell, taste, or touch. Simple movements provide a wonderful object for mindfulness practice. Chances are you already use awareness of the body to reduce your stress! Mindfulness can help you take that process a step further.

In This Chapter

- Why mindfulness of the body is so important
- How body awareness is part of all mindfulness training
- Exercises for cultivating physical awareness
- Tuning in to physical sensations without reacting
- Increasing comfort with your body

Why Mindfulness Begins with the Body

It's become clichéd to say there is no separation between mind and body, but a realization of how this is true is deeply important. It may sometimes seem as if your mind thinks it can carry on a life of its own, dependent on the body merely for nourishment and transportation. On the contrary, it's when the mind is present in the body—when body and mind are unified and directly experiencing your life—that you're most clear, at peace, and effective.

At a simpler level, the body provides an excellent object for beginning mindfulness practice because it's always available and always in the present moment. No matter where you are or what you're doing, you can shift your attention from stimulus-independent thinking to your sense of posture, your breathing, or the movement of your hands. This simple practice can be incredibly helpful at stressful times.

The Body Is Always in the Present

As discussed in previous chapters, mindfulness involves consciously maintaining awareness of your present experience. While your present experience includes your thoughts and emotions, it can be quite difficult to realize those thoughts and emotions are happening right here, right now. It's certainly possible (see Chapters 5 and 6), but you're likely to get drawn into the *content* of mental phenomena, which point to the past, future, or somewhere other than where you are.

With awareness of the body, this tendency to get drawn away from the present moment isn't a problem. Of course, your attention will still tend to drift away from awareness of the body, and from the present moment, but it's generally not because of any distraction the body itself provides. If you're able to keep your mind on basic physical sensations and experiences, you can taste the clear seeing of mindfulness principle #5, and the stillness and silence of principle #11 (see Chapter 3). While mindfulness of the body is a practice for beginners, it's also a complete practice in that it can allow you to fully realize all 12 of the mindfulness principles.

Body and Mind Are One

The direct experience we are aiming for in mindfulness always involves the body. Even if the only thing you're doing is sitting still in meditation, direct experience is fully embodied. This is the reality of your life. Of course, this doesn't mean your physical manifestation is *more real* than your mind, or that you should ignore your thoughts and emotions! That mindset just subscribes to the old body-versus-mind dualism. Body and mind are one functioning organism.

In order to directly experience your life, body and mind have to be in the same place, at the same time. Obviously, your brain never leaves your body, so in a sense your mind (the complex functioning of that brain, including the flow and processing of information) is never literally apart from your body. You are no doubt intimately familiar, however, with how the focus of the mind can be very far away from the body.

 MINDFUL EXERCISE

Either keep the body still or engage in a very simple physical task. Make an effort to keep your attention in the present, focused on what is happening right now. When you realize your mind has wandered, take special note of where it went. Did it leap to something you're anticipating? Did it return to something troubling or exciting that recently happened? Did it start abstractly analyzing what mindfulness is, or how well you're doing it? Just observing this process can tell you a great deal about how your mind works, and what you're concerned about. A big part of learning mindfulness is learning how your own mind operates.

I used to resist choosing mindfulness over mind wandering. It seemed to me keeping my mind present in my body was just choosing one kind of mental experience over another, and frankly, I preferred the endlessly fascinating content of my thoughts. "Why should I choose a mindful experience of drinking my tea over thinking about my next project?" I wondered. Sure, mindfully drinking your tea is nice. It lets you appreciate the taste and all the other sensations, which you would probably otherwise not even notice. But why forgo all the thinking in favor of a bunch of very simple, mundane experiences?

Over time, I have come to realize the most responsible and profound action we can take on behalf of the world is to be fully awake in our lives. Being fully awake means experiencing your life with both body and mind, and not walking around on autopilot while your mind amuses itself with stimulus-independent thoughts and concerns. When you meet a loved one with body and mind together, you truly meet them. When you respond to needs with body and mind together, your best response arises naturally. When you contemplate a project with both body and mind, your true potential is realized.

You can recognize people who are unified in body and mind. It may be difficult to describe how you can tell, but they seem present. They generally manifest a basic calm and dignity no matter what they are doing. They seem to know who they are. They respond honestly and spontaneously. They know when they don't know something, and take responsibility for their lives. Who would have thought this could be achieved simply by making sure your body and mind were in the same place? Of course, doing that is not necessarily easy.

Tuning in to the Body

As described in Chapter 3, attention is deliberately focusing your mind on something, while awareness is an unfocused but receptive state. Eventually, you will want the ability to maintain awareness of the body as you go about your daily life, but in order to get there you work on paying attention to physical sensations and experiences.

Training yourself to pay attention at will can be difficult. You naturally pay attention to things that interest you—things that are fascinating, entertaining, or of personal concern. In fact, there are probably at least a few things you find so engrossing that your attention stays glued to them to the exclusion of everything else! Perhaps it's video games, cooking, playing a sport, or bird watching. You might do these things for hours and forget about all the other things you're supposed to do.

Tuning in to the body in a mindful way is unlikely to be something you find quite as fascinating as your favorite pastimes. However, it's possible to train yourself to pay just as close attention to physical sensations and experiences as you do to those things that naturally interest you. The more often you bring your mind back to the body, and the longer you're able to keep the mind and body unified, the more interesting the experience becomes. It takes time and effort, but eventually it becomes its own reward, as stated in mindfulness principle #12 (see Chapter 3).

Attention to Breathing

Many people find that returning to the sensations of the breath for even just a couple of inhalations and exhalations helps them feel calmer. The breath is always available for this practice, and often it can tell you something about your mental and emotional state. Sometimes, as you pay attention to breathing, you notice the breath feels constrained because of tightness in your chest or abdomen. At other times, the outbreath turns into a sigh. In your mindfulness practice, you simply notice these things without jumping into an analysis of them. (Analysis quickly takes you out of the present moment again.)

In the simplest kind of mindful breathing, you do not try to change the pattern of your breathing at all. Instead, you simply notice the sensations of breathing. You are aware you're breathing (something you usually don't even notice), and you pay attention to the state of the breath at each moment: "This moment I'm breathing in, this moment I'm breathing out. Breathing in a shallow breath, breathing out a shallow breath. Breathing in a deep breath, breathing out a deep breath."

If you want to strengthen or deepen the practice of mindful breathing, it helps to keep the body still and minimize the distractions around you. To give yourself something to do, and get some feedback on your concentration, you can count your exhalations from 1 to 10 and then start again at 1. When you notice your mind has wandered, you let go of any judgment about that fact and simply return to one again. Doing this for a prolonged period can settle the mind in a deep way. However, if you find counting agitates the mind, try expanding your awareness to everything around you and simply holding your breath at your center in a physical way.

KEEP IN MIND

In Buddhism, mindfulness starts with the deceptively simple practice of following the breath. For thousands of years, Buddhists have treasured the instructions from the Satipatthana Sutta: "when [a practitioner] breathes in a long breath, he knows, 'I am breathing in a long breath,' and when he breathes in a short breath knows, 'I am breathing in a short breath' ... He uses the following practice: 'Breathing in, I am aware of my whole body. Breathing out, I am aware of my whole body. Breathing in, I calm my body. Breathing out, I calm my body.'" (From *Transformation and Healing: Sutra on the Four Establishments of Mindfulness*, by Thich Nhat Hanh)

There is no limit to how deeply and intimately you can pay attention to breathing. You can work on keeping the attention on the breath continuously—following the exhalation to its end, noting the pause before the inhalation, staying aware of the inhalation the entire time, and noting the pause before the next exhalation. When you do this, you become aware of how your breath is, in a sense, your life itself. In even deeper states of mindful breathing, there is no longer any separation between you and your breathing. Instead, there is only breathing. This invites you to consider what it would be like if there were no separation between you and your life at other times.

Attention to Position of the Body

One of the most accessible and useful forms of body awareness after attention to the breath is *proprioception*, or awareness of your body's overall position, movement, and acceleration. You can be aware you're sitting up, lying down, walking, or running. You know which leg is on top of the other, and can sense whether you're slouched over or sitting up straight. Turning your attention to proprioception can be very grounding.

It's important not to add an agenda of good posture to this kind of mindfulness of the body, or your attention will linger only momentarily on the body before it gets distracted by an ideal and an evaluation of whether you fulfill it. If you realize you're slouching, you can change your posture if you like, but try to do it only after really checking in with the reality of your body position first.

If your sense of any of the different objects of mindfulness becomes slack or static, your mind is likely to wander. Fortunately, there are many ways to keep a sense of energy and movement in your effort to maintain awareness. Mindfulness of the breath can be coupled with awareness of body position in order to give you something moving (your chest as you inhale and exhale) to hold your attention. Alternatively, you might try to generate and keep a sense of energy flowing throughout the body, or imagine a process of relaxing the body more and more. Use any technique that keeps you engaged in awareness of the body in the present moment.

Attention to Sensation

You can feel sensations inside the body (*interoception*) as well as those arising from contact with things outside the body (*exteroception*). You probably pay lots of attention to sensations, but rarely in a sustained way. Your mind tends to immediately identify, evaluate, and decide how to react to every sensation. You take brief note of a pang of hunger before thinking of when you're going to eat dinner. For a split second you enjoy the taste of a chocolate before thinking, "This is delicious! I'll have another!" As soon as you hear a sound, you decide whether it's relevant to you. If it's not, you tune it out; if it is, you listen while anticipating how to respond.

 **DEFINITION**

Proprioception is awareness of your body's overall position, movement, and acceleration. **Interoception** is awareness of sensations inside your body, such as pain or hunger. **Exteroception** is awareness of the world outside your body. All of these kinds of perception can serve as objects for mindfulness practice.

Mindful attention to sensations requires you to take the time to experience the sensations in and of themselves, before you interpret, label, or react to them. This can be a very fascinating practice! If you turn your attention toward one sensation, let's say the cold in your hands, you're likely to notice other sensations, like the relative warmth in your wrists, or the light sensation of touch in your fingertips as they rest on your computer keyboard. You can explore the sensation of cold. What is it? Is it pain? Is it constant, or does it throb? Is it inside your hands or outside?

One of the classic sensations used for meditation and mindfulness practice is sound. Even in the quietest of places you can hear some sound, even if it just the "ringing" of the silence in your ears. You can attend to sounds for a few moments at a time in order to relieve stress, or you can work on holding your attention on listening for longer periods. To deepen the practice, you can pay attention to the ever-changing texture and tone of the sounds you hear. If your thinking mind is very still, you can experiment with "perceiving the sounds with other senses" (exploring how the whole body-mind is involved in the experience), or trying to locate awareness within you. (You can't.)

Sights, sounds, smells, tastes, and touches are much more complex and unbounded experiences than you may realize. If you can sense them directly without thinking about them or categorizing them, even briefly, you're practicing mindfulness. Not only will you notice more, you will also learn that sensation does not necessarily need to be analyzed or acted upon. Hardly any of the sensations you feel are informing you of immediate danger! Noticing this fact can be very helpful in learning to tolerate annoying or unpleasant sources of stimulation when you need to do so.

The Body in Motion

Generally speaking, the more you physically move, the harder it is to maintain mindfulness. As long as you're very still, you can concentrate hard on trying to remember to stay present (and it's still not easy). As soon as you start to move, your mind usually figures it's time to get busy.

The possible exception to this is when you engage in a physical activity that requires all of your energy and skill, such as a challenging tennis game, playing a musical instrument, or rock climbing. To truly succeed at these kinds of activities, you can't let your mind wander—so mind and body are unified. In a sense this is natural mindfulness, which is one reason why such activities are very attractive to people.

The practice of mindfulness aims at being able to be fully present at will, not just when you're doing something that demands your full attention. However, you can learn something by investigating your experience when you're engaged in such an activity. Chances are you feel energized in mind and body. There is a wholeheartedness to your movements. Your responses have to arise in you before you think them through, so your ordinary thinking mind is bypassed. In fact, if thinking gets in the way, you're likely to make a mistake or not function at your best.

Physical Awareness During Simple Tasks

In mindfulness practice, you attempt to be similarly present, wholehearted, and free of stimulus-independent thinking while doing simpler, less demanding tasks. Remember, this is when your brain is likely to check out. The task doesn't demand your full mind-bandwidth, so you're likely to use the extra brain power to daydream, ruminate, or plan. "Oh," your mind thinks, "we're just doing the dishes. *Boring.* Let's think about something else."

It may not seem that important to pay attention to a simple task like washing the dishes, but as Zen teacher Thich Nhat Hanh writes, "If we can't wash the dishes, the chances are we won't be able to drink our tea either. While drinking the cup of tea, we will only be thinking of other things, barely aware of the cup in our hands. Thus we are sucked away into the future—and we are incapable of actually living one minute of life."

 MINDFUL EXERCISE

Pick a simple, mostly physical task like cleaning, gardening, cooking, or fixing something. Set a period of time during which you want to practice mindfulness—10 minutes, 20 minutes, or as long as the task takes. During this time, as much as possible, try to keep your attention on the movements of your hands, or on the position and movement of your body. Or, if it works better for you, try to maintain such an open awareness that you notice every smell, visual texture, and touch. When your mind wanders, gently return it to the task with a minimum of fuss. Return to the present over and over, reminding yourself you want to appreciate each moment of your life.

Like most people, you may find your attention wanders away from simple tasks over and over. You may even find you entirely forget your intention to be mindful during the task until later in the day! Mindfulness is so different from your habitual mode of operating that it will take a long period of diligent effort—perhaps months or even years—before you see a noticeable change in your ability to be mindful. If this is the case, try not to lose hope! The mere intention to be more present in your life begins to change things, and if you can strengthen that intention, it will definitely have an effect.

It may help you to keep your mind on a simple task if you come up with something to "do" with your mindfulness as you work. You could decide on a very precise way to cut carrots and then cut them as quickly as possible without getting sloppy. You could try to pull weeds carefully so the roots always come up with the stem.

You could imagine basing your consciousness in your lower abdomen, allowing the physical activity to occur without you directing it, and see how completely you can do this and still complete your task. You could imagine energy flowing out of your hands into whatever they touch—and the more energy that flows, the more effective the action. Pick something that requires you to keep up an effort: more and more, or deeper and deeper, or less and less. This approach can inspire you to put energy and forward momentum into your mindfulness so it doesn't stall with a sense of "that's enough."

Walking Meditation

Putting your full attention on the activity of walking is one of the classic forms of mindfulness practice. It's a great option if you want to work on your concentration but don't want to sit in meditation. (See Chapter 8 for more on meditation.) It can be very calming if you're agitated. The idea is to do this very simple physical activity, which requires the whole body, and to keep the mind as much as possible on the experience—particularly on the sensations on the bottoms of your feet.

Mindful walking is typically either done very slowly, or on a short, repetitive course so you don't have to think about where you're going. You generally don't look around, as that is too distracting. Instead, you keep your eyes on the ground or floor in front of you. You may also want to keep your hands clasped in front of you so your physical movements are fairly contained.

In slow walking, you take one small step with each exhalation. If you like, you can coordinate your entire movement with your breathing: slowly and gradually shifting the weight off your back foot as you inhale, moving the foot, and then gradually shifting your weight onto what is now the front foot until your weight is evenly balanced between your two feet. Then, repeat. Pick two spots to walk between; when you reach one of them, turn around and head back to the other. This is a lovely practice to do outdoors.

Fast walking is the opposite of slow walking in that you want to move very quickly, perhaps as quickly as you can if you have the space to do it. This makes the activity challenging and engaging as you try to keep up the pace and still maintain awareness of the physical sensations of walking. It's good to pick a longer course, or a circuit, for fast mindful walking. It can also be done on a path. From the outside, it may appear that you're merely doing an energetic hike, but internally you're working to let go of mind wandering and focus on being completely receptive to the here and now.

Mindful Body Practice

You can also combine mindfulness practice with a body practice like yoga, tai chi, running, or weight lifting. As with the practices already described in this chapter, the goal in a mindful body practice is to stay in the present instead of indulging in stimulus-independent thinking. If you already have a body practice, you may or may not already do it mindfully. If you do, congratulations! You already have some experience with mindfulness.

Chances are good, though, that unless you're learning a new position or move, or you're really striving to achieve a new level of skill or ability, your brain isn't totally occupied by your physical activity. You can think about all kinds of things while doing a body practice if you want to (depending on the practice, of course). You may just view your activity as physical exercise for the body, and you may never have used it as an opportunity for mindfulness practice. If you aren't used to it, it will probably seem strange to work out without listening to music, reading a book, carrying on a conversation, daydreaming, or otherwise using up your spare brain bandwidth.

 TAKE CARE

If you have decided to work on mindfulness during a particular activity or time of day, try not to get frustrated if it seems like it's nearly impossible to keep your mind on what you're doing for more than a few seconds at a time. Many people find this to be the case at first. It might help to set smaller goals for yourself. Decide you're going to really give mindfulness your best effort for a certain period of time—10, 20, or 30 minutes. Or see if you can slightly lengthen the time you're present. Three breaths? Four? Perhaps for the duration of an entire short activity?

Deliberately being mindful during your body practice isn't just an opportunity to work on mindfulness; it's also a great way to get positive reinforcement for how satisfying and effective it is to have body and mind operating together in the same place, at the same time. When you really pay attention while moving, you'll probably notice a difference in all kinds of aspects of your physical practice, including improved balance, endurance, and strength.

Awareness of the Body as a Body

There are two other benefits to cultivating awareness of the body: 1) learning to treat it better; and 2) getting more comfortable with having one. As you make a practice of tuning in to the body, you notice more about it. You notice how you feel about it, how concerned you are about its comfort, and how you're inclined to set it about achieving the goals set out by the mind.

Given our language, even in this discussion so far I'm referring to your body as something other than "you." Of course, it's not, but it often feels that way, particularly when your body isn't how you would like it to be. When the body is too fat, too weak, too ugly, ill, in pain, aging, or dying, it can feel more like an adversary or burden than an inseparable part of who you are.

Simple mindfulness of the body—awareness of posture, movement, and sensation—in a mindfully receptive mode means you pay attention to it without the usual cloud of judgments and ideas that arise when you worry about your physical well-being. In this present moment, there is only the physical experience. In the direct experience, there is a simplicity and cleanness that can make things much more acceptable and manageable.

Treating the Body Better

The first step toward treating the body better is noticing what it needs and doesn't need. This can be very difficult. You may tend to ignore or altogether miss your physical sensations. This may make you forge on ahead even though what you're doing is taking a physical toll, or may delay your recognition that you're exhausted, ill, or hurting yourself until considerable damage has already been done. Alternatively, you may be so fixated on your physical safety and comfort that you can't differentiate between a real physical need and something that's just a desire.

If you're someone who tends to ignore or miss what your body needs, try doing a body scan when you think you might need to check in with what's going on for you physically. Get into a comfortable position, seated or lying down, and take a few deep breaths. Start by placing your awareness on the top of your head. Slowly move your awareness down through the head, touching all its parts on the way—eyes, ears, nose, scalp …. Pass the awareness over everything, inside and out.

Continue down through the neck and the rest of the body, moving on to a new part whenever the mind wanders. You can listen to guided meditation 1 that accompanies this book to walk you through the process. Take note of any places where you feel tension or pain. You don't need to evaluate or explain any of it during the meditation, just take note of it. Chances are the reasons and remedies for most of your pain or tension will become obvious over time—as long as you notice and acknowledge them first.

Identifying Real Physical Needs

If you're someone who tends to be overly concerned about your physical sensations—to the point that you can't stand the slightest draft, or pang of hunger, or risk of slight injury—you can gain some perspective on your physical well-being by attending to your sensations with mindfulness. This means just experiencing them for what they are, and *momentarily* letting go of your fears of what damage or physical suffering *might* happen to you if you don't react to the sensations immediately.

I remember being on the verge of an eating disorder when I started practicing mindfulness. I noticed that at the slightest hunger pang—or even anticipation of such a pang when the clock told me it had been a couple of hours since I had eaten—I was overwhelmed by thoughts about food and anxiety about deprivation. Ironically, I had brought this on myself by dieting. It took many months of mindfulness practice before I was able to endure the sensations of mild hunger without this overreaction. It then took over a year before I could eat more slowly and mindfully, with less anxiety, and subsequently notice the subtle physical signs of being sated *before* I had eaten so much that they were masked by the feeling of being overfull.

 KEEP IN MIND

In many spiritual traditions, including Buddhism, there is emphasis on not being too attached to the body. All this means is that if you want to achieve greater happiness in your life, it's a good idea to do so in ways that do not depend on your health, physical attractiveness, or the pleasure that can be obtained through the body. These can all be sources of joy, but the body is fragile and subject to change. Still, anything you do depends on the body—so your happiness naturally involves taking good care of it.

You can not only survive but even thrive through many of your physical sensations of discomfort. Mindful attention to the feelings of being mildly cold, hot, hungry, fatigued, or in minor pain can let you experience these things with more equanimity. Uncomfortable sensations become just another interesting part of the landscape of your present moment. When conditions get bad enough that you need to take care of yourself, you'll know.

Getting Comfortable with Embodiment

In the old Buddhist text on mindfulness, the Satipatthana Sutta, the next exercises that focus on the body have to do with contemplating its composition and death. They include calling to mind, one by one, all the different parts of the body, inside and out, including the skin, bones, organs, and substances like blood and sweat. A monk is then advised to compare his own body to a corpse in various stages of decay, all the way to a collection of bones and then dust.

These meditations may seem unpleasant or extreme, but they can help reveal to you where you're still uncomfortable with being in a physical body. When you see, feel, or contemplate a certain part of your body and feel judgment, revulsion, or worry, this is very useful to note. Can you let go of these reactions (which have to do with the present, past, or comparisons) and tap into a simple, receptive awareness of your body? When you're troubled by seeing yourself or someone else growing old, getting sick, or dying, try to turn toward your discomfort instead of away. Can you simply observe such inevitable processes, and perhaps even notice how much can be learned from them?

Sometimes it seems better to try to hold on to physical attractiveness or youth any way you can, and avoid thinking about how fragile your body is, or about how you will inevitably grow old, get ill, and die. However, at some level you know this is going to happen, so it can actually be a relief to increase your comfort with these realities by working on mindfulness of the less pleasant or beautiful aspects of embodiment. A body appreciated in a mindful way—directly experienced in the present, without evaluation or commentary—is an amazing gift that makes living possible.

The Least You Need to Know

- Body-based awareness is the fundamental mindfulness practice—great for beginners, but indispensable no matter how long you've been at it.
- Even in other kinds of mindfulness training, you try to keep body and mind in the same place—so in a way, physical awareness is always involved.
- Exercises in body mindfulness include paying attention to breathing, posture, movement, and sensations.
- Whether sitting, standing, walking, lying down, or engaged in a physical activity, what makes it mindful is keeping your attention on the here and now instead of letting your mind wander.
- Cultivating a receptive awareness of your body can also help with things like aversion to discomfort, negative body image, anxiety about pain and illness, and fear of aging and death.

Awareness of Your Feelings

Feelings are your immediate emotional responses to the things you encounter, or to your own thoughts or actions. They tell you whether you like something, dislike it, or feel neutral about it. If you tend to give your feelings lots of weight, they obviously have a significant effect on your life. If you tend to dismiss your feelings, you probably find they end up having an effect on your life anyway—when you're unconsciously influenced by them, or when suppressed feelings manifest in physical or emotional problems.

In this chapter I explain how to cultivate more awareness of your feelings, and how developing a mindful awareness of your feelings allows you to see them more clearly. Mindfulness also gives you some freedom of choice around how to respond to your feelings, because receptive observation of them means you fully acknowledge them and take enough time to understand them. This process requires you to refrain from automatically believing your feelings reflect some kind of fundamental truth about you or your circumstances that you therefore need to act on.

In This Chapter

- A mindful view of feelings
- Learning to watch feelings arise and pass away
- Acknowledging feelings but not letting them control you
- Studying emotional reactions mindfully
- Gaining relief from troubling feelings

Feelings Versus Emotions

The way I define *feelings* in this chapter reflects the Buddhist way of looking at them. Feelings are your immediate responses to stimuli and come in three flavors: like, dislike, or neutral. Feelings in this sense are distinct from *emotions*, which are more complex emotional experiences that include thoughts and memories.

The distinction between feelings and emotions is very useful when you're practicing mindfulness. Feelings are much simpler, and arise very quickly. In the moment, there is little you can do about what feelings arise in response to something. Emotions, on the other hand, generally have more of a narrative associated with them, and often invite you to nurture that story or argue with it. Emotions require some involvement from your mind, and can persist for a long time.

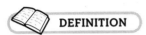 **DEFINITION**

> **Feelings** are your immediate emotional response to stimuli, including external things as well as your own thoughts and actions. Feelings fall into three categories: like, dislike, and neutral. They usually arise before conscious thoughts. **Emotions**, on the other hand, are more complex experiences that involve thoughts, memories, and narratives.

Of course, there is no clear line between a feeling you dwell on for a while, and a subsequent fully developed emotion. It's more like a continuum. There are lots of experiences that are usually identified as emotions that can actually begin as feelings, arising in a very immediate way in the moment. These include unpleasant feelings such as anger, fear, resentment, annoyance, or sadness, as well as positive feelings like appreciation or joy. These feelings develop into emotions when you engage or identify with them. (Not that this is a negative thing; it's just different.)

Here's an example of how feelings and emotions differ: let's say your child throws his breakfast on the floor and you feel an almost instantaneous experience of annoyance. This is a feeling that says, "Dislike!" As you pick up the food from the floor and think about how you've tried to stop your child's behavior again and again, and how you're busy and tired and don't have time for this nonsense, the feeling develops into emotions like anger, resentment, or a sense of inadequacy or being overwhelmed. You might feel that emotion for hours—long after the initial feeling of dislike was triggered by your child's breakfast ending up on the floor.

Paying attention to feelings as they arise in the moment is the second fundamental mindfulness practice, after cultivating awareness of the body and physical sensations. You can certainly practice mindfulness of emotions (see Chapter 14), but it's much more difficult because emotions tend to be so complex. Feelings, on the other hand, arise as a present-moment experience without reference to the past, future, or abstract concepts. They are easier to observe in the nonjudgmental, receptive space of mindfulness.

The Nature of Feelings

As discussed in Chapter 2, your body-mind evolved to protect you and look out for your best interests. Your feelings are the results of your initial judgment about whether something is useful, dangerous, or irrelevant to your well-being. Of course, most of your feelings aren't about things that are critical to your survival, but you're wired to evaluate just about everything you encounter: "What does this mean to *me?*"

Feelings usually arise before any intellectual decision about what you think of something. They are partly based in body memory, and are heavily influenced by experience, conditioning, and personality. Sometimes you don't know why you react emotionally to something the way you do, and you may have a different feeling-reaction than someone else in response to the same experience. Perhaps for some reason you can't stand organ music, traffic, or olives, but you love flute music, political podcasts, and dogs. Some of your preferences you can explain, but others you can't.

The Problem with Feelings

Most of your feelings may not matter much in the grand scheme of your life, but the problem is you probably give them more weight than you need to because you believe your feelings are *right* in some way. If you feel aversion to something, you'd better avoid it, right? If you really like something, you'd better try to get more of it. If you feel neutral about something, it's not worth your attention.

Because humans are naturally very concerned about themselves, they often don't bother to question their feelings but instead take them at face value. If you do this, you probably let your feelings dictate your decisions at times when more objectivity would be beneficial. You probably also let your unpleasant feelings cause you stress or suffering in the unfortunate situations where you can't get away from something you dislike, or can't get something you like. When you believe your feelings of dislike reflect reality, you're also more likely to dwell on them and build them up into persistent negative emotional states.

 KEEP IN MIND

It may help to change the way you talk and think about your feelings. If you stop saying, "I *am* angry," and instead say, "I am feeling some anger right now," it may be easier to cultivate mindful awareness of your feelings. By thinking or speaking different words, you acknowledge your feeling is just part of your experience, and that it will inevitably change or pass away.

Another problem with feelings is that it's easy to become identified with them. As children turn into teenagers and develop a more complex sense of self, one of the primary ways they define themselves is through their preferences. You probably did this, too, transforming a simple experience ("I like spicy food") into an identity ("I'm someone who likes spicy food"). This may not be a big deal when you're identifying with food preferences, but it can get you into trouble if you decide you're someone who can't stand academic work (and therefore shouldn't go to college), has a bad temper (so there's nothing you can do about your angry reactions to things), or hates your mother (so there's no point in working on your relationship with her).

There may also be feeling-reactions you wish didn't happen for you. Perhaps you get irritated at small things, impatient with loved ones, or repulsed by people when they are ill. These feelings end up being a problem because you feel guilty about them or struggle against them. Chances are when you experience a petty or less-than-noble feeling, you're triggered into an internal monologue about how you *shouldn't* feel that way. As you've probably discovered, these monologues are rarely effective at preventing feelings.

Feelings Just Arise

Actually, feelings themselves aren't a problem. They are just a response of your body-mind, like salivating when you eat, smiling back when someone smiles at you, or identifying the sound you hear as a dog barking. A particular feeling is simply information about how your body-mind perceives something—and your perceptions aren't always correct!

A classic example of a feeling arising in response to a misperception is the man who wakes up in the night and steps on a rope on his way to the bathroom. A strong feeling-reaction of fear arises in him as he thinks for a moment that he has stepped on a snake. When he looks down and realizes it's just a rope, the feeling disappears. Stress hormones may continue to course through his veins for a little while, but his startle response is quickly dismissed as a mistake.

In everyday life it's much more difficult to recognize whether or not your feeling is legitimate. Most situations are more complex than mistaking a rope for a snake. For example, when a strong negative feeling occurs in you because your boss seems to be implying you were neglectful in your work (and you weren't), are you right to feel the way you do? Perhaps you ask your boss and clarify, but chances are good you feel defensive and then look for ways to justify your feelings.

Working with Feelings

An alternative approach is to use mindfulness simply to note that you're feeling something. You can attend to the feeling in the present moment, and see whether the feeling is like, dislike, or neutrality. In the Buddhist text on mindfulness it recommends that you think, "I am experiencing a pleasant/unpleasant/neutral feeling," or, "There is feeling here." Then, with receptive aware-ness, you can investigate the feeling further and observe as objectively as possible what percep-tions it's based on.

Letting Feelings Pass

If you neither grasp nor push away the feeling, it will usually pass or change all on its own. This is the remarkable thing about mindfulness. It's kind of like you hold your mind still instead of dancing around with your feelings. This holding still is not a rejection of feeling, because that's just another kind of dancing around. Instead, the stillness of mindful observation lets you see the whole situation more clearly. Perhaps you're feeling something *very* strongly, and perhaps some action really needs to be taken. Mindfulness can help you see this is the case, and set you up to respond in the best way you can.

> **MINDFUL EXERCISE**
>
> The next time you find yourself feeling an unpleasant response to something—such as irritation, aversion, impatience, or frustration—turn toward your response with mindful awareness. Simply note what you're feeling, and say to yourself silently, "I am feeling (whatever it is you're feeling)." Don't judge your response or try to change it. Then explore a little further. How strong is the feeling? Where does it manifest in your body? Ask your feeling what it's about, without worrying about whether or not the feeling is justified. Don't suppress the feeling, but notice at some future point when you realize you've forgotten all about it in the interim.

It isn't necessary to hold on to a feeling in order to learn whether it has anything important to tell you. In the previous example where your boss may be judging you unfairly, you can notice your feeling—perhaps resentment, anger, or shame—and realize your body-mind feels threatened in some way. Okay, that's good information. However, it may or may not be true. Maybe your boss didn't even mean to imply you were neglectful, or maybe you forgot to file the report that would have shown him how hard you worked.

Letting Feelings Be

If you can mindfully observe your feeling-reaction, you're much more likely to be able to see it as just one part of a whole unfolding scenario, instead of becoming completely wrapped up in it. With this little bit of perspective, you can see more clearly, stay calmer, and make better deci-sions. In the example we've been using, you may be able to ask your boss, in a tone of voice that is neither defensive nor apologetic, what he or she thinks you did or didn't do. Chances are good this will be much more effective than speaking in anger, or stewing in silent resentment.

You may think maintaining equanimity or responding calmly is something people can only do if they don't experience strong feelings. Fortunately, this is not the case. You may experience a powerful emotional response of anger, for example, but if you pause for a moment to take a couple of deep breaths and do the mindfulness exercise, "I am feeling anger right now," you'll already have taken a step back from your feelings. You can gain some sense that you aren't defined by, or bound to act out, your anger, and recognize it's just something you're experiencing.

On the other hand, you may be someone who tends to ignore your feelings, or perhaps misses them altogether. Perhaps you've learned to mistrust emotions, or, because so many feelings are negative, paying attention to them seems pointless or indulgent. This approach has its strengths, but it can deaden your emotional life or encourage you to suppress feelings (which is when you make yourself stop feeling them instead of letting them pass on their own). Mindfulness can help you acknowledge and accept your feelings without requiring you to let them control your life. You can just let them be.

Looking More Closely at How You Feel

Feelings can be uncomfortable. This is obvious in the case of negative ones, but even positive ones can make you feel a little giddy, confused, or vulnerable. Strong attraction to another person may be disturbing, a surge of inspiration can make you worry about the possibility it will disappear, and being deeply moved can make you tearful or speechless.

Some people are addicted to feelings in general and focus intently on how they feel at every moment, but most of us have a more ambivalent relationship to our emotional responses. You may pay attention to some feelings but not others—particularly looking away from the painful ones, or the ones you're embarrassed to feel. It may help to keep in mind the feelings are there, whether you like them or not. You may dismiss, suppress, or distract yourself from them, but at some level they affect your thinking, actions, and stress level. It's better to have them in front of you, out in the open, where you can keep an eye on them and maybe even deal with them!

Not Censoring

If you're going to be more mindful of your feelings, it's essential not to censor them. If you're like most people, you do this a lot. As a small child you burst into tears when faced with disappointment and whined when you didn't get what you wanted. Then you were socialized to understand that the older you got, the less acceptable certain feelings were. Note: not only did you learn not to express or act out certain feelings, you learned *you weren't supposed to have them*. That is, not if you were mature, self-sufficient, unselfish, and worthy of respect.

 **TAKE CARE**

Looking more closely at feelings, or suggesting they "just arise" and you don't have to identify with them, may seem to suggest you should dissociate from them. Be careful not to do this, as if feelings have nothing to do with you. They do and they don't. What's important is to notice what would be most useful for you: gaining some perspective on your feelings because they tend to overwhelm you, or noticing and acknowledging them because you tend to push them away?

Of course, as adults we still have all kinds of emotional responses that are immature and selfish. As mentioned earlier, feelings are your body-mind's initial judgment about whether something is beneficial, harmful, or irrelevant to your well-being. This isn't to say you don't have compassionate or generous feelings, but most of them probably aren't. Unless you tell me, I'll probably assume your feelings are fairly noble or at least neutral, but I know what mine are: a desire to avoid someone panhandling for money, anger when I see someone has eaten the last cookie, and annoyance because there are other people walking on the sidewalk and I have to move to one side.

Many of our feelings are petty, selfish, negative, needy, judgmental, and irrational, so it can be pretty ugly when we start to look more closely at them. In order to see them clearly, you need to generate some courage and some willingness to bear the discomfort of experiencing feelings directly. As mindfulness principle #10 suggests (see Chapter 3), you're unlikely to be able to look at your feelings honestly as long as you fear or reject any of them.

Fortunately, with mindfulness you can learn to watch such feelings arise pretty much automatically in response to things, and realize you don't have much to do with them. They just happen and don't define who you really are. You can also watch the feelings pass without acting on them, which allows you to feel freer of them. Rather than thinking, "I am a mean, selfish, pathetic person," you can think, "Sometimes I have mean, selfish, pathetic feelings." There's a big difference.

What Was the Trigger?

There's a great deal to be learned by paying attention to what triggered a particular feeling. Again, this is done with mindfulness: cultivating receptive awareness of the trigger in the present (or very recent) moment. The purpose is to see clearly what is going on (mindfulness principles #4 and #5, Chapter 3), and you do this by dropping below the level of ordinary thinking in order to experience things directly.

For example, let's say you're in a meeting and you feel a strong aversion arise in you as someone begins speaking. Typically, without mindfulness, you might subsequently think, "That person is such a creep." You're inclined to believe your feeling reflects a reality, and so if you're feeling aversion it must be because that person is a creep. Therefore, your feeling was triggered by that person's creepiness. Subsequent meetings with this person are bound to be annoying, and should you end up having to work closely with the person, her creepiness could be a real problem.

Observing your aversion with mindfulness is different. You note, "As this person started speaking, I starting feeling aversion." To maintain receptive awareness, you don't leap into justification of your feeling, but you also don't dismiss it. ("I shouldn't feel aversion for this person.") Instead, you try to open your awareness even more—to become even more receptive. What is it about this person that is triggering your aversion? Is it a memory of past interactions with her? Is it her clothing, which suggests she has lots of money, and therefore suggests she might be arrogant about that fact? Is it her tone of voice, which makes her sound as if she's a know-it-all?

What's Behind the Feeling?

Just being able to see more clearly what triggered your feeling, you're likely to be able to see more clearly all the things—assumptions, memories, beliefs—behind the feeling-reaction you experienced. Again, to see all of this with mindfulness, you need to suspend judgment and just look. Your tendency will probably be to notice one thing that seems either right or wrong, and then run with it. If you discover a poor assumption, you may jump into arguing against your feeling. If you discover a dearly-held value, you may jump back into justification for your feeling.

KEEP IN MIND

Mindfulness principle #9 is, "The first step to learning something new is admitting you don't know." When you take your feelings at face value, you usually assume you know what they're about. They're *your* feelings, after all! However, if certain feelings are causing you problems or stress, a fresh, open-minded approach may be necessary. Maybe you don't yet see a feeling and its causes clearly. If you're lucky, you can learn something new that will help the feeling shift.

To continue with mindfulness in the example I have been using, if you noticed you were reacting to the person's know-it-all tone of voice, you would try to look more carefully at that. You might turn your attention to your breath for a few moments in order to keep yourself in the present reality instead of in abstractions. After all, *what's behind your feeling is in the present,* even if it has its roots in the past! You listen to the supposed know-it-all and experience directly your feeling-reactions.

Perhaps, as you listen, you recognize that a feeling of being offended arises in you because if this person thinks he knows it all, he thinks you *don't* know it. Presumably, you disagree! But then you might realize that although this person's tone is annoying, you don't actually really care what he thinks of you. Just seeing things more clearly, as suggested in mindfulness principle #3 (see Chapter 3), may give you some relief from your feeling of aversion for the person in question. Nothing about the person has changed, but he might cause you less distress.

Reliving Experiences with Mindfulness

Sometimes you don't have a chance to investigate feeling-reactions until after the fact. There may be too many things going on in the situation in which they were triggered to have the space to look more closely at them. Or you may have gotten caught up in strong or compelling feelings and forgotten to be mindful. It may seem counterintuitive that you can practice mindfulness retroactively, but fortunately it's possible. It's not as effective as being able to maintain mindfulness as a situation unfolds, but it can still let you see things more clearly.

If you have a feeling-reaction you would like to understand better, you can take some time when you have no distractions to review a past event. You try to recall your actual experience of the event—your physical actions, feelings, and thoughts. What happened? What triggered what? Can you look more closely at what was behind your feeling? What really happened?

This is very different from the usual way you think about past events in the abstract. Typically such recollection involves a narrative about what unfolded, who was right, who was wrong, and whether or not you liked the situation. In mindful recollection you try as best you can to relive the scenario, with your mind open to noticing new aspects of the events.

The Significance of Neutral Feelings

So far I haven't said much about neutral feelings. They tend to get lost in the mix; feelings of like and dislike naturally seem more interesting or troublesome. However, most of our feelings are neutral, and this turns out to be very interesting *and* troublesome.

The thing is, having a "neutral" feeling about something is not the same thing as mindful awareness of it that simply refrains from deciding whether it's good or bad, pleasant or unpleasant. Instead, a neutral feeling involves deciding something is of no importance to you. Remember how feelings are your body-mind's initial evaluation of whether something is beneficial, threatening, or irrelevant to your well-being? When you feel something is irrelevant, you tend to tune it out. Only things you like or dislike are worthy of your attention—so you can move toward what you like and away from what you don't.

Is it really the case that most of what you encounter or experience over the course of your day is unimportant? If this is the case, most of your life is unimportant, which seems like a sad conclusion. The alternative to a kind of deadened, blank neutrality is mindfulness, which involves maintaining a receptive awareness of the present regardless of how you feel about it.

> **MINDFUL EXERCISE**
>
> The next time you're doing something you feel neutral about—like waiting for a
> doctor's appointment, cleaning the house, or sitting through a rather boring meeting—
> notice what's happening. Chances are your mind is wandering because you're not
> very interested in the activity, but you also aren't particularly averse to it. Notice
> how your mind resists maintaining awareness of the neutral activity. Holding your
> attention on it may actually start to make it seem unpleasant. See if you can notice
> something interesting about the situation, though. People watch, or take note of sights
> and sounds, or play some kind of game like counting how many times someone says,
> "Ah." Anything to keep yourself from dismissing your current experience.

Mindful awareness is energetic, engaged, and generally appreciative. In his 2006 book *Transformation and Healing,* Thich Nhat Hanh suggests practicing mindfulness with neutral feelings can change them into pleasant feelings. He then gives an example of where a father is mindfully aware of sitting in a field with his son, appreciating the sounds and sensations and happy just to be present with his companion. The son, on the other hand, is bored. What the son really feels is that sitting in the field is irrelevant to him—so having to continue to sit there actually becomes uncomfortable, and as soon as he can, he returns home and turns on the TV. So neutral feelings can also turn into unpleasant feelings, depending on whether you choose mindfulness instead.

Influencing Your Emotional Responses Long Term

While it's true that feelings arise quickly, usually before you can do anything about them, that doesn't mean you can't influence what kind of feeling-reactions you have in the long term. To change feeling-reactions takes patience and determination coupled with mindfulness. Basically, you practice mindfulness of feelings as I have been discussing in this chapter. Some shifts in your feelings will happen naturally as a result of seeing them more clearly, but you may also need to make some changes in your life.

Keeping a Lid on It

While it's not a good idea to suppress or deny feelings, if you want to influence the kind of feeling-reaction you have to something, it's a good idea to limit the extent to which you express or act out the feeling you want to change. When you react to your feeling, you tend to lend it a sense of permanence and reality. It also makes it more difficult to maintain mindfulness and see things clearly because you're busy generating more activity, reactions, and feelings.

The classic example of the importance of keeping a lid on feelings (if you want to change them) is working with anger. If you act out your angry feelings by yelling, throwing things, or launching into a vehement argument with someone about how wrong they are, it makes it much more difficult to see your anger clearly. If others are involved, you now probably have to defend your position or deal with their reactions. Even if others aren't involved, you've momentarily acted as if your feeling is justified, and then you have to deal with your own judgments about your acting out (which in retrospect is rarely pretty).

Without suppressing or indulging a feeling like anger, you can try to stay present with it without venting it. This can make it feel difficult to contain, and can make you very uncomfortable until the intensity of the feeling subsides. However, each time you can manage to keep a lid on a feeling that is urging you to act (by losing your temper, bad-mouthing someone, complaining, going shopping when you can't afford it, etc.), your body-mind gets the message that this feeling can be endured and does not have to control you. Usually the feelings end up decreasing in intensity over time as your body-mind learns new alternative ways to be.

Decentering

As discussed in Chapter 1, decentering is becoming less identified with your feelings or emotions. This means that you learn to see them as *part* of your overall experience rather than as the defining aspect. When you can do this, you gain some maneuvering room around emotional experiences like depression, anxiety, and anger, which can sometimes seem to be taking over your life.

In a sense, decentering is about recognizing your feelings aren't *true*. This doesn't mean your feelings are wrong, or that you don't or shouldn't have them. Instead, it simply means that feelings, in and of themselves, aren't right *or* wrong, true *or* false. They are simply your response to something. In a sense they are very real, and denying, arguing with, or trying to invalidate them can actually be harmful. The first step in decentering (as opposed to dissociating) is always mindful awareness and acknowledgment of a feeling.

 TAKE CARE

As you set about trying to influence or change a feeling-reaction, it can be very difficult not to judge or reject the feeling. You'll know you're doing this if you start to feel disgust at the pace of your progress, or despair that you'll ever be able to change. It's natural to feel a little impatient, but the more you can make your peace with the ways things are *right now* (without comparison to others, ideals, or a possible future), the more mindful you'll be able to be as you work with a feeling you would rather not have.

After acknowledging a feeling, however, you can try to maintain a receptive awareness of your whole experience, rather than jumping to the conclusions the feeling invites you to (life stinks, something terrible is going to happen, that person betrayed you). A simple way to do this is to pay attention to how the feeling manifests in your body. How are you breathing? Are you tense? Slouched? Is there a knot in your stomach? This lets you keep the feeling front and center but also keeps your awareness open to other things.

The most important thing to keep your awareness open to is the passage of time. Inevitably, your feeling is going to change. Even if your life is generally characterized by depression or anxiety, you don't feel anxious or depressed every moment. If you can mindfully observe how feelings arise and pass away, how they change, and how they are affected by your circumstances, you can begin to see even powerful or oppressive feelings as part of the shifting landscape of your life. You start to notice other parts of that landscape, including other feelings, and simply by turning your attention there you can gradually influence the kinds of emotional experiences you tend to have.

The Least You Need to Know

- It's useful to differentiate feelings, which arise as spontaneous responses, and emotions, which are more complex experiences that usually include some kind of narrative.
- Mindfulness of feelings involves maintaining a receptive awareness of your responses as they arise and then continuing to stay in the present moment instead of jumping to conclusions or reactions.
- Feelings are information about whether your body-mind perceives something as being beneficial, potentially harmful, or irrelevant to your well-being.
- The perceptions, assumptions, and beliefs behind some of your feelings may be incorrect. Mindful awareness helps you see this more clearly—and may even free you from some troubling feelings.
- It's difficult to change the kinds of feeling-reactions you have because they happen so quickly, but using mindfulness you can influence the kinds of feelings that tend to arise for you over the long term.

Awareness of Your States of Mind

An important object of mindfulness is the state of your own mind. I covered some of this in the previous chapter on awareness of your feelings, but while a mind state may have an emotional tone, it's something very different from your immediate emotional response to something. How is your mind operating? Is it attentive, dull, agitated, calm, scattered, or focused? Do you know if you're being mindful or not?

In this chapter I explain how to recognize mind states and deepen your awareness of them. I describe a number of classic mind states to help you get a sense of what to look for, and discuss how mind states relate to your life and to other objects of mindful awareness.

The main thing to know is that mindfulness of mind states is about cultivating an awareness of *how* your mind is working, not about studying the content of your mind. Content may certainly be relevant to your life, and mindfulness can help you see the content more clearly. However, learning to recognize your state of mind is essential to conducting yourself wisely—and to improving your mindfulness. Unless you pay attention to your mind states, you can't learn how to work with them, and if you don't know how to work with your mind states, it's a little like having a car you don't really know how to drive.

In This Chapter

- What mind states are and aren't
- Becoming more aware of what's happening in your mind
- Various kinds of mind states you may experience
- Learning to look more deeply at your mind
- How to cultivate the mind states you want

Depending on your personality and experience, you may be surprised to find out the degree of variety and subtlety in mind states. Once you start to pay attention to your mind itself, you'll notice at one moment you feel dull and sleepy, while the next you feel refreshed and energized (maybe it's the end of the work day and you have a date). One day your mind is settled and receptive, while the next it feels like you can't concentrate on anything. The crystal clear mind you achieve after a long, energetic hike in the woods is very different from the cramped, stressed mind you had in the middle of your workweek.

Becoming Mindful of Mind

Mind states may briefly become the subject of your attention, but you probably tend to quickly evaluate them and move on, immediately trying to do something about them. If the feeling-reaction to a mind state is "like," you probably focus more on the pleasure than on the state of mind itself. If the feeling-reaction is "dislike," you probably start thinking about a way to alter your circumstances in order to bring about a more desirable state. If you feel neutral about the way your mind is working, there's no motivation to look at it more carefully.

Whenever you practice mindfulness, you need to pause long enough to be able to perceive what is going on in the moment. In the case of mind states, it's not enough to decide whether you like a mind state or not and move on. You have to "turn toward" the mind state, and work on your receptivity. You want to see the state clearly. You want to taste it, spend some time with it. What is its shape and texture?

 MINDFUL EXERCISE

Close your eyes and pay attention to your breathing. What happens to your mind? Does it leap away from the breath, to something you need to get done? Does it get drawn into thinking about something from the past, or drift toward something random that isn't even that important to you? Does it feel sluggish, or does it respond to your intention readily? Is it fairly easy to keep your attention on the breath, or is it a struggle? Do your senses open up to the things going on around you, or does your consciousness stay more or less focused on your own body-mind? Just note your answers to these questions, trying not to judge good or bad, like or dislike.

It may seem strange to contemplate mind with your mind. After all, mindfulness principle #5 states, "To see clearly, you have to drop below the level of ordinary thinking and experience things directly." How do you experience mind directly, without thinking? It can be tricky, but it's possible. The essential thing is to avoid getting caught up in the content of your thinking, and instead become conscious of your whole body-mind at once. There you are, and your mind state is only one part of your experience. There is also your breathing, the sounds you hear, and your feelings.

Remember, what you're trying to do is become more mindful of different kinds of states, not judge them or get rid of them. After practicing mindfulness of mind for a while, you naturally begin to get familiar with how your choices influence your mind states, so it's possible to cultivate more positive or useful ones. If you set off with an agenda of change right away, however, you're liable to interfere with your ability to observe your mind clearly.

Various Mind States to Look For

If you really pay attention to something, you'll start noticing all kinds of things about it—and then you'll need some language to describe what you notice. This is why the Buddhists are really good at describing mind states: they've been studying the subjective experiences of the mind for centuries.

In Western culture we tend to use just a handful of words to describe our mind states, and most of these address our emotional states more than our mind function: good, bad, sad, anxious, depressed, stressed, excited, bored, and fine. Our limited use of vocabulary in this area may reflect the fact that we don't think about mind states much. Psychologists have names for various illnesses and neuroses of mind and personality, but we don't often study the intricacies and aspects of normal mind function. When is the last time you heard someone at the bus stop ask another person, "Is your mind very collected today?"

Because of this, I thought I would explore a number of different mind states, explaining what they are like so you get a sense of the kinds of things you're looking for. Note that while feelings and emotions may cause, come along with, or be caused by states of mind, the states themselves are more or less independent of emotion. For example, your mind could be calm while you're happy, or calm while you're very sad.

You can cultivate awareness of mind states in and of themselves. Awareness of psychophysical factors, covered in Chapter 7, overlaps awareness of mind states somewhat, but has a different focus. Paying attention to a psychophysical factor like desire, for example, is starting to examine the content of your mind. When you're working on awareness of mind states, on the other hand, you try to notice the *way your mind is functioning* in an objective way—rather like examining how a computer is processing information, instead of caring what kind of software is running on it.

Grasping/Aversion or Calm

One of the most common mind states is one dominated by grasping or aversion. Actually, grasping and aversion are just two sides of the same coin: you want something to be other than how it is. There may be something you desire that you're fixated on obtaining, or something you dislike that you're determined to get rid of, but either way it's about what you want.

Grasping and aversion may sound rather extreme or negative, but they really just describe much of your ordinary daily routine of setting goals and planning how to attain them. Perhaps you want to complete a project at work, or stop a leak under your sink. You may be hungry and thinking about what you should eat, or pondering how to get your child to study more in order to do better in school. You identify things you want to have happen, and set out to make them happen.

KEEP IN MIND

It's perfectly natural, and probably unavoidable, that you have preferences about the way things are. These preferences aren't a problem in and of themselves. What starts to generate stress and suffering is when, "It would be nice if such-and-such would happen," becomes, "Such-and-such has to happen, or else." With the second way of looking at things, you've made your happiness (or sense of self-respect) contingent on a particular outcome.

Generally speaking, the more you want something, the more grasping or aversion are going to dominate your mind. When you're just doing your daily tasks, the desire or dislike you experience will probably be quite mild. However, if something seems very critical, or is either extremely attractive or extremely unpleasant, chances are good you'll experience a strong grasping/aversion mind state. You won't be able to think about anything except what you want or don't want.

Grasping/aversion mind is characterized by a fair amount of determination and energy, but also by stress. It has a single-minded focus that can easily lead to irritation or anger when you encounter any resistance to attaining your goal. When you're in this mind state, you're fixated on the future and likely to ignore or dismiss most of what is going on in the present. Requirements that arise in the present are simply annoying interruptions to your planning and anticipation.

By contrast, when your mind is calm, you aren't worried much about the future. You may have plans and goals, but none of them seem so compelling that you need to dwell on them right now. You're more receptive to the present, not because you make a particular effort to be so, but because you aren't being drawn into the future by grasping or aversion. A calm mind state can seem rather unremarkable, which is why people so often sacrifice it in favor of daydreaming, anticipation, or ruminating on the past. However, once you start being mindful of mind states, you'll probably start to appreciate the natural receptivity and relaxation of a calm mind.

Stuck or Free

If your mind is being drawn to the same thing over and over, it is stuck. This is different from grasping/aversion mind, even though in that mind state you might say your mind is stuck on a future project or goal. In a grasping/aversion state, your mind generally feels fairly energetic and hopeful about attaining its desired outcome. When your mind is stuck, it is often returning again and again to something in the past, or something you have no obvious way to address or resolve.

The stuck mind state can lead to depression or worry. You seem to have no way to fix things, and perhaps you recognize this, but still can't stop thinking about the subject of your concern. It can get exhausting and discouraging having certain thoughts continually intrude on your experiences. This is especially true if they are about painful events in the past you can do nothing to change, complex situations that aren't going to improve overnight, or concerns about possible future disasters there is no guarantee you can prevent.

A free mind is one that can shift its attention at will, and let go of a thinking process when it has ceased to be useful or has even become painful and counterproductive. It isn't easy to move from a stuck mind state to a free one! However, the first step is recognizing that your mind is stuck, and what it's stuck on. Then, if you can maintain mindful awareness of your mind state, you may be able to see clearly how it really isn't helping things for your mind to be stuck. A motivation to move on may arise naturally.

Dull or Bright

There are lots of reasons why your mind may end up feeling dull. Lack of sleep or nourishment, too much stimulation, depression, heat, or humidity can all lead to a dull mind state in which your thinking processes are slow and fuzzy. You also may be experiencing lethargy (see Chapter 7). A dull mind isn't very receptive, but not because it's busy looking to the future or stuck on something. Instead, it's like your mind is a submarine and it can't be bothered to send up the periscope to see what's going on above the water. The lines of receptivity just aren't open.

A dull mind state is characterized by lack of energy, disinterest, inattention, forgetfulness, and slow reaction times. There are also not a whole lot of resources available in a dull mind for doing anything about getting more wakeful or clear. It's not a particularly uncomfortable mind state and it's certainly not stressful, so it's pretty easy to just endure it and wait for it to change. Still, it's good to recognize if your mind is dull; that's probably not the best time for making big decisions or meeting short deadlines!

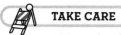 **TAKE CARE**

It's good to think of mind states as arising more or less on their own, like the weather—except that in the case of your mind, you can influence what kinds of weather tend to occur over the long term. It's worth learning about your mind states and what tends to bring about more positive, energetic states, but in the moment there's usually not a whole lot you can do about your mind "weather" other than be aware of it.

It's only in contrast to a bright mind state that a dull state can seem unpleasant or distressing. A bright mind is sharp, energetic, and clear. It responds quickly and is capable of sustained activity. It's receptive because it's wakeful and watchful—ready and waiting, like a dog waiting for you to throw a ball. When, through mindfulness, you notice what kinds of things tend to brighten your mind, you'll probably want to incorporate more of them into your daily life.

Scattered or Concentrated

Sometimes your mind is scattered even though you aren't thinking about the future or stuck on a particular subject. This means it is jumping around from topic to topic, sensation to sensation, without any particular purpose at all. Over the course of 30 seconds, you may think about what you're going to eat for lunch, a bird you see flying through the air, a line from an old song, the fact that you still mean to read that book, and who you should invite for dinner next week.

A scattered mind state is fairly typical when you're engaged in stimulus-independent thinking. As discussed in Chapter 2, this is when you're letting your mind wander because it isn't completely engaged in whatever activity you're currently doing. When you're letting your mind wander, you probably don't even notice how scattered it is.

A scattered mind becomes more obvious when you finally decide to concentrate on something, especially if it's as boring as a typical object of mindfulness like your breathing. Despite your intention, the mind continues to jump around fairly randomly, or it strings together superficially related thoughts in a chain that goes nowhere. A scattered mind is restless and easily distracted.

A concentrated mind, on the other hand, is very conducive to mindfulness. All of the energy and faculties of a concentrated mind are in the same place. Instead of feeling like your thoughts, intentions, and desires all have minds of their own and are pulling in different directions, you have a sense that all parts of you are collected and working together. You can focus, be present, and sustain your attention over time.

A concentrated mind state can be very difficult to achieve, although sometimes it happens spontaneously, particularly when you're doing something you really enjoy. Practicing mindfulness of scattered and concentrated mind states can teach you about all the various aspects of your mind and how they can either cooperate or work at cross-purposes.

Anxious or Composed

An anxious mind state may seem a little like a scattered one in that the mind tends to be fairly restless, but an anxious mind state is one characterized by doubt and tentativeness. While a scattered mind jumps from one topic to the next somewhat randomly, an anxious mind easily abandons a topic because it isn't sure of itself. Perhaps a given line of thinking is wrong, or the important data is being missed, or the anxious mind isn't up to the task of taking care of you.

In an anxious mind state, you're easily pulled away from a particular topic, line of thinking, or activity because of generalized worry. The concern behind the worry may not even be clear! This is how an anxious mind state differs from one that is stuck on something specific. Sometimes an anxious mind results from excitement (even about something positive), and sometimes it is a more pervasive experience arising from lack of self-confidence. Basically, an anxious mind is trying to anticipate problems and has no idea where those problems might come from—so it is stressed and jumpy.

At the other end of the spectrum from an anxious mind is a composed one. A composed mind state is confident that it will rise to any challenges it encounters, or at least it is unwilling to jump around in anticipation of them. There is a settled quality to a composed mind because it recognizes the most effective thing it can do is stay in the present. Another way to describe it is upright and dignified, although it gains these qualities from being ready and willing rather than from (necessarily) being especially knowledgeable or skillful.

MINDFUL EXERCISE

If you're trying to maintain mindful awareness of your breath or a simple task and you're finding it difficult, see if you can turn your attention to your mind state. What is going on in your mind? Does your mind drift because you just don't feel enough energy to keep it focused? Is it hard to avoid thinking about some particular thing? Is that thing in the past, present, or future? Are random thoughts, memories, and images intruding on your mindfulness? When you start thinking, are you contemplating your life, criticizing yourself, or worrying? Make an observation and then bring your mind back to its mindfulness task; make another observation when you notice you have started thinking again.

Internally Focused or Receptive

An internally focused mind state is one bound by your skin, limited to what is going on in your own body or mind. When your mind is internally focused, you may not even notice what is going on around you unless it intrudes in a very obvious way. Internally focused states can occur for many reasons, including physical pain, being absorbed in a complex creative or problem-solving process, or because you're reading.

Most of the time, however, your internally focused states are probably due to the self-referential, stimulus-independent thinking I discussed in Chapter 2. You basically are absorbed in thoughts about the past, future, or places other than where you currently are. This includes ruminating on past events, imagining alternative scenarios for the past or future, evaluating how you think and feel about things that aren't directly in front of you, and fantasizing.

Stimulus-independent thinking, as discussed in Chapter 2, is a favorite pastime of human beings whenever their minds aren't fully engaged with a task. Most of the people you pass on the street are more or less internally focused on these kinds of thoughts. They pay just enough attention to avoid bumping into things, and to be able to get where they're going, but they miss the majority of what's going on.

A receptive state of mind is centered in the body-mind, so it is also aware of your "self," but it includes the outside, present-moment world in its frame of reference. When your mind is receptive, it senses all kinds of things, and it is available for sensory data to come from anywhere, at any time. This kind of receptivity is incompatible with stimulus-independent thinking, because once your attention gets drawn into your head—to contemplation of the past, future, abstract concepts, or imagined scenarios—your ability to pay attention to what's going on around you is compromised. You may have good reasons to spend some time internally focused, but chances are you spend less time in a receptive state of mind than you would like. Practicing mindfulness can help you cultivate receptivity.

Capable of Reaching a Higher State (Or Not)

Finally, a very interesting mind state is one that the Buddhist Satipatthana Sutta calls "capable of reaching a higher state." There are many different mind states you can experience, and some of them are more calm, concentrated, clear, and pleasant than any you've ever experienced before. Some mind states are quite blissful—so much so that getting attached to them can be a problem (if you're lucky or determined enough to experience them).

It isn't the goal of mindfulness to achieve blissful mental states. However, the fact remains that "higher" mental states exist, you may end up in them at times, and these states can be useful for seeing your life more clearly (see mindfulness principles #3-5, Chapter 3). These states are called "higher" not because they are better (although you might argue that), but because the achievement of one state is dependent on another. For example, you have to be in a concentrated state of mind in order to achieve a *more concentrated* state of mind.

Generally speaking, you're able to taste a more refined or higher state when a whole bunch of mental qualities are present at once: you're in a mind state that is calm, free, bright, concentrated, composed, *and* receptive. This kind of state is rarely achieved in any kind of sustained way except through deliberate effort and long-term practice. These states can be extremely inspiring and energizing; your body-mind can feel full of vitality, potential, and great curiosity about experiencing the world in a new way.

This isn't to say that higher mental states belong in a special, inaccessible category that is largely irrelevant to your daily life. Everything is relative—so even if you're just beginning mindfulness practice, there are "higher" states available to you. These might be experienced as moments of particular clarity, or as new levels of centeredness and calm in the midst of activity. Part of the process of mindfulness is recognizing and celebrating these states of mind that are new—to *you*.

Noticing What Affects Mind States

As you get more familiar with different mind states through mindfulness, you also end up learning about what affects your mind states. This can let you make different choices about how to live your life and use your mind, depending on what mind states you would like to cultivate and which you would like to spend less time in.

 TAKE CARE

Be careful about judging too quickly which mind states are "bad" and which are "good." This will interfere with the process of becoming more aware of your mind states, and of the factors that influence them. Try to spend some time in each mind state as you encounter it, exploring it and noticing everything you can about it. If you feel dislike for a state, or frustration about not being able to get out of it, just notice these reactions as part of your overall experience.

Be forewarned that mind states can be frustratingly persistent when you don't want them to be, and frustratingly elusive when you really want them. If you want to change your typical mind states over time, be patient and understand that you'll need to experiment with all kinds of internal and external factors. You'll also have to build up new habits, which takes lots of work and time.

External Factors

The external factors that can influence your states of mind are practically infinite. Your genetics, hormones, history, and personality affect the state of mind you tend to have, and how easy it is to concentrate or let go of certain trains of thought. Mind states are also influenced by conditions that may be largely out of your control, like your physical and mental health, the weather, or political and economic circumstances. Obviously, things like the state of your relationships and the level of stress that tends to go along with your job affect your mind states as well.

People often focus on trying to change whatever external factors they can in order to feel better, be happier, and experience less stress. Doing this may be wise and helpful at times, but sometimes it can make your mind state completely dependent on your conditions—and if you can't make your conditions ideal, it means you're doomed to walk around in a scattered, stuck, dull, or anxious mind state.

Fortunately, there are many external things you can do to support the mind states you would like to cultivate. Getting enough sleep, eating well, and exercising are all extremely conducive to having a calmer, clearer mind, and to having some influence over your mind states. Many people find that a clean, fairly organized environment helps their state of mind, as does not overindulging in TV or intoxicants. Spending time with other people who are attentive to their own states of mind can also be very beneficial.

Healthy daily rituals and routines can help you experience calmer, collected mind states, especially if they involve some periods of silence, simple mindful activity, or meditation (see Chapter 8). You've probably found that it doesn't help much to just "tell yourself" you shouldn't be stressed, scattered, anxious, or obsessing over a particular thought. Momentarily putting aside all of your work and distractions can make it much easier to be present, and this ends up affecting your mind state throughout the rest of your day. This doesn't have to be a big deal: you might have a quiet cup of tea, spend 5 minutes simply petting your cat, or look out the window and follow your breathing for 30 seconds.

Internal Factors

You might have guessed by now, but practicing mindfulness can help a great deal with cultivating more calm, aware, collected, and energetic mind states. Building up the habit of being aware of the state of your mind means that you'll start to notice it more often, which is of course the starting point for doing anything about it. This doesn't mean you can practice mindfulness to instantly "fix" states of mind you don't like, but with practice you learn to direct your attention in ways that encourage more presence and receptivity.

For example, when you're caught up in grasping/aversion mind and would like to be calmer, take note of the effects that this mind state has on you. Chances are it stresses you out and makes you impatient and irritable. Observe: does the grasping/aversion mind help you achieve what you want? What happens if you slow down a little, take a few breaths, and remind yourself that the world is probably not going to end if things don't turn out exactly as you would like them to? You'll probably find that your stress decreases a little, and you actually become *more effective*. These mindful observations will make you just a little less captive to grasping/aversion mind—as long as you keep paying attention, and don't just tune out once you've told yourself to calm down.

Similarly, with sustained mindfulness you can start seeing more clearly how stuck, dull, scattered, anxious, and internally focused states of mind affect your experience of your life, your decisions, and your actions. When you realize that certain states are uncomfortable, wasteful, or limiting to your appreciation of your life, you'll start to question the choices you're making when you sink into dullness, obsess over something, let your mind wander, or try to anticipate every problem that could possibly come your way.

KEEP IN MIND

When you mindfully experience more positive states, you develop a natural preference for them. Mindfulness principle #3 is "Change occurs naturally when you see clearly what leads to greater happiness." This isn't about bad or good mind states, or about trying to live according to some ideal. This is about you becoming more mindful of *your* mind and *your* life, and doing what you really want with them.

Intention and Motivation

Your intention and motivation are two of the major factors that affect your mind states and your ability to have more influence over them. Many times, if you find it difficult to break out of a particular state, it's because you have reasons to stay there! Sometimes it's just about sticking with what you know, as opposed to facing the potential discomfort of something new. Sometimes it's just laziness. At other times, part of you is still convinced that grasping, obsessing, or fantasizing is going to get you what you want.

In these cases it is important to include your *entire* experience in your mindfulness. Your experience includes your reactions, intentions, and attachments. It can be essential to see clearly how a particular mind state is attractive, compelling, or self-perpetuating. It doesn't matter if part of you "knows" that replaying a scene from the past over and over in your mind isn't helpful, if another part of you continues to derive great satisfaction from recalling when you told someone off. This internal resistance to change is an important factor to consider if you're trying to cultivate different mind states.

Usually you won't have to argue with the parts of yourself that are drawn to unwholesome mind states. Instead, you can just challenge them to a mindfulness audit: "Okay, fine. You say it doesn't matter if we lay around in a dull mind state all afternoon. Let's just watch this experience unfold." Later in the evening, if you keep paying attention, you may find self-disgust, disappointment, or mild depression result from languishing in a dull mind state. Maybe not, but if you do, you'll have learned something very valuable that can fuel your intention to get up off the couch and take a vigorous walk next time your mind is feeling dull.

It's also important to push yourself to experience some of those "higher" mind states I discussed earlier. Basically, until you experience what the fruits of mindfulness can be, you don't know what you're missing, so the joy and pleasure of these states can't serve as motivation for your practice. It's generally not a good idea to describe wonderful mind states at length because then people will just compare them to their present state of mind and feel discouraged. However, in the interest of strengthening your intention to practice mindfulness, I'll just say that when I'm able to experience a particularly bright, concentrated, receptive mind state, it makes me feel like I'm awake to my life. In that state, if I think about my normal states of mind, it seems like I spend most of my time asleep.

You've probably tasted these kind of states as well, if you think about it. Perhaps you were hiking, spending time with a loved one, or maybe the sunshine just happened to come through the window in just the right way. Pay attention to and celebrate those experiences—and then go ahead and try to have more of them!

The Least You Need to Know

- Mind states are about how your mind is functioning. While they may tend to occur along with certain feelings and emotions, they operate independently of them.
- It's possible to directly experience the state of your mind in the present moment, without getting caught up in the content of what you're thinking.
- Typical mind states are grasping/aversion or calm, stuck or free, dull or bright, scattered or concentrated, anxious or composed, and internally focused or receptive. Real mind states fall somewhere on the continuum between extremes.
- It's important not to think of particular mind states as being inherently good or bad, but instead observe as mindfully as possible how they feel to you, and how they affect your life.
- You can influence the kinds of mind states that you tend to experience over time by adopting healthy habits, practicing mindfulness, and strengthening your intention to appreciate your life.

Awareness of Psychophysical Factors

The term *psychophysical* may seem specialized (and in some kinds of psychological research it is), but I use the term here simply to make it clear that the factors I'm presenting in this chapter are things you experience with your whole body and mind. They aren't just mental, *or* emotional, *or* physical. Instead, they tend to be associated with a number of different things at once, including characteristic body sensations, energy levels, feeling tones, mind states, thoughts, and impulses.

Cultivating mindful awareness of certain pervasive and influential psychophysical factors is essential to improving your mindfulness, seeing more clearly, and subsequently increasing happiness for self and other (see mindfulness principle #4, Chapter 3). The first five factors presented in this chapter are the major ones that obstruct and interfere with mindfulness. The next seven factors are those which support mindfulness, and are therefore associated with increasing clarity and happiness.

In This Chapter

- Introduction to the concept of a psychophysical factor
- Learning to recognize factors that affect mindfulness
- The five hindrances of desire, ill will, lethargy, restlessness, and doubt
- The seven factors that support being mindful
- Studying the function of psychophysical factors in your life

Investigating Psychophysical Factors

Imagine you're a scientist, and you're using the tool of mindfulness to make useful observations about the way the world works. According to the scientific method, you start with a hypothesis you want to test. This guides your inquiry and gives you specific things to look for. A scientist may have reason to believe his hypothesis is true, but he won't accept it until he has tested it to his satisfaction.

This is how you should approach the things that are presented in this chapter: as theories to test using mindfulness. Here you find many observations about how various psychophysical factors affect human experience, and how these observations have been proved valid by many mindfulness practitioners over the centuries. Just because others have found them to be true, however, is no reason to just accept them or adopt them as beliefs. It's much more effective to explore them in your own experience, and prove them true or false for yourself.

Just as most scientific studies aim to prove something that will be useful in guiding practical decisions in the physical world, the mindfulness study encouraged in this chapter should result in information that will be useful in guiding practical decisions in your life. These theories are about how the human body-mind functions, the factors that lead to clarity and happiness, and the factors that obstruct such happiness. They're based on Buddhist teachings but are general observations that are applicable to anyone.

Staying Objective and Receptive

If you want approach any of these theories about classic human psychophysical factors with receptive awareness, it's important to take the objective attitude of the scientist as much as you can. Inevitably, as you experience these factors they will be up close and personal—and you can easily get carried away by them and start making your habitual assumptions about them. If you stay rooted in the present through mindfulness of the body, you have a chance to watch with curiosity as these factors unfold in your experience, and learn something new.

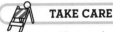 **TAKE CARE**

The psychophysical factors presented in this chapter aren't a list of mistakes and virtues you're meant to adopt as guidelines for the way you should feel and think. They're simply the things mindfulness practitioners throughout the centuries have discovered are either conducive to seeing your life clearly or make clarity difficult. Cultivating awareness of these factors and their effects helps you to provide the best possible psychophysical environment for your mindfulness.

As you contemplate something complex and potentially provocative like a psychophysical factor, you need to apply the mindfulness principles of awareness and attitude (see Chapter 3). To begin, you consciously decide to make a factor the subject of your mindfulness—that is, to cultivate a receptive awareness of it in the present moment in order to see it clearly. As stated in the principles, in order to do this you have to let go of your ordinary level of thinking in order to experience the factor directly. Rather than leaping to conclusions, judging, or making generalizations about the factor, you stay present with it as long—and in as sustained a way—as you can.

It's very helpful to maintain light awareness of your breathing as you turn your attention to a psychophysical factor. You want to keep your receptivity open to any kind of information, whether it is physical, energetic, emotional, or psychological. You might take note of a thought or a feeling, but as long as you maintain some awareness of your breath you won't get completely drawn into the content of your body-mind. Instead, you try to be aware of your experience as a whole and keep a large enough perspective that, ideally, you can see the arising, persistence, and passing away of the psychophysical factor. You can notice the effects it had on you, and what thoughts, mind states, feelings, or actions were supported by the factor.

An Example of Mindful Observation

For example, let's say you want to explore the experience of humor (this isn't one of the factors, I'm just using it to illustrate the process of mindful exploration). Someone tells a joke that immediately makes you laugh. Rather than focus on why the joke was funny, you try to be as aware as possible of the whole experience of humor.

You note there was some lag time between the end of the joke and your laugh, showing mental understanding was a necessary component. You notice warmth and buoyancy arising from the area of your stomach and moving into your chest. The sides of your eyes lift up, and as you laugh you experience a release of stress, and a brief sense of light-heartedness. Once the laugh has died down you see the whole experience has made you rather giddy, and you make a raunchy or sarcastic comment you probably wouldn't have made at another time. You find yourself looking for a likely person to share the joke with, judging the likely sense of humor of each person you encounter. If you stay mindful throughout, you'll learn something about how you experience humor, and perhaps even something about humor in general.

Psychophysical Factors versus Mind States

As discussed in Chapter 6, there is some overlap in cultivating awareness of mind states and psychophysical factors. Certainly, a mind state is something you might notice when examining a factor, and a factor might be one of the causes of a particular mind state. The difference is that awareness of a mind state is about paying attention to the way your mind is functioning, regardless of what thoughts, emotions, motivations, or factors might be present. A psychophysical factor, on the other hand, is something that may affect many aspects of your mind and body. It can be a force that builds or diminishes, affecting your life over time.

For example, a scattered mind state may occur because of overstimulation. Restlessness, a psychophysical factor, may produce a scattered mind state, but it's also characterized by certain emotions, motivations, and views. Basically, there's no clear-cut difference between mind states and psychophysical factors—they're more like different threads to follow with your mindfulness, with different results.

 MINDFUL EXERCISE

Choose a simple mindfulness practice, such as paying attention to physical sensations while you wash the dishes, or staying present while driving. Make an effort to do this practice many times over the course of a week, and note whether the practice seems difficult or easy in any given session. If you're finding it hard to stay present or keep your attention on the mindfulness practice, see if you notice any of the hindrances: desire, ill will, lethargy, restlessness, or doubt. If the practice is relatively easy, do you sense the presence of curiosity, energy, joy, ease, concentration, or equanimity? Don't try to change your experience, just note the factor and how it affects your mindfulness.

The Five Hindrances

The psychophysical factors that get in the way of your mindfulness agitate you, distract you, confuse you, or make it difficult for you to pay attention in a sustained or receptive way. As is the case with all of the psychophysical factors, they come from inside you. They may be triggered and affected by things around you, but you have to *participate* in them in some way in order to make them truly come alive. This is good news, because it means you can make different choices about that participation and subsequently become freer of the five hindrances.

As we consider factors that get in the way of your mindfulness, it's important to remember this isn't about dividing up your experience into categories of good and bad. Doing that can be frustrating and counterproductive when you find yourself experiencing something "bad" and aren't sure what to do about it. If instead you're able to keep some of the objectivity of the mindful scientist, you can simply note that there are some experiences you'd rather have less of, and investigate what you might be able to do about it.

Treatment of Each Hindrance

As I discuss each psychophysical factor that is considered a hindrance to mindfulness, I'll present it in three parts:

1. Theory for you to test: what causes the factor to arise, and how it affects your ability to see your life clearly

2. Tips for cultivating mindful awareness of the factor

3. Typical habitual assumptions about the factor that you can challenge through mindful observation

As you read, pause after each section to ask yourself whether and when a particular factor tends to appear in your life. See if you can recall particular situations in which the factor played a major role. In Chapter 5, I discussed how you can relive a past experience with mindful awareness, and that is something you may want to do here. Of course, you can also keep a factor in mind as you go about your day or week, noting when it occurs and what happens.

Desire

The theory about desire is this: to the extent you're fixated on something you really want (or something you really want to be different, or to go away), you won't be able to achieve the calm required for mindfulness. Instead, you're likely to experience a grasping/aversion mind state (see Chapter 6). You're also likely to experience stress and even suffering if the object of your desire eludes you. This stress and suffering can further fuel your desire, creating a cycle that keeps you emotionally upset, obsessed with certain thoughts, and dismissive of any experiences that don't have to do with obtaining what you want.

Note that the theory about desire says it interferes with your mindfulness "to the extent that" you're caught up in it. There is a spectrum of desire all the way from a minor preference to complete obsession. Generally speaking, the more you desire something, the bigger the disturbance to your ability to see your life clearly. A minor preference probably isn't a big deal, and even if you really want something, it doesn't present much of a hindrance as long as you aren't fixated on it.

Awareness of Desire

When you turn your mindful awareness toward desire, note how it feels. There will usually be some kind of tension or excitement in the body. When you desire something, you lean toward it—physically as well as mentally. Your whole body-mind becomes oriented toward it, and you usually feel motivated to start acting to obtain the object of your desire. It's like desire causes an itch that demands to be scratched. Until you relieve your desire by obtaining the object or outcome you want, there is a sense of discomfort (at the very least).

KEEP IN MIND

Mindfulness teacher Tara Brach recommends using RAIN (an acronym for the steps below) when you want to see something more clearly, particularly if it's something you'd rather not be experiencing, or would rather not examine carefully. The steps are: 1) recognize what is happening; 2) allow life to be just as it is; 3) investigate inner experience with kindness; and 4) nonidentification (you're not defined or limited by what you're experiencing). In her 2013 book, *True Refuge: Finding Peace and Freedom in Your Own Awakened Heart*, Brach says, "RAIN directly deconditions the habitual ways in which you resist your moment-to-moment experience ... Your attempt to control the life within and around you actually cuts you off from your own heart and from this living world."

As you stay rooted in the actual experience of desire (rather than thinking abstractly about it), ask yourself questions. What do you want? Are you making up a story about why you *must* have the object or outcome you desire? Are you tempted to compromise your own principles to get what you want? Is it difficult to think of anything else? Whether or not you act on your desire, try to maintain your mindfulness. If you don't get what you want, how long does the desire last? If you do get what you want, how long does the satisfaction last? After the desire dissipates, do you have any regrets?

Assumptions About Desire

The assumptions you usually make about desire are that your desire reflects a real need, and that the desire will persist in causing you discomfort until you get what you want. Are these assumptions true? With mindfulness you can challenge them. Observe whether desires can arise and pass away without your acting on them or taking them too seriously. Note how often a desire really reflects a serious need, and when it does, whether your desire has fixated on a particular way to meet that need, to the exclusion of other possibilities. Watch whether it's possible to let a desire go without suppressing it. (It is.)

Depending on what your internal research reveals, you may be able to gain a little bit of space around your desires. Instead of believing and feeling compelled to act on them, you can gain some freedom of choice to decide what would be the best thing to do in a given situation, and what would bring about the greatest happiness (that which applies in the longest term and at the largest scale, and includes the happiness of others, as stated in mindfulness principle #2, Chapter 3).

Ill Will

Natural anger arises in the present moment when your body-mind perceives there is something it needs to protect. It distorts your perceptions in order to focus all of your energy and attention on the perceived object of threat. Natural anger can provide useful information as long as you let it arise and pass away, and you question your angry perceptions. It causes only a momentary disruption in your mindfulness.

Here's the theory about anger as a major hindrance to your mindfulness: *ill will* is a deliberately nurtured psychophysical factor that results when you believe the distorted perceptions you experience while naturally angry, and then subsequently preserve them in a narrative and defend them. The concern that you or something you care about is under threat is very compelling, and maintaining ill will requires a great deal of your attention and energy. It keeps you stuck on a story that is based in the past, so your ability to be present is compromised. It encourages you to keep reviewing a particular narrative, so you spend lots of time thinking instead of settling into a direct experience of your life.

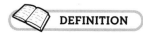 **DEFINITION**

> **Natural anger** is a feeling that arises in your body-mind in the present moment, in direct response to a perception that you, or something you care about, is under threat. **Ill will** is a psychophysical factor that requires active maintenance of negative feelings over time, and a narrative that justifies them.

Awareness of Ill Will

As you investigate ill will with mindfulness, keep in mind ill will can be extreme or very subtle. It can be aimed at people and clearly based on past episodes of anger, but it can also be focused on groups of people, ideas, or activities. The defining characteristic of ill will is rejection. Perhaps you're satisfied just to get the object of ill will out of your life, or avoid it as much as possible, but when things get more extreme you start hoping for its (or their) misfortune or downfall.

Ill will is almost always accompanied by tension in the body. As you investigate it with mindfulness, you may also notice bitter emotions or a sense of righteousness. Your mind is likely to be stuck on stories from the past, justifications of your feelings, and arguments you'd like to have with people who prove the validity of your feelings and thoughts. You probably gravitate toward people and situations that support your ill will, and avoid anything that will challenge it or suggest you might be being unreasonable. Speech based in ill will tends to be harsh and dismissive, stating things in absolutes instead of making calm observations, or disclaimers about speaking only from your own limited experience and perspective.

Assumptions About Ill Will

A typical unscientific assumption about ill will is that the more powerful and consuming the experience of it, the more right you are to feel the way you do. Strong feelings of aversion and anger are believed and interpreted as hard evidence that some kind of threat is coming your way.

Your body-mind convinces you that you have to hold on to, nurture, express, and even act on your ill will or suffer terrible consequences.

All of these assumptions can be tested with mindfulness simply by trying to stay fully present for your anger and ill will over time, so you have a chance to see what happens with it. What happens if you refrain from expressing or acting on your feelings? Does the anger or ill will dissipate if you don't fuel it? If you let go of anger or ill will, does disaster strike, or do you start thinking things aren't such a big deal after all? Any space you can create around anger and ill will—even if you don't let it go but at least *wonder* about it—can free you from the compulsion to act on it.

Lethargy

The theory about lethargy is this: while sometimes lethargy has physical causes (insufficient rest or nutrition, or illness), much of the time it's a psychophysical factor you indulge because—consciously or unconsciously—you aren't feeling motivated enough. You forget life is short, that the end could come at any time. You forget each moment is a precious opportunity to appreciate your life, take care of it, and give something back to the world. You dismiss your current experience as being boring or unimportant, your energy flags, and subsequently your mindful awareness almost disappears.

Awareness of Lethargy

Lethargy—also referred to as sloth, torpor, drowsiness, or laziness—can be a very tough psychophysical factor to deal with. When you're really lethargic, you forget you ever wanted to be mindful, or else paying attention to each moment seems like an insurmountable task. It can literally be painful to drag yourself out of bed, or off the couch, in order to force yourself to do something to break your lethargy. It can even be hard to take the steps to end physical lethargy (other than sleeping), let alone deliberately change your mind state.

 TAKE CARE

As you examine lethargy with mindfulness, remember not to judge it. There's no point in beating yourself up for not feeling energetic—this will probably just make you less inclined to work on arousing energy and mindfulness! Judging yourself can just make you discouraged or depressed, and make you liable to distract yourself with something that encourages even more lethargy. One typical pattern involves a brief struggle against lethargy, followed by rewarding yourself by taking it easy, followed by more lethargy. There may be less reactivity in the process if you view lethargy like a mild illness, and just get to work on things that will improve your health.

Assumptions About Lethargy

The assumption you probably make about lethargy is that it means there really isn't anything worth rousing your energy for. You think, "If life was interesting, if life needed me, if there was anything worth doing, then I would feel motivated." When you challenge this assumption through mindful observation, ask whether this is really the case. Can you find any part of yourself, in the present moment, that aspires to more? What do you really care about? When you force yourself to do something energizing (taking a walk, reading an inspirational book), watch very carefully what happens before, during, and afterward. Take special note of positive changes in your physical energy and mental outlook. It's the same world; if your view of it is so dependent on simple things like your level of activity, can any view be taken as truly reflecting reality?

Restlessness

The theory about restlessness as a psychophysical factor is that your mind gets overly agitated in its efforts to figure out and fix things, often to the extent you cease to be effective in those efforts. The more restless you become, the less effective your thinking and the more anxious your emotions—and because you aren't figuring things out, you become more restless. You get caught up in the content of your body-mind experience, rather than dropping below the level of ordinary thinking in order to experience things directly and see clearly (mindfulness principle #5, Chapter 3).

Restlessness can be caused by many things, but they primarily fall into two categories: worry about the future and remorse about past or current actions. When you're worried about the future, you're trying to figure out the best way to anticipate what's going to happen, and how best to fix it. When you're feeling remorse, you're trying to figure out what went wrong in the past, or how to improve the life you've ended up with (which is due at least in part to the choices you've made).

Awareness of Restlessness

Like all of the hindrances, restlessness is self-perpetuating and difficult to let go of. As you turn toward it with mindfulness, you're likely to notice an internal reaction, "I don't have *time* to be mindful! I've got to worry, analyze, and plan!" Even if part of you realizes you really aren't making any headway with all of your thinking, another part is determined it's the only way. Restless actions follow restless thoughts: jumping from one activity to another without follow through, or acting just for the sake of acting, without any results that really solve your problems.

Assumptions About Restlessness

The assumption inherent in restlessness is that more mental or physical activity is the only way to achieve happiness and avoid suffering. This assumption is directly challenged by mindfulness, and particularly by meditation (see Chapter 8). What happens when you take the risk of momentarily setting aside all the activity? What happens when you turn your attention to basic receptivity of the present, and let go of the worry and analysis? Do you lose track of your problems, or are they right there waiting for you when you turn your attention to them again? Does your thinking become less effective, or clearer? Do you benefit from the mental and emotional break, and afterward continue taking care of your life with renewed determination and energy?

Doubt

The theory is the psychophysical factor of doubt hinders mindfulness because you question the validity or effectiveness of the method itself, or your own ability to practice it. This isn't the same thing as *wondering* about whether and how mindfulness works but trying it anyway, with an open mind. The kind of doubt that hinders is doubt that thinks it *knows* mindfulness is a waste of time, or that you'll never be any good at it. You may waver between faith and doubt, but the doubt is always there in the background, undermining your efforts.

Awareness of Doubt

Sometimes doubt is very obvious, but sometimes it can be tricky to notice it. You may simply observe over time that your commitment to practice mindfulness is lukewarm, or that you form intentions about practice but don't really follow through on them. In the moment, you may find yourself lacking the motivation and determination necessary to do the work of letting go of ordinary thinking and just being present. Basically, if your mindfulness feels hindered and you can't sense much desire, ill will, lethargy, or restlessness, you're probably experiencing doubt.

 KEEP IN MIND

If you recognize doubt is starting to get in the way of your aspirations, it can be helpful to recall what has inspired or encouraged you in the past. Has it helped to read certain books, listen to particular teachers, or participate in a group with like-minded people? Has it helped to go on a meditation retreat or a long hike? Is there a friend or family member you can talk to who encourages you to have faith in yourself? Deliberately turning toward inspiration rather than doubt can enliven your mindfulness practice.

Doubt can manifest at different levels of intensity. At the most obvious level, you may be skeptical about whether mindfulness helps at all, or be holding on to an idea that you are incapable of concentrating. At a more subtle level, you might be convinced some mindfulness helps, but doubt there's sufficient reason to try to be mindful most or all of the time. A very subtle level of doubt isn't even conscious: your body-mind decides for you that business as usual is better than mindfulness.

Assumptions About Doubt

The assumption behind the psychophysical factor of doubt is that you already know. You know the way you experience the world is more or less all that is possible for you. You know your habitual ways of operating are good enough, and it's risky to try something new. You know practices like mindfulness are just fads without real substance, or that efforts to change always end in disappointment.

It takes courage to challenge your doubt! Who knows what might happen if you give up your cherished notions (and you can cherish notions even if they're painful to hold). Challenging your doubt also requires faith, although I hesitate to use such a loaded term. The faith that's required in this case is just enough to take the next step, which is momentarily setting aside your doubt and giving mindfulness your best shot. Fortunately, mindfulness is its own reward, so over time its simple practice starts to allay your doubt.

The Seven Factors of Awakening

The next seven psychophysical factors are the ones Buddhists call the factors of awakening. They're the ones that tend to support and deepen mindfulness, and therefore help you wake up to what's going on in your life. If you don't experience a particular factor very much, don't despair! You *do* experience it—perhaps briefly, or only in certain circumstances—but you can pay attention to whenever it arises. Notice how nice it is, and ask yourself what usually gets in the way of its arising. Take note of what helped bring about the experience, and see if any of the causes are things you can choose to bring about more often.

Mindfulness Itself

It may seem strange that mindfulness appears on a list of factors that support mindfulness, but here mindfulness is being talked about on two levels. As I discussed in Chapter 1, the meaning of mindfulness in modern secular usage has been expanded to describe a whole process of living: paying attention to your present experience, cultivating a receptive attitude, seeing clearly, and subsequently increasing happiness for self and others. This is what is referred to in the title of this traditional Buddhist list of factors as *awakening*. Within this list, mindfulness refers specifically to being able to direct your attention at will, keep it there, and remember to do it.

Mindfulness as a psychophysical factor is also called strength of mind. Without it, it's hard even to know if you're being mindful. If you can't pay attention to the state of your own body and mind when you want to, you won't be able to work on your mindfulness—so, in a sense, you need mindfulness in order to work on mindfulness! The same goes for cultivating awareness of, and working with, the other psychophysical factors. For purely practical reasons, it also helps to be able to pay attention to the world around you, so mindfulness is a powerful thing to cultivate.

Mindfulness as a factor often amounts to being aware that you're aware. This doesn't require a whole lot of self-consciousness, although that may happen when you're first practicing mindfulness. Eventually you want to have a simple sense of whether or not your mind is receptive to your present experience. This takes work, but eventually it's as natural as knowing whether your eyes are open, or you're standing upright.

Curiosity, Energy, and Joy

The next three factors—curiosity, energy, and joy—are particularly useful to have around when you're being hindered by lethargy or doubt. However, it's important to see these factors as positive things you cultivate in and of themselves, not as merely being antidotes to "bad" factors. The idea is that you work on strengthening these factors whenever you can, so you can arouse them when needed. It's good to become familiar with the experience of these factors and what supports them in your body-mind and in your life.

> **MINDFUL EXERCISE**
>
> Think of a time when you felt unusually mindful. It's often easy to recall such experiences because, at the time, you were fully present and aware instead of being caught up in your thoughts. You ended up with perceptions grounded in that moment that could serve as memories. What were you doing? Did the activity or setting inspire curiosity, energy, or joy in you? Were you involved with something or someone you care deeply about? Did the situation invite your joyous participation in some way? Recall the presence of curiosity, energy, or joy, and how they influenced your mindfulness.

Curiosity could be said to be the opposite of doubt, which was discussed earlier. Instead of getting stuck in what you think you know at a gross or subtle level, you try to recall the open, excited, wondering curiosity you experienced naturally as a young child. This doesn't require you to dismiss what you have learned. Instead, it encourages you to acknowledge you'll never know everything, and to push the boundaries of what you know. When you're curious, you willingly engage the inevitable change and growth life brings instead of resisting it (more on curiosity in Chapter 10).

Energy is, of course, the fuel for everything. How much of it you naturally have depends on many physical and mental factors, but you can probably access more energy than you usually do if you need to, and you can probably use what you access more efficiently. Energy generally arises when you perceive a real need for it—you need to obtain something you really want, or need to take care of something you care about. The deeper the desire and the more you care, the more energy arises, and the more focused you are when you apply it. If you can discover and remember your deepest aspirations, and keep in mind how brief and precious life is, chances are you'll have more energy. (See Chapter 10 for more on accessing your life energy.)

Joy is a great thing to see on this list of factors of awakening, isn't it? In order to wake up to your life, you need some joy. Of course, this isn't saying that in order to awaken you need *pleasure*. Joy is a lightness of heart and buoyant appreciation for life that doesn't depend on having particular possessions, relationships, or experiences. Instead, it's the French *joie de vivre*, or joy of simply living. In the midst of difficulty it can be hard to access or remember, but it's possible. (See Chapter 12 for more on cultivating joy.) Joy leads to a warm, personal engagement with the present moment that makes mindfulness a way of wholehearted living instead of just a mental skill.

Ease, Concentration, and Equanimity

The psychophysical factors of ease, concentration, and equanimity are important to calming the mind when you're caught up in desire, ill will, or restlessness. They may seem a little less positive (and a little less fun) than curiosity, energy, and joy, but they're similarly rewarding to experience if you give them a chance.

Ease is also referred to as serenity or calm. It is a deep inner, unworried stillness that can be seen as the opposite of restlessness. Sometimes it's also called relaxation, but this psychophysical factor isn't the same as passively giving up any effort. Instead, ease ends up being something you can access at any time, no matter what is going on in your life, even if you need to take action. You access ease by being completely and wholeheartedly present right here, right now. There is a timeless quality to being completely present; in this very instant there is no movement, no noise. Everything is completely still (instantaneously), and you can touch this stillness to achieve real calm. You can strengthen your sense of ease through mindfulness. (See Chapter 11 for more on ease and stillness, and how to cultivate them.)

Concentration can be one of the most difficult psychophysical factors to cultivate if it doesn't come naturally to you. Most people are only trained to concentrate on problem-solving tasks that involve the ordinary thinking mind. Concentrating in a mindful way means having the same disciplined focus you have when trying to solve a practical problem you find fascinating, but you aim that focus at directly experiencing something (such as the factors I have been discussing). If mindfulness is presence of mind, concentration is putting your energy behind that mind and focusing its power on a particular object. (See Chapter 8 for how to work on concentration.)

Finally, equanimity is about not being bothered by things because you're viewing life from a broad perspective. The idea is that, in the grand scheme of things, very few (if any) of the things you get upset about really matter—even to you. When you see clearly what leads to the greatest happiness for all (see mindfulness principles #2-4, Chapter 3), things like traffic, insults, or lost possessions seem unimportant. When you're able to experience things directly, without the filters of assumptions or expectations, even painful and difficult things are just part of an amazing unfolding of life. Equanimity isn't about not caring about things; it's about having enough insight about life to remember what you care about *most*. (See Chapter 9 for more on cultivating equanimity.)

The Least You Need to Know

- Psychophysical factors are things you experience with your whole body and mind. They can affect your feelings, emotions, thoughts, mind states, and behavior.
- The psychophysical factors that tend to hinder your mindfulness are desire, ill will, lethargy, restlessness, and doubt.
- The factors that support and deepen mindfulness are mindfulness itself (awareness of whether you're aware or not), curiosity, energy, joy, ease, concentration, and equanimity.
- Awareness of the psychophysical factors in your life requires you to suspend judgment and simply be present for a full experience of them (and their effects) over time.
- You influence the factors active in your life by watching what causes them to increase or decrease, and then feeding the ones you want and starving the ones you don't.

Deepening Mindfulness with Meditation

The modern secular understanding of mindfulness includes meditation, sometimes called "formal mindfulness practice." It's formal in the sense that it's something you take the time to do, setting aside any other activities. There are specific postures, settings, and techniques you're likely to use for meditation. This is in contrast to informal mindfulness practice, which involves trying to be present with your experience as you go about your daily life.

Practicing informal mindfulness as you go about your daily activities can be done diligently and can have a significant effect on your life, but there's nothing like doing meditation to improve your mindfulness in general. Meditation is intensified practice of all of your mindfulness-related skills, including the ability to direct your attention and keep it on something, the ability to drop below the level of ordinary thinking and experience things directly, and the ability to shift out of the default mode of self-referential processing (see Chapter 2 and Chapter 3).

In This Chapter

- What meditation is
- How meditation relates to mindfulness
- Why it's a great idea to meditate
- Instructions for three types of meditation
- Tips for when meditation is difficult

In this chapter I explain what meditation is in the context of mindfulness practice, and why it can be so helpful in your life. I also give basic instructions for a number of different ways to meditate, including silent seated meditation but also practices you can do if you find it hard to concentrate or sit still. This chapter also has tips for dealing with challenges in meditation, and ways you can improve or intensify your meditation practice.

A Description of Meditation

In mindfulness meditation, you choose a very simple activity— mental or physical—and try to maintain wholehearted awareness of that activity for the entire meditation period. The point is to practice intensive mindfulness: consciously maintaining awareness of your present experience with a receptive attitude, in order to perceive things more clearly and consequently increase happiness for self and other. You don't try to change the feelings, thoughts, and emotions you experience during mindfulness meditation, you just observe them as part of the overall landscape of your present moment.

 KEEP IN MIND

There are lots of different kinds of meditation in the world. In a broad sense meditation is just about consciously working with your mind, so there are obviously many ways to do that. In some kinds of meditation you chant something over and over, in others you engage in elaborate visualizations, and in others you try to cultivate particular mind states or attitudes. If you're interested in meditation, you may want to try different kinds and see what works best for you; they can all have benefits.

Keeping Things Simple

The objects of mindfulness meditation (what you turn your attention to) are aimed at calming or concentrating the mind, so they tend to be very simple. You might be focusing on one kind of sensation, your sense of posture, your breathing, or the sound of someone's voice doing a guided meditation. You aren't trying to achieve or *do* anything, so there's no need to engage in ordinary thinking (although you'll tend to do it anyway). You're trying to create the most conducive circumstances possible for allowing your mind to let go of all of its usual activity and just be aware of the present, moment after moment.

For a similar reason, meditation is generally associated with practices in which you keep the body still, or move it in a very slow or simple way (such as mindful walking). The emphasis is on calming, concentrating, and observing your mind. Generally speaking, the more you move your body, the busier your mind gets. If you want to be able to settle the mind, it's very helpful to minimize your physical movement.

Generating Awareness of Yourself as a Whole

You can also think of meditation as cultivating awareness of your functioning body-mind as a whole. In the previous four chapters I introduced the classic things to pay attention to as you work on mindfulness: your body, feelings, mind states, and the psychophysical factors at work in your body and mind. These things may serve as objects in your meditation, but in the background is always your experience of your own body-mind. Is it busy, distracted, or dull? Does it resist meditation, or is it eager to engage in it? Do you avoid or get stuck on certain thoughts? Do you feel frustrated, bored, sleepy, or self-conscious? When you put everything else down and devote yourself to an extremely simple activity like meditation, there's not much to distract you from what's going on in your body-mind.

Do I Have to Meditate?

You certainly don't have to meditate in order to practice mindfulness, but it's strongly encouraged. Keep in mind you don't have to meditate every day, or for long periods of time. Just putting aside your usual activities in order to meditate for 5 to 10 minutes on a regular basis can make a big difference in your life. Just attending a meditation group once a week can anchor and deepen your mindfulness.

In some ways it's difficult to explain why. Meditation affects you at every level—physical, emotional, and psychological. It can influence your attitude, world view, and understanding. It's a complex process that engages your whole body-mind, so its effects can't be explained by simple, linear, cause-and-effect relationships such as, "You try to focus your mind in meditation, so it helps you concentrate better." Instead, your experience is more likely to be something like, "I try to focus in meditation but it's very hard. Still, after I meditate I find I'm more patient in traffic." It's difficult to predict what your meditation is going to be like, or what effects it's going to have.

Just about any reason you have for resisting meditation is based on a misunderstanding of what it involves. A big reason you might not want to meditate is because you think it requires you to take awkward physical postures that are either impossible for you or will lead to discomfort. Fortunately, you can meditate in any posture that allows you to stay fairly still yet remain alert. (Instructions on posture are given later in this chapter.)

Perhaps you think meditation has to be done a particular way, and if you do it "wrong" it will be useless, harmful, or you'll end up embarrassed in front of people who do it "right." The good news is after reading this chapter, you'll know everything you need to know in order to start meditating. You can keep improving your meditation for as long as you live, but the techniques themselves are extremely simple. Plus, no one else knows what's going on in your mind when you meditate, so no one's going to be able to judge your practice unless you share your experience verbally.

TAKE CARE

There are probably lots of things competing for your time, so why choose to spend it meditating? Beware of comparing meditation to other enjoyable, enriching, or healthy pastimes like playing a musical instrument, learning a language, or even exercise. These other kinds of activities make you happier, healthier, or smarter in incremental ways, which is why you may feel like you should do a whole bunch of them in order to have the kind of life you want. Meditation, on the other hand, affects the way you see and do everything else in your life. It's like recalibrating your whole body-mind, so even a modest meditation practice can make you happier, healthier, or smarter in everything you do.

Finally, you may worry meditation will be emotionally or psychologically uncomfortable. Perhaps it will be excruciatingly boring, weird, or like lifting the lid off a Pandora's box of suppressed thoughts and emotions you'd really rather not deal with. I won't lie. Occasionally meditation fits these descriptions, but very rarely. It's also extremely unlikely these descriptions will match your *first* experience of meditation. The vast majority of people find meditation is sometimes *slightly* boring, and some people find it *a little bit* weird at times. And your suppressed stuff? Your mind is very skilled at suppression! A little meditation isn't likely to blow things wide open, even if you want it to.

Reasons to Meditate

Hopefully I've convinced you to at least temporarily overcome any resistance you might have to meditation, but you may still want to know *why* you should meditate. (I talked about some of the empirical evidence of the benefits of meditation in Chapter 1, so here I'll concentrate on your subjective experience.) It can be hard to find lists of reasons why you should meditate. This is because meditation teachers often resist trying to convince you to meditate by telling you all the wonderful benefits it has—not because it doesn't have benefits, but because it's so easy to get impatient or start judging your experience if you have expectations about it (or even hopes).

The best thing to do is just keep meditating regularly for at least a year or two and see what happens. Still, it's human nature to be curious, so in this section I give you some reasons to meditate. Reading them also gives you a sense of what you're trying to do (or not do) in meditation.

Stepping Off the Hamster Wheel

It's fine to try to keep certain principles in mind as you go about your day, such as, "It's good to appreciate the simple things in life," or, "It doesn't pay to get upset." Often, however, you can find yourself upset and stressed despite all of your best intentions and despite all of the wise things you understand about life. You end up caught up in the momentum of taking care of your responsibilities and working on your projects and start to lose touch with the insight or calm you might have been able to cultivate in the past.

Often, when I sit down to meditate, I feel like I'm a hamster that has just stepped off one of those little exercise wheels that goes around and around. A hamster on a wheel runs with frantic determination, but it isn't trying to exercise like a human on a treadmill; a hamster really thinks it's getting somewhere. Similarly, I get caught up in my daily activities with an overriding sense of imperative and expectation—and I only realize this once I put down those activities and sit down to meditate. The full effect of the "I'm getting somewhere" trance is extremely difficult to break out of unless I stop doing *anything* for at least a brief period of time.

 KEEP IN MIND

Most of the empirically proven benefits of mindfulness listed in Chapter 1 are the result of mindfulness practice that includes a significant amount of meditation. Research subjects often take the 8-week course on Mindfulness-Based Stress Reduction (MBSR) and then are compared to control subjects who have not taken the course. MBSR course participants spend 45 minutes every day doing either mindful yoga or meditation, or some of each. The meditation practices include listening to guided meditations, doing body scans, and sitting in choiceless awareness.

It isn't that your daily activities are as pointless as a hamster running on a wheel; it's just that if you really think about it, where are you trying to get to? Your life is happening right here, right now. You may want to improve or experience certain things, but that doesn't mean you want to write off the present. If you take the time to meditate, you're sending yourself this message loud and clear, regardless of whether or not you enjoy the meditation. Your effort to focus your attention on a simple, ultimately purposeless activity (such as following the breath or walking slowly back and forth) is a potent antidote to the strange intoxication of busyness. Your meditation session may end up being the one time over the course of your day that you realize, "Hey, look. This is my *life.*"

Challenging Your Default Mode

In Chapter 2 I discussed how your brain has a default mode. Basically, whenever you aren't engaged in a task that requires your full attention, your mind uses the spare bandwidth for self-referential processing. Usually without even realizing it, you analyze the past, fantasize about things you'd like, and imagine future scenarios in anticipation of problems or opportunities. If you're like most people, you spend an immense amount of time in this default mode as you go about your daily life, and lots of the stuff you think about doesn't end up being useful in any way. In fact, some default mode thinking ends up being repetitive and dysfunctional (such as dwelling endlessly on a past event that made you angry, or worrying yourself into a state of anxiety).

As you meditate, you will become conscious of the endless stream of self-referential thoughts that bombard you when you try to do something simple like focus on your breathing or on the sensations on the bottoms of your feet as you do slow walking meditation. You'll be distracted by anything from planning your grocery list to reviewing a bad memory from 20 years ago to imagining what a great meditator you might turn out to be. On and on the mind goes, generating thoughts about what has happened or might happen to you. Some of what you think about in default mode is important, but chances are you'll recognize you'd rather be attentive to your present experience than pay attention to much of what your mind is dwelling on.

Your efforts in meditation are the direct opposite of operating in default mode. You are deliberately guiding your attention toward certain objects and trying to keep it there. This is very different from engaging in an activity that naturally requires your full attention, or in which you are naturally very interested. In those cases, your brain bandwidth is more or less fully used, so you are unlikely to operate in default mode. During meditation you are focusing on something very simple or on nothing at all—precisely the kind of situation where your mind is likely to start active self-referential processing.

Fortunately, although it takes time, meditation and mindfulness can help you spend less of your life in default mode, as stated in mindfulness principle #7 (see Chapter 3). Research has shown default mode activity decreases during meditation, as I discussed in Chapter 2. Additionally, in experienced meditators the areas of the brain used in default mode are actually connected to the rest of the brain differently, perhaps reflecting the general shift in perspective described in their subjective reports. This physical change in the brain is due to its amazing plasticity, or its ability to "rewire" itself based on experience. Your meditation can have a lasting effect on your life.

Achieving Comfort with Simplicity

When I first started meditating, the idea of deliberately spending my time essentially doing nothing seemed quite radical to me. I remember looking over at my cat, who was dozing peacefully in the window without a care in world. I wondered, "Is that what I'm trying to do here? Become that simple?" At the time the idea of becoming as simple as my cat seemed quite ridiculous. It seemed synonymous with becoming stupid or passive (apologies to my cat).

Fortunately, the simplicity you are trying to cultivate in meditation doesn't require you to become passive or stupid. Even though you are setting aside all of your concerns and efforts for a time, even though you are letting go of your ordinary thinking and just trying to *be* much the same way as a placid cat, it doesn't actually require you to deny the parts of yourself that are smart, ambitious, determined, active, or passionate.

> **MINDFUL EXERCISE**
>
> Pick a *very* simple activity you really enjoy, such as petting your dog, drinking your morning coffee, or taking a walk on a beautiful day. Try to let go of thinking about anything other than exactly what you're doing—not because you *should,* but in order to fully appreciate this activity. Maintain mindfulness in this way for just a minute or two. How often do you naturally stop all other mental and physical activity in order to do only one thing? You'll probably find mindfulness greatly increases your ability to enjoy something.

Instead, in meditation you are giving a different part of yourself some time—a part that tends to be highly neglected. This part aches to just *be.* It wants to relax in the silence. It doesn't need to have answers; its very existence is the only answer it needs to offer. It longs to *just* drink tea, *just* sit in the sunlight, *just* kiss the top of a baby's head slowly, taking a moment to catch the subtle scent of her hair. This part of yourself really is as simple as a cat.

This simple part of yourself is surprisingly important to your ability to function effectively in the world. It's the part that will give you strength when things fall apart and nothing else makes sense. It's the part that finds reasons to go on making an effort when things get really discouraging. It's the part that lets you take a few deep, calming breaths in the midst of a busy, demanding schedule. The simplicity of meditation gives the quiet, spacious part of yourself a chance to refresh and renew itself. I'll go into more detail about embracing simplicity and stillness in your life in Chapter 11.

Identifying Less with Content

After you have spent many hours in meditation, you will have watched the arising and passing away of countless thoughts, feelings, emotions, and mind states. Because you have decided to do nothing for a time, you can't act on any of the stuff that arises in your mind (except by engaging in more thinking, but you've also decided not to do that). During meditation, you are trying to stay present, or stay focused on a particular thing, but your mind generates all kinds of stuff in spite of "you." You begin to get a sense of yourself that is not synonymous with the content of your mind.

For example, perhaps you are meditating and you remember an interaction you had the day before with a family member that made you very angry. You will tempted, as usual, to think about why you're right, why the other person is wrong, and what you can do to make all of this clear to everyone involved. But then, because you are meditating, you try to bring your attention back to the breath. In that moment you become aware, "I am feeling angry," and you take a step back from the anger. You don't have to stop making yourself feel anger, and you don't have to decide you are wrong after all. All you have to do is notice, "Ah, anger," and you have become less identified with your emotion. Now you have more freedom of choice around it. Maybe you act on it, maybe you don't, but once you gain a slightly broader perspective you don't *have* to. I'll discuss more about changing your relationship to your thoughts and emotions in Chapters 13 and 14.

Building Concentration

Concentration is holding your attention in one place, and concentrating *intensely* is generating lots of energy and focusing it all in one place for a prolonged period of time. Concentration is what unlocks the answers to questions and takes you to the next level of understanding something. You need a little bit of it to decide what to eat for breakfast, and a moderate amount to complete a project at work. You need an immense amount of concentration to respond to an emergency or finish a complicated task in a short period of time.

DEFINITION

Concentration is focusing everything you have on one thing, including your attention, will, interest, and energy. The more of yourself you can bring to the object of focus, and the smaller (or more specific) that object of focus is, the more concentrated you are. Concentration is a tool for obtaining answers to questions and solving problems.

Most people assume building concentration is one of the primary things you are trying to do in meditation, and in one sense it is. Concentration is a very powerful tool, and you can improve your concentration if you work on it by … well … concentrating. However, meditation is unlikely to dramatically change your ability to concentrate. If you're already good at it, you'll find yourself experiencing extra deep concentration during meditation. If you're no good at concentrating, trying to do it during meditation is likely to be somewhat frustrating. Even if you don't give up, you'll probably still find it challenging after many years of meditation.

The good thing is you don't need to learn to achieve amazing levels of concentration in order to meditate, practice mindfulness, see clearly, or work toward more happiness in your life. What you need to learn is *appropriate* concentration. When you recognize what is really worth paying attention to, the necessary concentration will be there.

Think of it like this: someone tells you to concentrate on a door. You don't know why you should. Perhaps they tell you it will make you a better person if you do, so you agree and set about trying to meditate on the door. If you're at all concentration-challenged, you'll find the task very hard. Now imagine someone convinces you there's a flash flood and at any moment the water is going to come crashing through that door. You need to pay attention so you can push a button that will channel the water elsewhere. *You will be able to concentrate sufficiently for the task.*

You learn appropriate concentration through meditation and mindfulness because, over time, you learn what is worth paying attention to. Habitually your mind may ruminate on the past, fantasize, or worry about the future, all because it thinks it's important to do so. Meditation and mindfulness challenge that assumption, and you begin to realize how important it is to pay attention to your present experience. In order to learn this you need to concentrate long enough to get the point, so you always have to push your concentration a little farther than is comfortable. How long and how hard do you have to concentrate? As long and as hard as you can. But don't get frustrated—every time you are able to concentrate, you are likely to learn something that will strengthen your mindfulness at least a little bit.

Basic Instructions for Meditation

In this section I give you the basic instructions you need in order to do just about any kind of meditation. I cover physical posture and give tips for when and where you're likely to find it easier to meditate. Keep in mind each person is different, so pay attention to what works for you and don't be afraid to improvise. Throughout the rest of the chapter emphasis will be placed on the most essential elements in each set of instructions, so you can tell what's most important and what's just a suggestion.

Physical Postures

There are four traditional "postures" for meditation, according to the Buddhists: seated, standing, walking, and lying down. *Any* of these postures can work as long as you're able to remain fairly comfortable but also alert and present. Lying down is a great option if you're experiencing physical pain or illness, but it can make it very difficult to stay alert. However, if you're able to stay awake while reclining and you prefer it, fine! Similarly, leaning back in a stuffed chair may make it more difficult to stay present than sitting upright on a meditation cushion on the floor, but if it works for you, that's okay. It's important to be comfortable enough so you can keep the body very still (with the exception of walking, obviously), so you may be able to meditate better in a chair, standing, or mindfully walking.

However, there's nothing like the classic meditation position of being seated on the floor to help keep you alert and present, as long as you can physically do it. The essential thing when you're seated on the floor is not to slouch. This can lead to pain and isn't conducive to meditation. If you're sitting cross-legged, you can put a firm cushion under your buttocks to help tilt your center of gravity forward so you're sitting upright. When sitting on the floor you can also help prevent your legs from falling asleep by making sure one of them isn't tucked under the other. If you're flexible enough, you can place one calf directly in front the other, without tucking either leg underneath you.

It may help your experience of meditation to sit on a cushion or bench made especially for that purpose. (You can order these online for $45-65.) Meditation cushions
are generally round and stuffed to be very firm with a cotton-like material, or filled
with buckwheat hulls to be like a bean bag. Meditation benches are about 1.5 feet
wide and less than a foot tall; you place them over your ankles while you're kneeling,
so you can sit on the bench instead of on your feet. These benches help you maintain
a nice upright posture without requiring lots of flexibility.

There are various things you can do to maintain alertness and presence in easier physical postures. If you sit in a chair, it helps if you sit on the forward edge instead of leaning back, and
perhaps even put a cushion on top of the chair to improve your posture. If you need back support,
you can place a cushion between your back and the chair so you can sit upright instead of leaning
back. If you need to recline, you can put yourself in some kind of formal position to help you stay
focused instead of feeling like you're napping. You can lie on one side with a folded blanket under
your head, the hand of your lower arm tucked under your cheek and the upper arm stretched
out along the top of your body. If you need to lie on your back, you can place something such as
a small cushion on top of your chest or stomach, and gently hold it there with one hand on each
side. This requires you to physically engage the posture to some degree, and can keep you more
attentive.

When and Where to Meditate

You don't need a perfectly silent, secluded, beautiful space for meditation. (Fortunately, or you'd
have a good excuse for not doing it very often!) All you really need is a time and place where you
aren't going to have to fight too many distractions. Now, what qualifies as a distraction is entirely
dependent on you. If something in your environment pulls you strongly into thinking about the
past, future, somewhere else, or something other than the object of your meditation, then it's
distracting you. Background noise, clutter, or the proximity of other people aren't necessarily distracting. Alternatively, even in the simplest of environments you can find something to distract
you, so you can't depend entirely on altering your environment to achieve a calm mind.

Generally speaking, when you meditate it's good to be alone in a room, or with other people who
are meditating. Try to situate yourself so wherever your gaze rests is fairly neutral or uninteresting, such as a blank wall or the floor. (It helps you stay more alert if you keep your eyes open.) It
also helps to pick a time of day when you naturally feel less stressed or more alert. Some people
find mornings best, others evenings. Neutral noises like traffic, or the buzz of human activity such
as you might find in an airport, can actually serve as an object for your meditation. Engaging
sounds like television or the details of an overheard conversation, however, are very difficult to
meditate through.

Three Types of Meditation

Once you're in a comfortable position but alert, situated in an environment that isn't too distracting, what do you do? Here I give you the instructions for three different kinds of meditation. It's recommended you try them all, and use them at different times depending on your physical and mental state.

Whatever kind of meditation you're doing, you'll choose an object for meditation. The object can be any of the things discussed in the last four chapters, including your sense of physical presence and posture, your breathing, sensations like sound or sight, feelings, mind states, or psychophysical factors. Depending on the type of meditation you're doing, you engage the object differently. It's good to experiment with different meditation objects to see what works for you, and it's fine to switch them up. However, choosing one and sticking with it for a while can help you get better at keeping your mind concentrated or aware. Ultimately, meditation should challenge your sense of boredom, so try to avoid changing things all the time just to keep yourself amused.

Guided Meditation

Guided meditation involves listening to someone speaking live or on a recording who guides you though a meditation exercise. One of the benefits of this approach is the guidance keeps bringing your attention back to the present. Another benefit is you can learn some techniques for calming or concentrating the mind that you can use at other times. Because of this, many people find guided meditations are a great introduction to the practice, or a support for their meditation if they find it very difficult to stay present on their own.

 KEEP IN MIND

There are eight guided meditations included along with this book: Body Scan, Awareness of Sensations, Awareness of Feelings, Awareness of Mind States, Awareness of Psychophysical Factors, Staying Focused on the Breath, Including Everything in Your Meditation, and Just Being. The first five walk you through the process of turning your mindful awareness toward the things I've introduced in the last four chapters. Obviously you can (and should) cultivate such awareness outside of formal meditation, but it tends to be much easier to notice and pay close attention to these things while meditating. The last three guide you through concentration and expansive awareness meditations, which I introduce in the next section.

As you listen to guided meditations, try to maintain some kind of physical awareness even if that isn't the subject of the meditation. Otherwise, you can get drawn into thinking abstractly *about* the guidance, instead of putting it into action in the present, with your own body-mind.

Throughout a guided meditation, if your mind wanders, simply bring it back to the sound of the voice and to the exercise. During the periods of silence it's up to you to try to stay present, but you'll only have to do that for a few minutes at a time.

Concentration Meditation

In concentration meditation you choose an object of awareness and try to keep your attention on it in a sustained way. Once you're able to do this, you can deepen the meditation by intensifying your concentration, the skill I discussed earlier in this chapter. This involves becoming very interested and absorbed in the object of your meditation. Another way to think of this is that you try to let the object fill your awareness. It's not that your awareness becomes small or confined, but that the incredible complexity of your meditation object becomes obvious and there is suddenly plenty to pay attention to in something as apparently simple as the breath.

Typical objects in concentration meditation are the breath (as used in one of the guided meditations that come with this book), sounds, and the sensations on the bottoms of your feet while walking. You can also use questions as objects, although these aren't typical kinds of questions you engage with your ordinary level of thinking. Instead, they focus your powers of observation on something, such as a psychophysical factor, by posing simple but passionate queries. "What is this?" "What is really happening here?" Or, "What is underneath appearances?" You ask and then you just observe—without trying to figure anything out.

Whatever your meditation object, in concentration meditation you keep bringing your mind back to the object over and over. Every time you do this, you strengthen your ability to direct your mind's attention at will. It requires energy and effort to increase your concentration, but the experience of being more concentrated can be very satisfying. It's as if certain aspects of life only reveal themselves to you if you make an effort to stop and experience them in a much more sustained and direct way than you habitually would.

Expansive Awareness Meditation

Expansive awareness meditation can end up getting you to the same place concentration meditation does (a still, present mind), but by using a different path. It requires the same amount of energy and effort, but the necessary energy and effort have a different flavor. You may find expansive awareness meditation works much better for you than trying to concentrate, or vice versa. It just seems to depend on the way your mind works.

When you do expansive awareness meditation, you try to open your awareness to *everything*. Imagine you're waiting for some unusual or miraculous event, but you don't know which of your senses you'll perceive it with. Will it be a sound? Will it be a sight? Will it be a thought? Whenever you find your mind has wandered, instead of bringing it back to an object, you open your awareness back up. Any time you latch on to a train of thought or a particular sensation, you're also closing down your awareness of other things. By opening your awareness as wide as you can, you're returning to mindfulness of the present, just as you would by turning your attention back to an object of concentration.

MINDFUL EXERCISE

Sit, stand, or lie down and keep your eyes open. Widen your gaze, including what's to the sides and above and below in your peripheral vision. (This will help keep you from getting distracted by particular things you can see.) Now watch your visual field as if it's a movie—a slow-moving movie, perhaps, but one of those quiet, visually rich, artistic ones. Just keep watching. When you stop because you have gotten caught up in thinking, note that you have tuned out the "movie" because it's boring, or because you think you know what's going to happen next. Ask yourself, "When I really stop to look, is anything truly boring? Do I really know what's going to happen next?"

If this kind of meditation seems distracting because you find your mind jumping around in response to different sensations, it may help to maintain awareness of one particular kind of sensation. It can be enough just trying to stay open to all sounds, or stay aware of everything in your visual field as if your eyes are video cameras. Curiously, you can also think of thoughts and feelings as sensations in this context—things your body-mind can perceive just like anything else. The goal in this case is to notice *all* thoughts or feelings as they appear in the body-mind, and watch them like a hawk. What happens to them? How long do they last? What arises in response to them? You try not to engage the content, but instead stay completely aware of all of it as it flows through you.

The results of diligent, energetic expansive awareness meditation can be similar to those of concentration meditation. When you're completely open, your mind can become very still. This facilitates seeing clearly, even if you aren't concentrating on a particular object or question with the intention of understanding it more fully. Exactly *what* you might end up seeing clearly with expansive awareness you may not know ahead of time, but that also allows insights to arise from unexpected places and in unexpected ways.

Dealing with Challenges in Meditation

Many people find meditation challenging. Of course, many people find it delightful and rewarding, but even they will acknowledge it takes effort. If you're wondering how to improve your meditation, or whether you're doing it right, it's good to keep in mind that such questions are all part of the process.

Think of improving your meditation as you would improving a complex skill such as playing basketball or a musical instrument. Even as a beginner, your playing will be rewarding, interesting, and enriching. At no point can it be said you aren't playing yet because you aren't doing it "right." However, you're aware there are always higher levels of skill possible. In your efforts to improve, you need to take many things into consideration, including your attitude, motivations, and assumptions. Tips that help certain players improve may not help you, but then you'll happen upon an approach that really opens things up for you. You can always improve, and this doesn't invalidate any of your efforts along the way.

Recognizing What "Good" Meditation Is Like

When you're meditating very deeply, you really are *just present*. Your mind isn't wandering at all. You're not shutting out or grasping after anything. If you're concentrating on something, such as a feeling or a psychophysical factor, you're doing it completely consciously and deliberately. Your concentration is sustained, and is motivated by pure curiosity, not by anger or anxiety. If you're practicing expansive awareness, you notice everything, and no part of you is bored.

 **TAKE CARE**

> Meditation experiences differ widely based on who you are, the technique you're using, how long you've been practicing meditation, and how you're feeling on a particular day—among many other things. It's not helpful to get stuck on the description of "good" mindfulness meditation I give in this chapter! For example, a perfect meditation session *for you, at a particular time,* might involve crying the whole time because you have gotten in touch with some grief. A great meditation might mean you intimately experience the dullness of your depression and finally realize you need to do something about it. Still, it can be helpful to know what kind of experience you're going for, so you can tell what you still have to work on.

Ideally, in mindfulness meditation you're alert, engaged, and interested in your life in this very moment. Your mind is calm but energetic. The simplest things—your breath, the wall, the birds singing—appear fascinating and beautiful. There is nowhere else you'd rather be. And yet, you're not in some transcendent realm, you're just here. If someone across the room needed your help, you would be able to spring up from your meditation seat and respond to the best of your ability. In fact, because of the stillness of meditation, your response would be quicker and more appropriate than it would ordinarily be.

Getting to Know Your Own Mind

So, when your meditation isn't perfect (and it never is), what can you do about it? The first step is to get to know your own mind. No one else can know how it works like you can, and your mind is also incredibly unique. It's grammatically incorrect to use the word *incredibly* to modify *unique,* but in this case there is a good point to be made by doing so. It's not just one or two features that make your mind unique; it's a lifetime of causes and effects that have added up and resulted in who you are. There is enormous variety in meditators, the techniques that work for them, and their experience of meditation. Even the advice of a meditation master might not address exactly what's going on for you.

The basic thing to keep in mind is this: cultivate mindful awareness of your meditation object, but also cultivate awareness of your experience of meditation. Eventually you'll want to drop the sense of separation between you and the meditation object, and you and your meditation. (You'll want everything to just be experience.) In the meantime, however, you have to pay attention to your experience so you can learn how to adjust your efforts in order to improve your meditation. You need to notice when your approach isn't working—when your meditation feels dull, you can't stop your mind from racing, or meditating is just making you feel inadequate.

Here's an example. For many years the only meditation instruction I remember receiving was for what I call concentration meditation (discussed earlier in this chapter). I very much wanted to learn how to meditate, so I spent countless hours trying to keep my attention on my breath, or on sounds. It felt like a constant struggle. I could only keep my concentration for a few seconds at a time before my mind would race off to make elaborate plans for things I never ended up doing. "What's wrong with me?" I wondered. "Either I must not want this badly enough, or I'm just a failure at this." Finally it occurred to me that maybe the instructions I received weren't quite right for me (even though they clearly worked for others). I started experimenting with other ways, and found that expansive awareness meditation (discussed earlier in this chapter) was a much better way for me to calm my mind.

Applying the Right Medicine

Here are some suggestions for how to address a few of the typical challenges in meditation. As I described earlier, you should try out recommendations but also feel free to improvise, interpret, and discover new ways to work with your own mind. Often, however, if you can get to know your own mind and diagnose what the problem is in your meditation, you can apply the right "medicine" to cure it.

Struggle: Meditation takes effort and energy, but if it feels like too much of a struggle you can get discouraged and start to avoid doing it. Also, a sense of struggle in meditation usually means you're holding on to some idea about how meditation should be. Sometimes just realizing this can relieve the pressure. If it doesn't, experiment with the different types of meditation described in this chapter and see if one works better for you. If there's still struggle, remember to include all aspects of your experience in your meditative awareness of "here and now."

> **KEEP IN MIND**
>
> The Buddhists have been teaching meditation for over 2,000 years, and have made it into quite a science. Just about any obstacle you might encounter in your meditation has been dealt with by someone else at some point. There are many Buddhist texts and online articles on meditation and the various ways to overcome particular difficulties you encounter in your practice. A Buddhist teacher can also point you toward resources and answer your questions about meditation.

Judging: You need to recognize when your mind is wandering or when you're stuck in rumination or worry. However, all you have to do is observe these things; when you see clearly the effect they have on you, you'll be inspired to let them go (see mindfulness principle #3, Chapter 3). Rejecting things just agitates the mind. Your resistance, frustration, random thoughts, or inability to calm the mind are just what's going on. Often, ceasing the struggle against something helps it subside.

Restlessness or dullness/sleepiness: If you just can't settle into meditation or can't rouse the energy to do it, try bringing to mind your deepest aspirations. These probably have to do with the things you care very deeply about: perhaps you want to be at your best for the people you love, clear and energetic in your work, or able to access your strength and creativity. Remind yourself that meditation helps you fulfill any aspirations you have. Recall that your life can end at any time, and think of how motivated you would be to be present for this very moment if you knew you had only one day left to live.

Stuck on negative thoughts and emotions: Sometimes all you end up doing in meditation is ruminating on past events or worrying about the future. You might be stuck in anger, feeling discouraged or depressed, or facing difficult circumstances. Try connecting with the part of yourself that really needs a rest from all the thinking. Promise yourself after meditation you will give any troubling issues your complete attention. If necessary, put a piece of paper next to you and jot down any thoughts you are afraid of forgetting—and then gently encourage yourself to let them go for now. Remind yourself that after a little meditation break, you will be in much better shape for dealing with any problems you have.

Getting Help with Meditation

Finally, it can really help your meditation to get some personal instruction. You can take a mindfulness-based stress reduction (MBSR) class, go to a meditation center, or seek out a meditation teacher. There are lots of people teaching meditation these days, even online! Some teachers are trained in MBSR, some are Buddhists, and others have simply found a method they want to share with others. Judge for yourself whether a class, group, or teacher is useful to you. Is your meditation improving, or at least how you feel about it? Do the teachers or other meditators give you tips that end up working for you?

Attending a meditation retreat can also be very helpful for developing and deepening your meditation. The eight-week MBSR class includes a one-day retreat, and most Buddhist centers hold retreats regularly. These generally involve maintaining silence throughout the day and spending many hours meditating. Meditation is broken into 25 to 40 minute sessions, and interspersed with other mindful activities like working together in silence, or guided yoga. The sheer amount of time you spend meditating at a retreat can help your mind settle more deeply than it ever has before. You can benefit from that experience in and of itself, but it also shows you what is possible in meditation. Eventually you can meditate in a similar way outside of retreat.

The Least You Need to Know

- Meditation involves taking time to set aside all of your other activities in order to practice mindfulness intensively.

- In mindfulness meditation you choose a simple object for your meditation such as your breath, or sound, and try to sustain awareness of your present experience.

- The many kinds of meditation include guided meditations, where someone verbally guides you through an exercise; concentration meditation; and expansive awareness meditation.

- The goal in mindfulness meditation is to be completely and energetically present in a sustained way. Ideally as your mind is not wandering, and you are so interested in your present experience that there's no place you'd rather be.

- Ideals can get in the way in meditation. It's important to get to know your own mind so you adjust your techniques and approach, and learn what works to calm and focus you.

PART 3

Developing a Receptive Attitude

An essential part of mindfulness is cultivating and maintaining your receptivity. Even if you can pay attention, if your mind is closed or biased because of judgment, lack of acceptance, or expectations, you won't be able to see things clearly. If you're complacent or fearful, you might not even be willing to work on mindfulness, let alone summon the energy and courage required to deepen it. If it's difficult for you to access joy, you miss out on the purest source of motivation for being present and receptive in your life just as it is.

In this part of the book I discuss the many ways you can identify obstacles to your mindful receptivity, and how to deal with them. You'll find out what it means to let go of judgments and cultivate acceptance, and how this is very different from passivity. You'll learn about how to generate more curiosity about everyday life and how to engage it with an energetic and fearless spirit of investigation. I discuss what stillness and silence are in the context of mindfulness, and the importance of increasing your familiarity and comfort with them. Finally, I suggest ways to access the joy of simply being alive in the present moment, free of expectations, and how this helps you to be even more mindful.

Nonjudgment and Acceptance

When you're working on mindfulness and trying to see your life clearly, it's not enough to be able to pay attention. That's a prerequisite and very important, but even if you're able to sustain awareness of something, your perceptions can be biased and clouded by your judgments about what you're perceiving. Lack of acceptance can prevent you from seeing something clearly because it's too uncomfortable to face it.

In this chapter I discuss how to practice letting go of judgment without letting go of your intelligence. It's possible to take a fairly objective view of things even while you understand some things are helpful, some are harmful, some you like, and some you don't. I also cover how to cultivate acceptance of difficult things without condoning them, and without giving up your efforts to make the world a better place. If you can function with a deeper sense of acceptance, it will be very beneficial to your mindfulness as well as reducing your stress.

In This Chapter

- How nonjudgment and acceptance support a receptive attitude
- New ways to relate to your judgments and assumptions
- Letting go of judging yourself
- Learning to operate without jumping to conclusions
- How to work on acceptance and equanimity

Receptivity and Why It Matters

Think of your mindful awareness as a video camera. When you work on paying attention and cultivating awareness, as discussed in the previous part of this book, you're learning how to aim the camera at an object, keep it still, and focus it. When you work on your receptivity, as will be discussed in this part of the book, you're learning how to clean your camera lens and shine the right light on your object so you end up with a clear picture.

As I talk about letting go of judgments and developing acceptance, keep in mind this isn't about trying to adopt nice feelings or optimistic views in order to make yourself feel better. Cultivating your receptivity is a very personal, challenging, gritty process of coming to terms with the way you view the world and your place in it. The more mindful you're able to be, the more you'll notice when, for some reason, you *can't* see something clearly. You start to realize when there is a smudge on the lens of your camera, or when the conditions aren't right for getting a good picture. Then you turn your mindfulness toward whatever is interfering with seeing clearly.

Recognizing Judgments Aren't Reality

Your brain is wired to perceive and process information efficiently in order to help you survive and be successful in life. Part of the way it does this is to quickly categorize all of your experiences so you don't have to think about them anymore. Once you know something is right, you can put it on the shelf with other "right" things and move on. You don't have to ponder the intricacies and ambiguities of the situation, except perhaps to get better at arguing for your conclusion. If something gets placed in the "ick" category, or someone is unreasonable, you can rest in your decision and turn your attention to avoiding the unpleasant person or thing.

 KEEP IN MIND

Judgment is intimately tied to the function of language. In a certain sense even looking down at your hand and identifying it as "your hand" involves judgment. You discriminate between your hand and the surface it's resting on, your hand and the rest of your body, your hand and anyone else's hand. You categorize it as a hand, a body part with a particular structure and function. When you become aware of your hand without judgment you see color and texture. You notice the shininess of the fingernails and the veins crisscrossing over the tendons. You feel coolness or warmth, and become conscious of your hand's position—without thinking "my hand," or attaching any other words to the experience of it.

Even when you aren't judging like from dislike, good from bad, acceptable from unacceptable, your mind is constantly discriminating between things. This is the "ordinary level of thinking" referred to in mindfulness principle #5: *to see clearly, you have to drop below the level of ordinary thinking and experience things directly* (see Chapter 3). The left side of your brain—often the most active side—is perfectly attuned to the relative differences between things: light versus dark, high versus low, ugly versus beautiful.

Of course, reality, which is what you're trying to see clearly in your mindfulness practice, doesn't actually fall into neat categories. Reality is rich, nuanced, and ever-changing. No one is always unreasonable, beauty is in the eye of the beholder, and there are at least two sides to every story. When you start to believe your judgments truly reflect reality, you're replacing direct experience and observation with ideas. You may have very good reasons for forming those ideas, but ideas are always less complex than reality; they're convenient glosses that lump things together in groups instead of acknowledging the infinite variety in manifestation.

Getting Perspective on Judgment

How do you avoid believing your judgments reflect reality? How do you minimize jumping to conclusions about things, but instead remain present with them, observing and learning? If you're anything like me, you don't even want to find out *how* until you have reassurance that letting go of judgment doesn't mean you have to ignore what your mind is telling you. So I'll give you that reassurance here: becoming more receptive to reality doesn't require you to become stupid or undiscriminating.

You don't have to suppress or ignore your judgments. They're part of your reality. The key is recognizing they're just *part* of it—and actually just a small part that is often unreliable because of bias and misperception. As you practice mindfulness, you simply notice when you're experiencing judgment. You don't try to get rid of it, argue with it, or feel bad about judging. You just note your judgment as you do any other aspect of a situation. "Hmmm," you observe, "I'm thinking this whole work proposal is ridiculous. I'm also hungry and it's 10 o'clock in the morning." Your judgment doesn't get any special weight among all the things that arise in your awareness.

Increasing Your Tolerance for Ambiguity

Not believing your judgments requires you to increase your *tolerance for ambiguity*. This is the ability to experience ambiguity without feeling compelled to avoid it or resolve it with a series of judgments. This is an extremely useful skill to have whenever you encounter things that are contradictory, confusing, unresolved (or unresolvable), or vague. Tolerance for ambiguity helps you stay present with your experience so you have a chance to see things clearly. You may or may not come to any conclusions about your experience, but you won't feel compelled to jump to them prematurely because ambiguity is uncomfortable or threatening.

DEFINITION

> **Tolerance for ambiguity** is the ability to experience ambiguous situations or problems without finding them too uncomfortable to bear, or perceiving them as a threat. A high tolerance for ambiguity allows you to remain calm and patient when faced with things that are complex, vague, contradictory, or unresolved. A low tolerance compels you to avoid or resolve the ambiguity by any means necessary.

It's quite amazing to experience the space before judgment and realize it can be completely legitimate to stop there. This is very different from taking refuge in ignorance, or not caring about the truth of things. Resting in nonjudgment in a mindful way means you're very aware of what's going on and ready to make a decision or take action if you need to. If no such action is required, you realize you can maintain more receptivity to reality by continuing to engage it directly than by relating only to your judgments about it. If you practice doing this over and over, you increase your tolerance for ambiguity because you realize you can survive it, and that leaving things temporarily unresolved doesn't necessarily mean disaster will strike.

Here's an example: your intimate partner makes a poor lifestyle choice, such as smoking. You've asked him not to, but he's unwilling or unable to stop even though he admits it would be a good idea. At this point you have two choices. You can continue to judge, either nagging your partner constantly or feeling stressed and angry whenever you see him smoking. The choice to judge will probably undermine the quality of your relationship and/or your own well-being.

The other choice is to let go of judgment because it isn't useful in this case. When you see your partner smoking, you stay grounded in your present experience. In the moment, you're aware of your partner and your affection and respect for him. You don't have to think about all the terrible things that might happen in the future because of his smoking. You don't have to get pulled away from your current experience by thoughts about how things should be other than how they are. You can rest in the place of nonjudgment—which ironically will make your partner less defensive and more likely to choose positive change all on his own.

Sifting Through Your Assumptions

Assumptions are judgments you have made in the past which have become part of the way you view the world. You lose track of them, forget they're judgments, and therefore tend to let them operate without question. To go back to the analogy of learning to operate a video camera, this is like putting a filter on the camera and forgetting it's there. Everything viewed through your mindfulness "camera" looks fuzzy or blue, and you assume that's the way things really look.

How do you challenge your assumptions when you often don't know they're there? First you notice something is getting in the way of your ability to see something clearly. This obstruction may be obvious in that you're aware you don't understand something in your life, or you don't feel like you're able to experience it directly. The obstruction may be less obvious. You may simply recognize there is a problem in your life you can't seem to do anything about. This can be a habit of thought, speech, or behavior, and it seems to resist change no matter how much you think about how to deal with it.

 TAKE CARE

> The practice of nonjudgment can be easily misunderstood. You might think it means holding yourself back from getting involved or committing to a position, but that kind of refusal to judge can just be a way of protecting yourself. Pondering the real truth of a situation can be troubling, and coming up with your best response can be challenging. Taking a stand puts you at risk for embarrassment or defeat. Nonjudgment isn't meant to help you avoid such responsibilities; it's meant to help you fulfill them with greater clarity and perspective.

When you suspect an assumption might be getting in the way of seeing clearly, it helps to calm down by doing a simple mindfulness exercise and then call to mind the issue you're working to understand. Quietly ask yourself what you think about it, trying not to judge or censor yourself. Let the truth of your assumption reveal itself even if it's obviously wrong, stupid, or outdated.

For example, perhaps you turn your mindful awareness toward your troubled relationship with your father and let yourself notice that you're thinking, "He's never liked me." You may not have ever realized before that you were carrying around this thought. Just recognizing it's there can open up new possibilities for you, such as asking your father whether your assumption is true, or recalling times you've previously overlooked when he has been supportive of you.

The Problem with Judging Yourself

If you want to be able to settle into mindful awareness and see clearly, you have to be ready to face some truths about yourself you'd rather not know. You may end up noticing attributes or behaviors that make you feel ashamed, embarrassed, or disgusted with yourself. You may remember things that fill you with regret. You may realize your life is way out of balance. Alternatively, you may see some positive assumptions you were making about yourself aren't as true as you thought they were.

You may not really want to see the reality of your life, and no one can make you. However, if you *do* want to see it, you'll need to learn to be gentler or wiser in your judgments of yourself. Otherwise, your mind is likely to refuse to let you see things in order to protect you from yourself! It may sound strange, but it's true. Without even realizing you're trying to avoid facing something, you can rationalize, distract yourself, and conveniently forget certain topics. If you finally face difficult realizations and then overindulge in judging yourself, you're likely to start avoiding mindfulness altogether.

Who Cares What You Think?

Instead, to develop more receptivity, you try to regard your judgments of yourself the same way you do your other kinds of judgments, as discussed earlier. Judgments are part of your reality, but only part, and they're a part that tends to be highly biased and oversimplified. It can be difficult to take this objective approach when you're considering judgments about yourself, because they seem to be especially true or right. After all, you know yourself, don't you? And who else should draw conclusions about your thoughts, speech, and behavior besides you?

 KEEP IN MIND

> Some of the most important judgments you need to let go of are those about your mindfulness practice itself. You can limit your progress by drawing conclusions about your own abilities or level of commitment, and use them as excuses for not making more effort, getting creative, or seeking support for your practice. You may find yourself thinking things like, "I just can't concentrate," or, "I'll never manage to get perspective on my emotions." Instead of believing these judgments completely, just notice them and respond internally, "Hmmm. Maybe." Opening up just a little space between yourself and the judgments can let you keep growing and learning in ways you don't expect.

The important thing to remember is that it doesn't really matter whether a judgment is true or false. In any case, it's never going to be entirely true or entirely false, but instead will fall somewhere on a continuum between fiction and fact. What matters is what the act of judging is doing to your body-mind, and whether or not it's useful. Your power of judgment is meant to help you survive and be successful, right? So when it's actually hindering you, obstructing your ability to see clearly, threatening your relationships, or resulting in anxiety or depression, it's time to let go of it and try something else.

Not Letting Judgment Derail You

An example may help illustrate the process of letting go of a judgment about yourself. Let's say you've been working on mindful awareness of your feelings and it becomes clear to you that you experience disgust and aversion when your child whines and throws a tantrum. With the receptivity cultivated in mindfulness you're able to see clearly how strong these feelings are, and how they affect your interactions with your child. Let's say this realization is something of a surprise to you. It's bound to be unpleasant, especially if you hold an idea about yourself as a good parent or a nice person. Seeing reality may be painful, and may provoke shame, sadness, and a sense of despair about being able to change.

If you don't let go of judgments about yourself at this point, they're liable to get in the way of learning more about your life, and taking positive action. What's needed now is for your mind to become even calmer and more receptive. Judgments, as discussed earlier, simply categorize things so you don't have to keep engaging them directly. In the case of a difficult realization about yourself, you may not *want* to continue engaging it directly, so the temptation to judge can be strong. However, if you manage to tolerate the ambiguity and stay present instead, you can examine your feelings more closely, as discussed in Chapter 5. You can learn to acknowledge your feelings and relate to them differently, so they don't affect your behavior as much.

Navigating Your Life Objectively

The receptive attitude you need for mindfulness is much easier if you can remain somewhat objective about your own life. This can be a challenge, because you naturally care very much about your happiness, the well-being of those you care about, and the success of your projects (including mindfulness). In fact, the effectiveness of mindfulness practice depends on your desire to be happy (see mindfulness principles #1–4, Chapter 3).

You can be more objective about your own life when you question the following assumption: in the pursuit of happiness, you *have to* get stressed, worried, or upset. Is this true? Most people believe, whether they realize it or not, the more they want something, the more willing they have to be to get upset about it. And yet, when you watch carefully, you can see how getting stressed or angry rarely helps anyone get what they want. Getting upset may initially motivate you to do something, or it may help you communicate to someone that you really mean what you say, but continuing to operate in a state of agitation tends to agitate others and compromise your ability to function effectively.

MINDFUL EXERCISE

Take a few calming breaths and then call to mind something in your life that presents a problem. Write down all the things you've tried in order to fix the problem. Then write down all the things you can think of that you haven't tried. Now set aside all of those solutions for a while and open yourself up to the possibility that real and lasting resolution will come from somewhere else. Is there anything in your mind or heart that resists change, and why? What longings or fears might lie behind your problematic choices? Is this really a problem, or do you just think it should be? Once you set aside ordinary thinking and just look, answers can arise from anywhere.

The mindful approach is to let your natural desire for happiness work with your intelligence, knowledge, and values toward the best result you're capable of achieving. There's a way in which you can "watch" this process unfold, without the involvement of your worried, judging mind. You do this by staying mindfully present throughout—staying grounded in awareness of sensations, tolerating ambiguity, and not jumping to conclusions. You don't forget about the issue in front of you; you keep observing everything with receptive awareness, including your thoughts and feelings. You let all of the information enter the supercomputer that is your body-mind and then give it enough time to process. At some point, a plan of action will present itself to you. Is it right? Will it work? The answers to these questions don't really matter as long as it's the best plan you have.

Less Upset About Results

When you've maintained mindfulness and responded to life in the best way you can, you can also let go of judging the results. You observe the results with mindfulness and learn from them, but you don't need to categorize a complex, unfolding experience as good or bad, a success or a failure. You definitely don't need to take judgment a step further and conclude that because of the results of your actions, *you* are good or bad, a success or a failure.

As discussed earlier, it doesn't matter whether these judgments are true or false, it just matters they aren't helpful to seeing clearly and managing your life. It's much more conducive to mindfulness if you can suspend judgment and just continue to experience your life directly.

Resistance to doing this is often due to your attachment to ideas about yourself. For example, perhaps you think of yourself as a good communicator who manages to maintain harmonious relationships with everyone. Then someone you're working with completely misunderstands what you were trying to tell them. They end up angry and hurt, and no amount of explanation or apology on your part can completely erase the harm that's been done. You can stress about this series of events at great length, trying to figure out whether you're actually not a good communicator or people-person after all, or whether this person is just unusually stupid or unreasonable. You'd like to make a judgment that will let you know whether you're right or wrong.

A mindful response to a scenario like this involves allowing your life to be ambiguous. Sometimes you're a great communicator, and sometimes you're not. Great communication is a vague categorization that requires the agreement of at least two people, and depends on a whole host of factors beyond your control. You do your best and hope for happy results for everyone involved, and sometimes you fail. Sometimes you fail because you're blind and selfish, but who isn't? Are you required to meet a higher standard than everyone else?

Lack of Acceptance as an Obstacle

It's much easier to maintain receptive awareness of your life when you've cultivated acceptance. Resistance to things as they are causes reactivity and agitation. When you encounter a reminder of something you don't want to accept, your mind tends to leap out of the present moment into justifications for your opinions, plans for how to fix things, or distractions that are more pleasant to think about. Lack of acceptance is like the ultimate judgment: no! You've put something squarely into a category of things that should not be considered any more, and about which no ambiguity can be tolerated.

 TAKE CARE

> When you're working on acceptance, try to avoid telling yourself how you should feel, and that you should get over it. First, that doesn't work. Second, mindfulness asks you to be present with reality—and part of your reality is how you're feeling, and the fact that you're finding acceptance difficult. Let go of any agenda; simply being mindful will move you closer to the place where you can embrace acceptance.

Acceptance is taking nonjudgment one step further. When you accept something, you make your peace with it. This does *not* mean making your peace with injustice, harmful actions, ignorance, etc., in the sense that you stop trying to do anything to create change. What acceptance *does* mean is you make your peace with the way things are right now. There is absolutely nothing you can do to change the way the universe has ended up being at this moment. Once you stop struggling against the mere fact of having to face what you're facing, you'll feel a lot less stress and unhappiness.

Working on Acceptance

Acceptance is much easier said than done. Your circumstances might be extremely painful physically or emotionally. You may be suffering as a direct result of someone else's greed or violence. You may be caught in a vicious cycle of addictive behavior that is destroying your life. It's natural to wonder whether there are some things that are just impossible (or unwise) to accept.

Fortunately, there are no circumstances in which acceptance doesn't help. It usually requires some mindfulness in order to arrive at real acceptance, but then the acceptance in turn helps you be more mindful. You'll be able to see things more clearly instead of resisting them, you'll be in the best position to take effective action in your life, and you might even be more appreciative of it.

For example, let's say you're struggling to make ends meet with a job you hate. You don't have enough money to get the training necessary for a better job because someone swindled you out of your life savings. It will be very tempting to dwell on the past injustice you've experienced, how much you hate your job, and how your life is never going to get any better. In the midst of all of this resistance to the way your life is, you probably aren't the slightest bit interested in mindful awareness of your present experience. You may get bitter and depressed, and your health may suffer.

What does acceptance mean in a circumstance like this? It means you'll make a valiant effort to be mindfully present for your life no matter how you feel about it. As you do this, you'll probably have to directly experience the grief, anger, and despair you've been carrying around inside. You'll have to acknowledge fears and how your hopes and dreams have crumbled. As unpleasant as all of this sounds, if you can stay present for all of it (not just thinking about it and how you can change it), you have a chance to make your peace with the way things are. It's not that things are okay or even acceptable; it's that they just *are*, and you don't have any life other than this one.

Equanimity

Acceptance relates to equanimity, the psychophysical factor of awakening discussed in Chapter 7. Equanimity is very conducive to mindfulness, but sometimes it gets a bad rap because people think it requires you to be cold or superior—as if the most important thing is that you aren't bothered (or aren't seen to be bothered). In real equanimity you aren't concerned about whether or not you're bothered. You remain receptive and open, without clinging to any particular feeling or mind state. You don't think, "Ah, look! This doesn't upset *me*!" You receive all the data pouring in from your life, but it flows freely through you because of nonjudgment and acceptance.

MINDFUL EXERCISE

Imagine you're standing in a line at the grocery store checkout and someone pushes their cart into you from behind. How do you feel? Irritated, maybe even outraged? Are you inspired to kick back at the cart and send it crashing into its owner, or do you want to yell about how inconsiderate and careless people can be? Take a moment to imagine your physical experience of this situation. Now imagine you look back and see the person behind looks faint and is struggling to stay upright. How do your feelings and thoughts change? Is it that you've suddenly become a better person who isn't bothered by being bumped, or is it just that your perspective has changed?

Here's an analogy: a powerful stream of water is coming your way. Judgment is like trying to redirect or channel the water so it goes where you want it to. This approach lets you control the landscape of your life, but it only works as long as the water doesn't come too fast or with too much volume (which is analogous to facing overwhelming or difficult circumstances). Lack of acceptance is like trying to build a wall to block the water. You might succeed for a time, but eventually the pressure will build and the water will burst through with even more destructive force than it would have to begin with.

Equanimity, in this analogy, is like learning to swim. You aren't trying to hold on to any position or contain anything. You aren't trying to control anything other than your own body-mind, because you've seen clearly that it's all you can ever do. This isn't distressing because you're confident of your ability to swim—which is simply being as mindful of your life as you can be, and letting your best responses arise naturally.

You may think equanimity sounds like a pretty high ideal, but of course it's not an all or nothing experience. Anyone can cultivate *more* equanimity in their life. It doesn't matter whether you achieve perfect equanimity, or whether anyone ever has. What matters is that you work on non-judgment and acceptance whenever you can. Over time, you can develop a taste for directly experiencing your life no matter what, instead of categorizing it or resisting it. You prove to yourself it's not only less stressful to operate that way, it's more effective. Each time you just breathe through something that might upset you and then come out intact on the other side, you increase your equanimity.

The Least You Need to Know

- Your mind is wired to produce judgments on the things you encounter so you can categorize them and deal with them more efficiently, but that means you end up dealing with ideas instead of reality.

- One of the biggest obstacles to mindfulness is the tendency to judge yourself harshly. This can prevent you from seeing things clearly—or even prevent you from looking.

- It's possible to refrain from judgment by staying grounded in mindfulness of the present moment. Unless you need to make an immediate decision, this is preferable to judgment because it leaves you open and receptive.

- Lack of acceptance makes it very difficult to stay present with your experience because you're resisting or rejecting something. Staying mindful no matter how you feel can help you find some peace with things as they are.

- Practicing nonjudgment and acceptance can lead to more equanimity, one of the great supports for mindfulness. Equanimity results from trusting you'll just do your best, instead of trying to control or resist your experience.

Curiosity, Energy, and Courage

Buddhists identify curiosity and energy as two of the essential elements in an effective mindfulness practice. These two psychophysical factors were introduced in Chapter 7, and together they provide the forward momentum that motivates you to keep improving your mindfulness. You also need courage in order to use mindfulness to look deeply at your life, because you never know what you might find.

In the last chapter I discussed the ways you can obstruct your mindful receptivity through judgment and lack of acceptance. In this chapter I explain how to increase the scope and reach of your receptivity, and develop an inquisitive, bold attitude. This kind of attitude gives your mindfulness vitality and opens you up to discovering new things about your own body-mind, your life, and the world.

In This Chapter

- The role of curiosity and energy in fueling your mindfulness
- How to avoid being complacent about your life
- How interest leads to curiosity and energy
- Developing fascination for anything—even challenges
- Facing uncomfortable realizations about your life

Continuing Education

In most cultures, the vision of a human life includes a period of intense growth and learning called childhood, followed by a long period of adulthood during which you get busy with responsibilities like family, work, and helping to run things. As an adult, you're expected to learn additional skills and information as necessary to fulfill your responsibilities, but it's generally assumed you know pretty much all you need to in order to function effectively.

You've probably realized how limited this view of human life is. As an adult, you find yourself constantly challenged to learn and grow. You've discovered it's no simple task to effectively use the infinitely complex organic machine that is your body-mind. You've recognized you always fall at least a little short of your ideals with respect to how you conduct yourself in relationships, manage your life, access your potential, contribute to the world, and stay in touch with your deepest aspirations.

 KEEP IN MIND

Albert Einstein encouraged people not to give up their awareness that there is much they don't know. In his essay "The World As I See It," he writes: "The fairest thing we can experience is the mysterious. It is the fundamental emotion which stands at the cradle of true art and true science. He who knows it not and can no longer wonder, no longer feel amazement, is as good as dead, a snuffed-out candle." (From the book named for the essay *The World As I See It,* translated by Alan Harris.)

The intensive learning and development that happens in childhood doesn't have to stop with adulthood. Hindu culture recognizes this by identifying a fourth life stage, after adulthood and retirement, when someone spends time in spiritual pursuits like meditation and seeking enlightenment. This acknowledges there is another level of learning to be experienced beyond the practical, including refinement of understanding of what it means to be human, and of one's ability to be mindful and see clearly.

In modern times people have the time and freedom to be able to work on their spiritual education throughout their lives instead of waiting until the end. If you don't like the word *spiritual,* just think of this as mastering the art of living a human life. Living as fully, deeply, authentically, and happily as you can is no simple undertaking. Instead, it's comparable to something like martial arts, playing a musical instrument, or working on a craft like fine carpentry. A higher level of mastery is always possible. Refining your skills and understanding isn't something you necessarily do because you're unhappy or inadequate; it's something you do because you want to take full advantage of being alive.

In mindfulness, the continuing education you're engaged in is about your own life. You keep examining your body-mind and getting to know yourself intimately. You become familiar with your tendencies, habits, obstacles, and strengths. You learn about your deepest aspirations and greatest fears, and come to terms with the past. You question your assumptions, explore living with less judgment, and experiment with new ways of being. You study carefully how your body-mind operates until you become more skilled at navigating your life.

The Obstacle of Complacency

The curiosity and energy you need in order to work on mastering the art of living a human life can be lacking if you become complacent. This is very easy to do, so this shouldn't be viewed as a terrible fault, or something extreme that you'll necessarily be aware of. As discussed in the previous chapter, it's human nature to categorize your experiences with judgments and make assumptions about life rather than observing it with receptive awareness. It's also human nature to settle into your life and just enjoy it as much as you can, without worrying too much about how you might refine it before it's over.

Tuning Out Versus Tuning In

If you really stop to think about it, complacency is about thinking everything is good enough as it is, and that you know everything you need to know. When things are going reasonably well, you're likely to feel at least a degree of complacency. There's little motivation to challenge yourself, make changes, or put lots of effort into working on mindfulness. You're likely to tune things out, let your mind wander, and forget about your deepest aspirations.

 MINDFUL EXERCISE

Pick up an everyday object you tend to use but tune out of your awareness, such as a coffee mug. Imagine you have to verbally describe the appearance, use, and significance of this object to an alien from another planet, where the beings don't have anything resembling our hands. You can't assume anything in your explanation. How do you go about this? You have to communicate size without comparing the object to something the alien isn't familiar with. To explain the use, you have to explain lots of other things. What aspects of the appearance do you mention that you haven't noticed in years? Compare this level of detailed observation with the complacency with which you usually regard the object.

Sometimes it's only when you experience something unusual or challenging that you recognize the complacency with which you typically regard your life. Perhaps you travel to a foreign country where every sight, sound, smell, taste, and touch is new and different. You find yourself paying much closer attention to your experience than you usually do; your interest and receptivity are naturally heightened. Perhaps, instead, your life changes drastically. One minute everything is familiar and routine, and the next you have to carefully consider everything you do. Many of the assumptions you used to make about life no longer apply. Again, your interest and receptivity are heightened—even if it isn't a pleasant experience.

Waking Back Up

The sad thing about complacency is that your life is short, and it can be even more rewarding and fascinating than you currently realize. (This is true for all of us.) You can't miss what you've never experienced, so just because things seem "good enough" right now doesn't mean you would feel the same way if you saw your life more clearly, or tasted it with new levels of intimate awareness.

For example, when people attend intensive meditation retreats they often find themselves getting snapped out of complacency. They wake up to new ways to engage their lives that are very inspiring, even if they're subtle (like sustaining mindfulness for longer periods). Life as a whole looks different—more significant, more full of potential. Then the "retreatants" return to their everyday lives and find complacency creeping over them again. They get comfortable or fall back into routines. They're no longer in a situation that encourages mindfulness, curiosity, and energy, so these things tend to decrease. It can be hard to sustain the wakefulness you're able achieve at certain times, no matter how you achieve it.

Fortunately, you can do things in your daily life to minimize your complacency and motivate yourself. One way is to establish habits that encourage you to be mindful and to keep investigating your life. Such habits can include regular meditation, participating in a mindfulness group, or study. Personal rituals can help if they encourage mindfulness or remind you of your aspirations. These can be simple things like reciting an inspirational poem in the morning, always holding your coffee cup with two hands, or driving to work without the radio on so you can pay closer attention to your moment-to-moment experience.

 MINDFUL EXERCISE

Choose an activity you do regularly that mostly involves observation. This could be driving to work, listening to other people in a meeting, or going for a walk. Do this when you don't need to carry on a conversation, and turn off the radio or music. Now imagine as vividly as you can that you have only one day left to live. This is your *last* drive to work, *last* meeting, or *last* walk—ever. You'll never have this experience again. Don't start imagining what kind of plans you'd make if you were at the end of your life, just try to be as incredibly attentive and appreciative as you would be if you had a very short time left to live.

Another way to avoid complacency is to remind yourself life is short, and that this moment will never happen again. It isn't necessary to make yourself anxious about dying, or gloomy about the inevitability of death. The impermanence of life is a simple fact that makes each moment you have precious. Just stop and think about the fact you'll never again experience *this* day, or this particular way the sun is lighting up the old oak leaves still hanging from the trees. You'll never be exactly this age again, or interact with people the same way twice. When you're complacent you might think you know pretty much everything you need to, but you don't actually even know what's going to happen when you walk down the hallway to the next room.

Interest Leads to Curiosity and Energy

Curiosity and energy arise naturally when you're really interested in something. Interest can stem from concern about your well-being, or the well-being of those you care about. You may want to avoid something that could be unpleasant or harmful, or obtain something that could be beneficial or pleasant. Interest also arises when things are brand new to you and—here's the essential part—you think they're relevant to your life.

If you don't find most moments of your life interesting enough to pay attention to, chances are you're writing them off as not fitting into one of the categories of interest listed above. You figure there's nothing to be gained from engagement in a particular moment, or lost by ignoring it. You've experienced lots of moments like this before, so you might as well think about something else. Maybe there's something novel going on, but it doesn't have anything to do with you. No one's going to test you on it later.

Fascinated by Your Life

To generate the necessary curiosity and energy for mindfulness, you need to experiment with a different way of calibrating your interest level. In contrast to the self-referential ways of determining whether to pay attention described earlier, think of something that, for some reason, you feel passionately interested in. Perhaps it's wild birds, astronomy, or masterful athletes. This subject of interest offers you no chance of gain, and has no direct connection to your everyday concerns and responsibilities. Still, you've no trouble at all concentrating on it whenever you encounter it. You're naturally fascinated.

It's entirely possible to find your everyday life as fascinating as the subjects or activities that naturally ignite your passionate interest. You won't be able to see things this way as long as you're judging and categorizing your experience, as discussed in the last chapter. When you do that, you stop interacting directly with reality and instead just interact with your ideas about it. Mindfulness helps you tune in to what's actually going on around you—and when you do that, you notice a whole lot more. Things that appeared dull, boring, or unremarkable when you only gave them a quick glance are revealed to have infinite layers of complexity and beauty if you look more closely.

Ordinary Things Viewed Mindfully

As an example, consider the simple activity of brushing your teeth. Ordinarily, this is a time to think about other things because you've brushed your teeth thousands of times and it's a boring activity. If you stay mindful throughout the experience, you'll notice all kinds of things. A toothbrush is an amazing invention—all those little bristles, firm enough to clean your teeth but not hurt your gums. The toothpaste tastes chalky and minty, and produces suds like soap. Your hand executes a complex series of movements as it applies the toothbrush to all the different areas of your mouth—and if you think too much about it, your hand is liable to make a mistake and jam the toothbrush into your gums. All of this is to clean your teeth, which are bones protruding out of your gums. Weird! Now, if brushing your teeth can be fascinating, how fascinating will it be to pay attention to your interactions with other people, or watch your mind state as you engage in a creative activity?

 **KEEP IN MIND**

Sometimes it can be hard to appreciate the simple things in life when you feel deprived of the important things. Some of those important things might even feel essential to your well-being, such as health, money, or companionship. It's important not to put your mindfulness in opposition to your needs. You aren't trying to console yourself with little things, or tell yourself you should be happy with what you have. Instead, think of it as not letting your lack ruin your life. You can appreciate the simple things in your life in spite of the fact that there are things missing from it.

This isn't about amusing yourself during boring activities. After all, you already do that by engaging in stimulus-independent thinking. This is about recognizing how your interest level is determined by you, not by your surroundings. It's the result of the choices you make about what's worth paying attention to. If you decide something is worth your interest, it opens up and becomes interesting. You can make a choice at any moment to make your life interesting if you want to, rather than waiting for fun, pleasurable, or exciting things to entertain you. If you're only interested in those experiences, your life will be composed of long worthless parts interspersed with brief periods of enjoyment.

Mindfulness, on the other hand, can help you appreciate *all* parts of your life. Greater mindfulness leads to greater interest; greater interest leads to greater curiosity and energy; greater curiosity and energy, in turn, inspire greater mindfulness. In Chapter 3 I presented three aspects of mindfulness: aspiration, awareness, and attitude. The feedback loop involving mindfulness, interest, curiosity, and energy is an example of how aspiration (the desire to see more clearly), awareness (mindfulness), and attitude (in this case, energetic curiosity) reinforce one another. You can work on any one of them to inspire and support your work on the others.

The Spirit of Investigation

It's very beneficial to your mindfulness if you can adopt the role of a scientist as you study your own body-mind and life. I introduced this concept in Chapter 7, where I talked about cultivating awareness of psychophysical factors. In that case, it was the scientist's objectivity that was valuable. In this case, it's the scientist's habit of relentless, energetic inquiry. A good scientist tries to make no assumptions. She is patient and deliberate, setting up experimental circumstances to test her ideas. She has an appetite for discovery and truth that drives her forward, even when one of her cherished theories might be in danger of being disproven.

A good scientist is also always on the lookout for things we don't know. Not knowing isn't seen as a shortcoming; it's recognized as being a permanent state because there's always something more to learn. This attitude is exactly the opposite of the one many people take, which is to be constantly on the lookout for all the things they know. It's tempting to see not knowing as a weakness to be hidden, or something to be fixed as quickly as possible. There's an alternative view that is much more conducive to seeing your life clearly: identifying something you don't know as an opportunity.

This alternative view may sound like a clichéd piece of advice you'd give to someone to encourage them to think positively when they're having lots of problems. However, this isn't about feeling positive or negative. Whatever your circumstances or emotions about them, you can learn to feel a subtle sense of exhilaration when you identify something you haven't mastered, or discover an aspect of your life you don't understand. This exhilaration can manifest even when things are painful or difficult, because now there's a possibility you can change things.

 TAKE CARE

If you try to embrace your challenges as opportunities, don't forget to cultivate mindful awareness and acceptance of your feelings first. The spirit of investigation should open you up to perceiving all aspects of the situation, and your feelings are part of it. Perhaps you've just encountered something you don't know or haven't been acknowledging, or some way you have of interacting with the world that isn't producing great results. It's natural to feel things like anxiety, defensiveness, frustration, or disappointment. These emotions don't have to dampen your spirit of investigation. In fact, they can even add fuel to it.

Cultivating Courage

Once you've followed the process of mindful investigation through to insight and positive change a few times, you start to anticipate how rewarding it is, and how it almost inevitably leads to greater happiness. This builds your confidence in the process, and leads to the courage you need to face difficult things and develop a truly receptive attitude. The ability to maintain mindfulness through discomfort is important when you have to face difficult realizations, come to terms with painful events from the past, or struggle with harmful habits. Common sense tells you if something makes you uncomfortable, you should move away from it, or at least try to distract yourself from the discomfort. Mindfulness recommends the exact opposite: if something makes you uncomfortable, it's especially important to open up to your experience of it and examine it closely. The things that inspire negative reactions in you—such as aversion, fear, anger, or shame—are pointing you toward areas for mindful investigation. These are your areas of not-knowing, where you do not yet see clearly what does and doesn't lead to greater happiness for self and others. (See mindfulness principle #4, Chapter 3.)

The goal of mindfulness is greater happiness, so it can seem contradictory that you're asked to investigate uncomfortable things in your life. However, this has to do with the "greater" and "lesser" kinds of happiness explained in Chapter 3. You may need to compromise your lesser (short-term) happiness in order to mindfully engage with something challenging, but the idea is that it will ultimately result in greater happiness—which is what applies in the longest term, at the largest scale, and includes the happiness of both self and other.

The need for courage in your mindfulness practice, like the need for curiosity and energy, can be obvious, but most often it's subtle. When you lack the courage to face things, you may find you are distracting yourself, avoiding mindfulness or meditation, or stuck in thoughts that justify your position or try to convince you that nothing's wrong. This is when you can rely on mindfulness principle #1: *you, and all other beings, just want to be happy.* Remind yourself that facing reality ultimately leads to greater happiness and then acknowledge it takes curiosity, energy, and courage to do it.

Here's an example of following a process of mindful investigation from beginning to end in a way that requires courage but also strengthens it. At some point in my mindfulness practice I found out I had a tendency to unintentionally offend people while I was speaking. I only discovered this because I was trying to pay more attention to my life. In the past I had been too caught up in my own thoughts and expressions to notice people's subtle reactions. The tools of mindfulness helped me notice that sometimes when I spoke, certain people would shut up and withdraw because of the abrasive, sarcastic, and insensitive ways I expressed myself.

It was difficult to face and examine this tendency of mine. It was tempting to dismiss this realization as unimportant, and rationalize that I was just being myself when I talked and other people needed to grow thicker skins. I tried to be honest with myself, however, and acknowledge that I felt saddened and embarrassed. At the same time I was also excited and hopeful. I knew the tools of mindfulness would help me examine this habit and understand it better. When I was able to see clearly why I acted the way I did, I had a chance to see alternative ways of behaving. I cultivated more mindfulness of my speech and of the emotional states of others. Eventually I became more sensitive and respectful when I expressed myself, and my relationships with people improved. (See Chapter 13 for how to mindfully make changes in your life.)

The Least You Need to Know

- Curiosity and energy provide the forward momentum in your mindfulness practice.

- Complacency hinders mindfulness. When you're complacent you figure things are good enough as they are, and you know all you really need to know.

- Mindfulness helps you become naturally fascinated with your daily life. Curiosity and energy arise naturally from passionate interest.

- It's very helpful to develop a spirit of investigation like that of a good scientist: staying on the lookout for things you still don't understand and then setting about finding the answers with exhilaration and determination.

- You can develop the courage to remain receptive to difficult realizations by following the process of mindful inquiry through to the end repeatedly. You'll discover it always leads to less stress and greater long-term happiness.

Comfort with Stillness and Silence

To cultivate the receptive attitude required for mindfulness, you temporarily stop trying to influence your circumstances and just open the doors of perception. You try to let go of activity, judgment, and trying to figure things out using your ordinary level of thinking. You momentarily set aside commenting on things and explaining your point of view to others. Your body-mind may generate thoughts and feelings all on its own, but you simply observe them as being part of your overall experience of the moment. You're just watching, listening, sensing, and perceiving. The subjective experience of this purely receptive mode is stillness or silence. The absence of activity or noise may be internal, external, or both. It can be very uncomfortable if you're not used to it.

Fortunately, you can increase your ability to let go of activity and be still. You might even end up liking the experience! The more familiar you get with this simple mode of being, the easier mindfulness will get. In this chapter I explain further what stillness is and why it's so important to mindfulness. I also offer ways you can become more still when you want to, and how to get more comfortable with the resulting silence.

In This Chapter

- The relationship between stillness and a receptive attitude
- How letting go of activity can help you make better decisions
- Why some people are uncomfortable with silence
- Learning to appreciate stillness and silence
- Ways to cultivate more stillness in your life

Letting Go of Activity

Stillness is simply letting go of all activity. The activity you let go of may be working to obtain something you want, trying to avoid or get rid of something you don't want, or escaping something you find neutral or boring. It can be obvious or subtle. Sometimes you're making decisions and taking actions in order to further your best interest (or that of people you care about). Sometimes you're just thinking about plans for the best actions to take. At other times you're just trying to make sense of things in your own mind so you can feel calm, secure, or happy.

 TAKE CARE

> Making an effort to be still when you're definitely not can be very frustrating if you go about it the wrong way. Try not to tell yourself, "I should be still!" Instead, acknowledge the reasons you have for wanting to act and think. Observe them with nonjudgment and acceptance. Then gently try to become curious about whether you need to think and act right now, or you can spare a few moments to cultivate stillness.

It can be very difficult to choose stillness over this kind of activity. Your mind usually does a good job of convincing you your concerns are very important and need to be dealt with *right now.* The vast majority of the time this isn't true, but you'll find yourself arguing you can't spare 10 minutes for dedicated mindfulness practice because you've got too much to think about. It helps to understand why stillness is useful so you can motivate yourself to explore it despite your habitual tendencies.

Joining Stillness and Receptivity

As long as you're focused on fulfilling your agenda, you aren't able to be fully present and mindfully receptive. As discussed in Chapter 5, feelings of like, dislike, and neutrality arise in you more or less automatically in response to anything you encounter. The feelings themselves aren't a problem, but when you feel compelled to act on them you compromise your mindfulness.

Active thinking in the mind or actions taken with the body set more things in motion: subsequent thoughts and feelings arise, and the reactions of others require you to respond. Having acted, you're likely to feel like you need to justify yourself—so you create arguments in your mind about how the perceptions you acted on reflect reality. At this point in the process you'll not only have lost track of the event that originally triggered your feelings, you'll also be busy juggling all the thoughts, emotions, and repercussions of your actions. Calm, receptive awareness is likely to be the last thing you're trying to cultivate.

When you're able to rest in stillness, you become much more receptive to what's going on in your life. It's as if your mental and physical activity create a whole lot of noise. When you let go of that activity, it's like turning off the noise. Suddenly you can hear. You're able to perceive what's going on around you. In addition, when you turn off your volitional actions and thoughts, you dramatically increase your ability to see, touch, smell, taste, and objectively perceive the feelings and thoughts that are present in your body-mind in spite of "you" (that is, the conscious, willful part of you).

Getting Still, Then Acting

It isn't necessary—or advisable—to choose stillness and then do nothing. Mindfulness isn't about becoming passive. What you're trying to do is see your life clearly so you can take better care of it. At some point action is necessary and wise, but you're unlikely to be able to know the best time to act or the best thing to do unless you take some time to rest in stillness first. This turns down the noise in your body-mind and opens up the doors of perception.

It's important to realize that stillness is not *ultimately* useless; it's only *apparently* useless at the moment. As you rest in stillness, your body-mind is still present and operating; it's just not being guided or censored by the part of you responsible for ordinary discriminatory thinking and judging. The information that you receive while mindfully aware goes into your body-mind and affects you. You're just temporarily suspending judgment and action. This actually gives you a chance to process things in a more holistic and deep way than you habitually do. Ironically, resting in stillness can help you make better decisions and be more effective in your life.

 MINDFUL EXERCISE

Look for a time when you're resistant to stillness. You may be excited about something, or you may believe you *have* to get something done or figured out. Despite your resistance, spend two minutes trying to be mindful of something simple like your breath or sound. (No matter how pressing your concerns, you have time for a couple of minutes of inactivity.) Observe the effects. Don't jump to conclusions about how you should or shouldn't cultivate stillness in the future, just let your experience inform you.

You know it's a good time to opt for stillness when you feel stressed, irritable, overwhelmed, or just stuck. These emotional states are signs that your ordinary thinking mind isn't quite up to the job. At some level you realize you're spinning your wheels, missing something, or unable to keep up. This is precisely the time when you're likely to work harder and think even more frantically about how to solve your problems, but it's also when some stillness will be most useful. Things may even start to resolve themselves if you take some time to cultivate mindful awareness or meditate.

How much stillness is enough? It depends on the circumstances and what you want to achieve. It might be beneficial to feel a little bit calmer after spending 10 minutes mindfully eating your lunch instead of chatting or reading. If you're upset about something, 30 minutes of meditation or mindful yoga might give you enough clarity to make a decision. If there's a more pervasive problem in your life, spending a week in a meditation retreat might dramatically shift your perspective and help you see a way toward resolution. Basically, "enough" stillness lets you continue going about your activities with sufficient calm and clarity to take good care of your life.

Stillness Results in Silence

Internal silence is what you experience when you're still. (Note that neither *stillness* nor *silence* is a technical term. They're just words that point to experiences which involve your whole body and mind, and which ultimately can't be described.) Using the metaphor from earlier in the chapter, when you manage to set aside your physical and mental activity and just *be* in a purely receptive way, it's like the noise that's usually present in your head has finally been switched off. You can concentrate on what's going on in the present moment without being distracted by your own agenda.

Overcoming Your Discomfort with Silence

This temporary cessation of noise may seem like a good thing, but the experience of internal silence, as well as the closely related experience of external silence, makes many people very uncomfortable. They fill any quiet moment with entertainment by listening to something on their headphones, reading, or carrying on a conversation. If no external stimulation is available, their minds are busy with fantasy or self-referential processing. Boredom ensues when neither daydreaming nor external stimulation is enough to keep the internal silence at bay—and some people will do anything to avoid boredom. Even if you tend to enjoy a quiet moment, it's likely you resist becoming *completely* still by dropping every last bit of commentary or evaluation.

It's as if deep inner and outer silence is somehow threatening. The reason for this becomes clearer if you look carefully at the experience of literal silence. When you encounter the absence of sound, you may notice how powerfully absence points to presence. It's like the old saying, "You only notice something once it's gone." The quiet seems to echo with all the sounds that aren't there. The silence can feel deafening because it indirectly highlights how rarely you're without some auditory input.

The absence of stimulation also highlights what's still very much present: *you*. If you haven't spent much time being mindfully aware of your body-mind, being left in silence with only your own sensations and perceptions can be disconcerting to say the least. If you have lots of thoughts and emotions you've been trying to avoid, silence can make them very obvious. Even if you think an hour or a day of silence is nice, how do you feel when you contemplate a week, a year, or three years of silence? (Many people practice silence that long or longer!) There's probably a period of silence long enough to make you think, "That's enough! Any longer and I'll go crazy."

KEEP IN MIND

You may resist choosing silence over having a conversation, surfing the web on your phone, or listening to music. These activities may seem like pleasant rewards for all the work you do, or like opportunities to relax and relieve stress. No one's saying you should give them up entirely, but you may want to experiment with choosing silence sometimes and observing what happens. You may surprise yourself and notice you feel happier and more relaxed after a little silence than you do after your usual choice of stimulation or entertainment.

External silence tends to encourage internal silence, and when the two are experienced together the effect can be quite profound. (This is why meditation retreats are usually silent, even when you're not meditating.) Internal silence isn't a state most people are used to, which is part of why it's uncomfortable—it's just new and different. Another reason is it can make you feel vulnerable because you aren't busy trying to take care of yourself. As mentioned earlier, the stillness required for internal silence also opens the doors of perception—and who knows what might come through?

Learning to Appreciate Silence

It's true that in silence you may notice things about yourself or your life that are unnerving or even disturbing. However, as discussed in the previous chapter, with time and practice you can build your confidence in the process of mindfulness. You can develop the courage to face difficult things because you've proven to yourself over and over that dealing with things directly ultimately leads to greater happiness than ignoring or suppressing them.

While internal silence may be uncomfortable at first, it can become something you enjoy and value. Think of when you were a child, and you were able to become completely absorbed in certain experiences. You went into a mode that was completely receptive—watching, listening, touching, and learning. You might have been able to watch an ant make its way across a field without feeling the slightest bit of boredom. You might have sat on a lakeside just listening to the waves lap the shore for an hour, without thinking about time at all. These were experiences of internal silence, although you probably didn't recognize them as being special. Even if you weren't physically still, you were still inside. You weren't actively thinking about anything.

There is a simple and contented part of you that longs for stillness and silence. It just wants to *be*, without having to worry or plan, and without having to justify the way it's spending time. You may be able to taste this simple state of being when you're relaxing in one of your favorite places. You just let the sun shine on your face, or let the background sounds wash over you. What you're feeling at times like this is the psychophysical factor of ease mentioned in Chapter 7. Mindfulness practice helps you experience it, and ease in turn supports your mindfulness because it makes you so receptive.

MINDFUL EXERCISE

The next time you're near a small child or an animal, try doing exactly what they're doing. (Choose a time when a child isn't talking.) If possible, mimic their physical position or activity. Chances are they're just sitting or lying there, or are completely absorbed in some simple activity. See if you can momentarily experience the same internal stillness and silence they have. See if you can settle entirely into the present moment the way they can.

Silence also increases your sense of intimacy with life because it gives life a chance to respond. When you've chosen stillness and let things inside you get quiet, you can perceive many things that are usually drowned out by the noise of your physical and mental activity. Another person's actions or speech may surprise and touch you. Ordinarily you might not even have noticed what happened, or given the person the time and space to express him- or herself. When you notice a tiny flower blooming outside your window, it can seem like part of the reason it's blooming is for you to see it. This isn't some kind of mystical experience. It's very down-to-earth and real. You simply become aware of all the activity and beauty around you.

Ways to Practice Being Still

The ability to be still and tolerate (or even enjoy) the resulting silence is an essential component of mindfulness. Like the other factors, attitudes, and qualities discussed in this book that strengthen your ability to be present and aware, stillness and silence are in turn strengthened by mindfulness practice. It's a nice feedback loop that keeps deepening your ability to be receptively aware of your life as it's happening. There are a number of practices you can do to support this process and cultivate more stillness and silence in your life and increase your comfort level with them.

Not Hurrying

When you're hurrying, you're not just moving quickly in order to get something done efficiently. You're also thinking about the future, wishing things were moving faster, and perhaps even wishing you didn't have to do whatever it is you're doing. Any obstacles to your efforts are likely to be irritating, and you're probably not enjoying or appreciating the present moment. Once you start feeling frantic or impatient, it's a sure sign that you've sacrificed internal stillness in order to achieve something.

Deliberately not hurrying supports internal stillness even when you need to be moving quickly. When you notice you're hurrying, turn your attention to something that's going on in the present moment. Try to be aware of your hands, your movements, or the objects you're using. Take a few deep breaths, and ask yourself whether you're going to be able to get things finished any faster by wishing they were already done. Even if you need to run to your next appointment, it's possible to do so mindfully! Cultivating mindfulness instead of hurrying may feel like slowing down, but ironically it helps you be more efficient. When you're mindful of what you're doing you'll not only feel less stressed, you'll make fewer mistakes and deal with challenges more effectively. You might also be able to appreciate the present moment even when you're busy.

Pausing

Pausing is taking "not hurrying" one step further. You consciously insert a moment or two of mental and physical stillness before acting, speaking, or continuing down a train of thought. You can do this before you answer the phone: look at the phone, listen to the ring, and take a deep breath before answering it. When you're physically stopped at a red light, make an effort to stop thinking for the duration of the light. When you feel upset and ready to speak or act, just stand still for a moment and cultivate awareness of your body.

 **KEEP IN MIND**

Pay attention to when you tell yourself you don't need to, or can't, pause. It's at times like these that it's most important to insert a moment of stillness. You're probably acting out a habit pattern that results in short-term satisfaction of some kind, but compromises greater happiness. You don't want to stop for a moment because you might see things more clearly and change your mind!

Pausing is a great practice because you can do it even if you're unwilling or unable to stop your activities for an extended period for formal mindfulness practice. It's a way to weave a little bit of stillness into your ordinary daily life. Despite the fact that the pauses don't add up to a great deal of time, they can make a big difference. Each time you choose to pause you're choosing stillness. You're reminding yourself that your mental and physical activity *can* stop, and the part of you that's always simple and content is there inside you, waiting to appreciate any moment no matter what's going on.

Leaving Space Before Answering

If you pay close attention to your mind when you're carrying on conversations, you're likely to notice that when someone else is speaking you're only listening with part of your brain. The other part is evaluating what the person is saying and its relevance to you, and formulating a response. To some extent this is natural and helps keep the flow of conversation going. However, it can compromise your relationships when you fail to *really* listen to others. It also gets in the way of intimacy. You don't end up noticing what is going on for others because your mental and physical activity interferes with your ability to be receptive to another person's body language and the subtler aspects of their communication. Instead of thinking back to a conversation with someone and remembering *them,* you just remember what you were thinking and feeling as you interacted with them.

How often do you leave space for silence when you're talking with someone? This means external as well as internal silence. You're just present with someone, waiting for the next thing to arise. It's a very intimate experience, but it can also make you feel rather nervous. In the silence questions can arise: "What is my relationship with this person? What do they really think of me? What if they express something in this space that is critical or disturbing?" If you can tolerate the silence for just a few moments, you'll find your relationships with people shifting. Everyone appreciates being listened to and truly seen, and often people will share something with you after a moment of silence that they never would have otherwise.

Achieving Complete Relaxation

How often do you *completely* relax? This means relaxation of body *and* mind. Perhaps you have trouble relaxing at all, but chances are there are at least some things you do that you think of as being relaxing. If you observe these situations with mindfulness, you may notice your body is relaxed but your mind is still busy processing. You may not be worrying, ruminating, or planning, but even a casual daydream is often connected to some subtle sense of dissatisfaction about your current circumstances. Part of you is still reaching for somewhere other than where you are, or something other than what you have.

 TAKE CARE

You may find a certain kind of relaxation in reading, or in watching movies or television. These kinds of activities give your mind a break from its self-referential processing, so they can be restful relative to your ordinary way of operating. However, they don't offer the same kind of relaxation for your mind as stillness and silence. When you're reading or watching something your mind is still engaged, and it isn't aware of what's going on in your present moment.

The best way to practice complete relaxation is to deliberately focus on releasing tension in the body and then on fully appreciating your present experience without thinking about the past, future, or anywhere other than where you are. Two of the audio guided meditations included with this book, Body Scan and Just Being, can assist with this process. On your own you may want to take a physically relaxing posture and then work on releasing tension throughout your body, starting with the top of your head and moving down to the tips of your toes. Once you've done this, see if you can close your eyes and temporarily let go of every last worry and concern.

Deepening Your Stillness

Even a slight increase in your stillness can make a big difference in your life, but if you're interested, it's possible to take it even deeper. There's always another degree of stillness and silence you can try in order to challenge yourself, and you may be surprised how rewarding it can be. You can taste some of the peace, clarity, and spaciousness that motivates some people to attend meditation retreats, spend years in remote hermitages, or even commit their lives to cloistered silence.

External Silence and Simplicity

As mentioned earlier, external silence supports and encourages internal silence. In Chapter 4, I discussed how minimizing the movement of the body helps calm the mind. As a result, no matter how diligently you practice internal stillness as you go about your daily activities, you're unlikely to experience it anywhere near as deeply as you could if you were externally silent and limited yourself to very simple activities. This is what you end up doing if you go to a meditation retreat, but you can also arrange situations in your life that allow you to do the same thing.

You might try designating a day, or part of a day, for practicing silence and simplicity. Plan ahead what you're going to do, so during your private retreat you can minimize decision making. Do only simple physical activities like cleaning, cooking, or gardening. Include some formal mindfulness practice like meditation or mindful yoga. If you're going to have a meal, try to eat it with full awareness instead of reading. If anyone else is going to be around, tell them you're going to try to keep quiet for a period of time, so you would appreciate it if they would write you notes instead of talking to you, or wait until later to tell you something.

 KEEP IN MIND

It can be very helpful to have the support of others in keeping silence and limiting your activity. Even if you aren't interested in regularly participating in a meditation group, you might want to attend a retreat. You can start with a one-day retreat, or one that only lasts a weekend. I like to call the support of a group "positive peer pressure"—when you reach a point where you would call it quits on your own, you stay silent and mindful because everyone else is. If they can do it, so can you!

Extended periods of literal silence and stillness can allow your mind to settle more deeply than ever before. Without new stimulation in the form of active thoughts or exciting input from outside, your mind runs out of stuff to do. It tends to keep rehashing certain things over and over, but eventually it seems to bore itself. Generally speaking, the longer you remain silent and still, the calmer the mind gets (although this isn't a linear process—sometimes the mind gets busier before settling). It's a remarkable experience on the third or fourth day of a meditation retreat when you realize you've *just* eaten your lunch instead of thinking about a million other things. And, perhaps even more remarkably, you didn't even have to struggle to do it!

Solitude

Some people love being alone, but almost everyone reaches a limit where solitude starts to feel oppressive. For you this might be a month or a weekend, or it might only be a few hours. Whatever your limit, your eventual discomfort with solitude is more or less the same thing as your discomfort with silence. Only in solitude does silence become complete. You have no need to express yourself verbally, so even internal commentary tends to fade away. In addition, just as silence is absence of sound, solitude is absence of relationship with others. Who are you when you're not a spouse, a parent, a co-worker, or a teacher? The absence of things can call extra attention to what's still present—and all of your questions about it.

Solitude can be challenging, provocative, and educational. For example, I once went on a solo backpacking trip. I planned it to last five days, and I didn't bring a watch or any reading material. All I wanted to do was hike, meditate, and mindfully go about the simple activities of camping. The first day and a half were okay, but then I suddenly panicked. I got very bored, and the prospect of another three days with nothing to do and no one to talk to seemed overwhelming. I packed up all my gear and hiked fast all day, and only had to spend one more night on the trail. Afterward I struggled with the question of why I couldn't tolerate the silence and solitude.

What I learned was there were depths of stillness I was not yet comfortable with. To settle into such a long period of silence, I needed to let go of keeping track of time and of who I was. These are both fairly subtle levels of mental activity, but just like other kinds of activity they can get in the way of directly experiencing the present moment. Letting go of *even more* activity and embracing *even deeper* stillness and silence can be scary, but despite what your mind might tell you, it's not actually dangerous. You can start thinking again at any time! Pushing the edges of your comfort zone may help you tap into the wonderful, spacious experience from childhood of just *being*. When I returned to the woods for another solo trip, I was able to relax in a whole new way.

The Least You Need to Know

- Internal stillness is letting go of all mental activity, and it's an essential component of mindfulness. It's as if your volitional thinking produces noise, and when you turn it down you can be more mindful of what's going on around you.

- Internal silence is what you experience when you're still. Many people are uncomfortable with silence because it can call attention to things they've been avoiding, or they're just not used to it.

- External stillness and silence support and encourage the same states internally.

- It can be very relaxing and enjoyable to let go of all mental and physical activity that's aimed at getting somewhere other than where you are, or obtaining something other than what you have. If you can do this at will, you can take a little vacation whenever you want to.

- There are many simple things you can do to invite more stillness into your life, such as making an effort to be mindful instead of hurrying, and pausing briefly before acting or speaking.

12

Accessing More Joy

Joy is one of the psychophysical factors that supports mindfulness and the ability to see your life clearly, as explained in Chapter 7. Obviously, joy is also a great thing to have in and of itself! It's a wonderful blend of calm happiness, simple pleasure, and a kind of energy that has nothing to do with a desire to gain or change anything. Joy brightens your life and makes everything seem a little easier.

Fortunately, just like the other things covered in this part of the book—nonjudgment, acceptance, curiosity, energy, courage, stillness, and comfort with silence—mindfulness is both strengthened by a sense of joy *and* a way you can access and increase it. It's another positive feedback loop. In this chapter I talk about how this process works and introduce practical ways you can use mindfulness to tap into more joy in your life just as it is.

In This Chapter

- What joy is and how it arises in the moment
- How mindfulness helps you access joy
- Cultivating appreciation for your life just as it is
- Identifying obstacles to complete satisfaction
- Joy as clean-burning energy for mindfulness

The Nature of Joy

When you do something joyfully, you feel engaged and willing even though you aren't going to gain any tangible benefit from what you're doing. Or, if you're going to get a tangible benefit, it's not the source of your motivation. You're doing something for the sheer pleasure of it, or because you're happy to benefit others. Joy is a simple state that has nothing to do with the past or the future. It's just a buoyant state of well-being right here, right now.

 TAKE CARE

> If you think joy is missing from your life, it may simply be that you're misunderstanding how the word is being used here. Joy isn't necessarily exciting, and it doesn't necessarily require you to be happy. It can be very subtle—just a lightness of heart when you hear a bird sing, or when you put your feet up after a long day at work. It's a moment of simply being glad you're alive.

There are many closely related words that describe states of well-being, including happiness, pleasure, contentment, bliss, and satisfaction. The joy that supports mindfulness can arise because of these other states, but it's also possible for them to be the *result* of joy. Joy is like a light that brightens your perspective on everything else, making it more likely you're going to find the things in your life acceptable or even good. It has an energetic quality that may be lacking in a state of happiness. Happiness may be subdued or excited, and has more to do with your relationship to life overall. Joy may arise when you experience something that makes you happy, such as getting a new job, but is has more to do with the present moment than anticipation of anything— a "yay, life is good right now" reaction.

Mindfulness Leads to Joy

Regardless of any evaluation of the state of your life and whether you like it or not, joy can arise all on its own when you engage things in a direct and mindful way. It's as if your natural life energy and enthusiasm bubble to the surface in response to a close encounter with the world. Much of this book is about how to use mindfulness to improve your life by reducing stress, becoming more attentive to your life, and seeing things more clearly so you can make better decisions. However, after you practice mindfulness for a while, you also notice being consciously and receptively aware of the present moment is rewarding in and of itself. Even if it didn't result in any tangible benefits, it would still be worth doing.

Being mindful—as present for your life as you can be, moment by moment—is really nothing other than living fully, but it can be difficult. As discussed in Chapter 10, it's easy to get complacent about life and start tuning out any experiences that aren't new, exciting, pleasurable, or particularly aversive. You can end up more or less sleepwalking through most of your life. It may not seem this way to you because you figure stimulus-independent thinking is also a nice way to spend your time. However, even though the occasional daydream or mental planning session might be enjoyable, there's just no comparison to being engaged directly with your life as it's happening. Spending time up in your head doesn't let you tap into joy the way mindfulness does.

A Short Time Left to Live

More than any explanation, the following example illustrates the inherent value of being present for all of your experiences. It's a common occurrence for someone who has only a short time left to live—let's say a few weeks or months—to experience a radical shift in awareness. Previously, like most of us, they let their mind wander, lived in anticipation of the future, and got annoyed about little things. Suddenly they find themselves paying close attention to the simplest things and deeply appreciating them, such as waking up in the morning, the smile of a loved one, or the comfort of a soft robe. Even things that were previously irritating, such as getting stuck in traffic or having an argument with someone, can seem infinitely precious.

Someone who knows they're close to death (and still fairly awake and free of pain) is often able to live mindfully simply because their perspective has changed so radically. They have no future anymore, so they're much less likely to tune out the present moment in anticipation of something better. Rumination on the past is usually motivated by a desire to resolve things, and when time's running out it quickly becomes obvious which things just have to be accepted as they are. Someone in this situation may be able to engage the present moment entirely without reference to what it's going to get them or whether they like it—and yet nevertheless maintain intense interest because they don't have many moments left.

Everyday Life as Precious

It's possible to access this kind of appreciation and joy even if you don't have a terminal diagnosis. Practicing mindfulness requires you to let go of thinking about the past or future and maintain receptive awareness of this moment. When you do this, you realize that when someone knows their end is near and they gain a great appreciation for life, it's not because their life circumstances have changed, and it's not because they're imagining things. They're simply waking up to the true nature of reality—they just weren't mindful enough to see it before. Over time, you can strengthen your mindfulness and experience more times when simply being alive is a source of joy.

This isn't to say that being mindful will always mean you're happy. You may go through terrible, painful times when happiness seems far away. Even when this is the case, you can access the subtle joy of being present. Perhaps you're facing all kinds of challenges, but you see the sun shining through your window and experience a moment of sincere appreciation. Perhaps you've had a miserable day at work but have to smile back at a cute little kid on the bus. The French call this *joie de vivre*, literally "joy of living," which can be ebullient and energetic but is probably more often subdued. It may be impossible to explain why we feel it. Maybe it's our subjective experience of the instinctual will to live, but looking at it that way might tempt you to dismiss it as invalid when in fact it's one of the great things about being human.

> **MINDFUL EXERCISE**
>
> Over the course of a day, pay close attention to whenever you feel even a little bit of joy. Be on the lookout for any positive feelings, but see if you can differentiate the experience of joy from being happy or satisfied after you evaluate something and decide you like it, or decide it's going to lead to a good outcome in the future. See when and how joy arises—a simple, buoyant feeling you have when you're just happy to be alive and aware in order to experience exactly what you are at a given moment.

Living with No Expectations

There is a lesson we can take from the natural mindfulness of someone facing death: living with no expectations lets you see simply being alive as very precious. When I suggest you live with no expectations, you may think I'm telling you to take a pessimistic approach, but that isn't the case. When someone says they have no expectations about something, it often means they have strong expectations—they're just *low*. Living with no expectations at all is very different. It means you're watching and waiting for things to unfold and then engaging them directly. You aren't focusing your attention based on expectations of what's going to happen, and you're not comparing results to ideas about what *should* have happened.

Identifying Preconceived Notions

There are an infinite number of ideas you can hold about life and how it should go, and each can interfere with your mindfulness. Simply identifying your expectations and ideas is the first step in getting free of them. Here's the kind of thoughts to look out for:

- If I work hard, things should go well for me.
- If I take care of my body, I won't get sick.
- If I'm nice to people, they will like me.
- As long I do my best, my efforts will be appreciated.
- The world should be free of injustice, violence, and greed.
- My life should be pleasant or fun.

- I shouldn't have to deal with this.

- That person is always _____.

Identifying your preconceived notions doesn't mean they disappear. You simply recognize them for what they are: thoughts. Thoughts are generated by your body-mind in response to a given situation, and they're just part of the whole picture. "Oh," you might observe when a new policy is announced at work. "I'm having a thought that this isn't fair." Your judgment is most likely based on preconceived ideas you have about fairness, or about your workplace. To practice mindfulness, you take note of your thoughts about things, but then try to stay receptive to all aspects of the situation instead of completely believing your ideas about it.

Engaging Life Directly

Holding on to expectations about how things are, or how they should go, not only interferes with mindfulness, it can also make you miserable. When you experience something, you immediately compare it to your expectation about it. Viewed objectively something may be unpleasant, disappointing, or even painful, but it seems even worse if you dwell on how it *shouldn't* be happening to you. Alternatively, it may be unfortunate that something you want is eluding you, but your expectation that you *should* have gotten it by now makes the situation even more frustrating.

 KEEP IN MIND

Sometimes, without realizing it, you may think you're influencing the outcome of things by holding on to your expectations. Perhaps you're afraid another person will surrender completely to some bad habit unless you maintain your sense of disapproval of it. When you're having a tough time, you may feel the need to walk around with a sense of resentment just in case some universal dispensary of bad luck notices you've let your guard down and it's okay to send even more trouble your way. If you really pay attention to the way life works, though, you realize most of the world cares very little about your expectations.

As mentioned earlier, sometimes the prospect of letting go of expectations sounds like adopting low expectations instead—as if you're sighing in resignation and inviting the world to walk all over you. On the contrary, letting go of all expectations leaves you even more able to engage life effectively and take care of your responsibilities. When you live your life directly instead of constantly comparing it to your ideas, you're more receptive and open-minded. You can adapt quickly when things surprise you, and are less likely to bias outcomes ahead of time. You'll deal with challenges as needed without getting caught up in resentment. All of your skills and intelligence will be available for your use—the only difference will be that you're paying more attention to the way things actually are than to your own ideas.

For example, consider the situation mentioned in the previous section, where you've had a thought that a new policy at work isn't fair. In the end you may indeed conclude that, in your opinion, things aren't fair, but you don't necessarily have to get upset, argumentative, or defensive because you're clinging to the idea life *should* be fair. It's also possible you'll come to see the wisdom of the policy, or realize its outcomes weren't what you expected. Not holding on to your ideas leaves you open to learning these kinds of things and adapting your opinions with grace.

Gratitude for Things as They Are

Life experienced without any expectations lets you access joy much more easily. It helps you feel sincere gratitude for the good things you already have or experience. Imagine if you replaced the preconceived notions above with these observations:

- I try to work hard, and it's great when things go well.

- I take care of my body, and it feels good to be healthy.

- I try to be nice to people, and it's great when they like me.

- I do my best, and appreciation is sweet.

- It's inspiring that there are so many people who voluntarily work for justice and refrain from violence and greed.

- I love it when my life is pleasant or fun.

- I don't really like this, but it's what I get to deal with right now.

- That person is sometimes _____; I wonder what they'll do now.

When you read this list, you may imagine that pervasive joy and gratitude are accessible only if you adopt positive (and perhaps naïve) ideas. However, this is about mindfully observing your life *without* attachment to ideas or expectations—even positive ones.

For example, when you allow yourself to be inspired by the fact that people are often kind, fair, and generous with one another, this has nothing to do with an idea about how the world is, on the balance, more wonderful than terrible. It doesn't require you to deny the prevalence of injustice, violence, or greed. But when you're not holding on to any idea about the way people *should* act—when you have no expectation that the world *should* be a place free from conflict or selfishness—what stands out is people's voluntary positive actions instead of how they fall short of an ideal. When you recognize an expectation as a mere idea (even if it's reasonable or good), it doesn't have to make you miserable.

 **TAKE CARE**

When working on appreciation and gratitude, be sure you stay honest with yourself. If you don't feel it, you don't feel it. Mindfulness is about becoming aware of things as they are, without judgment. If you notice expectations that are hard to let go of, or things in your life you just can't accept, that's okay. As long as you stay mindfully aware of your life, you'll keep learning and things will keep shifting. Just keep your mind open—at least a little bit.

In fact, you can find reasons to be grateful no matter how circumstances are measuring up to your plans and hopes. For example, when you get sick even though you always eat well and exercise, you simply deal with being sick instead of getting discouraged. When you feel healthy again, you're grateful instead of feeling as if health is something you're owed because of your efforts. When someone dislikes or mistrusts you despite the fact that you've tried to treat them well, you continue to treat people well because that's what you want to do—but you shrug and acknowledge that human interactions are mysteriously complex and impossible to predict. When people end up liking you, you appreciate it as a pleasant outcome instead of thinking of it as payback for being nice.

Complete Satisfaction

You may feel like you have enough appreciation, gratitude, and joy in your life already. However, if you really stop and ask yourself whether you're *completely* satisfied with your life, what's your answer? If you were to die right now, would your heart be filled with gratitude for all you have, or would there be lingering regrets about the past? Is some of your current happiness contingent on the fulfillment of hopes for the future? Few of us can honestly say we are perfectly satisfied with all aspects of our lives, all the time, but if you're able to live mindfully and free of expectations, it's possible to experience a deep sense of peace about the state of your life.

What Are You Waiting For?

Try asking yourself honestly about what's lacking in your life. What keeps you from being completely and utterly satisfied, right now? Mindfully observe what arises in your body-mind, remembering not to censor or judge. Notice things you're hoping or expecting will happen in the future. Perhaps there's a project you want to complete, a skill you want to master, or a trip you want to take. Perhaps you want to nurture a community, further a cause, or see your kids get into college. Notice things you intend to change for the better. Do you plan to lose weight, get fit, improve your relationships, get financially sound, or give up a bad habit?

Now pay attention to whether you're postponing your complete satisfaction with life until these things are experienced or achieved. When you contemplate never doing so, what is your internal reaction? Maybe it's an unvoiced, "Nooo!" Does it seem impossible to contemplate resting in complete satisfaction without experiencing the things you hope for? Do you imagine unconditional contentment would be settling into laziness or complacency? (It isn't, as mentioned earlier, that living with no expectations leaves you even more able to deal effectively with your life. But it's good to notice whether part of you is concerned about this.)

The Joy of "This Is Enough"

Mindfulness can help you, at least at times, to see your life in such a way that you can sincerely say, "This is enough." This doesn't mean it wouldn't be nice to see certain things come about, but you stop postponing the joy, ease, and peace of being completely satisfied with your life as it is. In this chapter I've discussed tapping into the joy of simply being in the present moment, and not being biased by your expectations. If you do both of these things, you'll find a source of satisfaction that is unconditional—that is, it doesn't depend on conditions or circumstances. As long as you're alive and conscious, you'll be able to appreciate your experience of the present moment.

MINDFUL EXERCISE

Sit down in a comfortable position in a quiet place. One by one, call to mind things in your life you'd like to achieve, experience, or improve. Imagine how things might change, what an ideal scenario would look like, and how you would enjoy it. Then ask yourself, "What if this never happened?" Stay present and receptive with any feelings of resistance or disappointment, but also explore what it might feel like to be content in your life without the outcome you desire. Sometimes you'll be able to access a part of yourself that will be satisfied even if certain of your hopes and aspirations never get fulfilled.

When you're able to find more joy and contentment in your life just as it is, you don't have to be so dependent on achieving conditional sources of happiness. More money, a new house, a better relationship, a thriving company, a relaxing retirement, successful children—all of these things can be great sources of happiness and pleasure. However, you're probably familiar with the stress that comes from a sense that you *must* achieve these things, *or else.* You may not even fill in the blank after "or else," but essentially it's "or else I'll never be truly and completely satisfied." The achievement of certain things becomes an imperative that can keep you driven, unhappy, or unable to appreciate your life as it is.

When your satisfaction isn't contingent on conditional things, you can still go about working hard to bring about the outcomes you know will make you and others happy. However, because it's no longer an imperative, you can be calmer and more easygoing about everything. You know that no matter what happens, you have a base of simple joy and satisfaction in your life. Even if such-and-such never happens, you'll be fundamentally okay.

How Joy Supports Mindfulness

Throughout this chapter I've talked about how to access more joy in your life through mindfulness, but this part of the book is also about factors you can cultivate in your life that support mindfulness—in particular by helping you maintain a receptive attitude. Joy does this by relaxing your sense of concern about your well-being. In Chapter 5 I talked about how your instinct is to evaluate everything you encounter in terms of whether it's a potential threat, source of benefit, or irrelevant to you and those you care about. This constant evaluation keeps your mind very busy. It also invites you to categorize your experiences (like, dislike, or neutral) and then relate to them through the filter of your ideas. Joy in simply being alive lets you meet each experience as if it has some value, regardless of how it relates to your agenda. Joy makes you more willing and eager to be receptive to whatever comes next.

Mindfulness takes effort, and joy can be a source of energy for that effort. The great thing is that it's a clean-burning energy source. You can get energy from other things, such as a determination to end your suffering and improve your life, or a passionate desire to understand something. However, these other sources of energy tend to generate by-products or leave residues. A determination to change your life can sometimes lead to frustration, discouragement, or burnout. A desire for something—even something "spiritual" like insight—can cause suffering if you don't attain what you want. It can also lead you to form ideas about your goal that end up getting in the way, or make you strive in such a way that leads to self-absorption and stress. Energy and motivation arising from joy, on the other hand, simply gives you enthusiasm and propels you forward. It's not contingent on anything—so always enjoy it when you feel it!

The Least You Need to Know

- Joy arises when you're simply glad to be alive. It makes you happy to be experiencing whatever is happening in your life at the present moment.
- When you're mindful, you let go of the past and future and maintain receptive awareness of this moment. Inexplicably, this can let you access joy—as if it's your natural response to direct engagement with life.
- Expectations and other preconceived notions get in the way of both mindfulness and joy, but you can identify them and learn to relate to them differently so they don't determine the nature of your experiences.

- It's possible to cultivate a deep, complete satisfaction with your life just as it is. You may still want to change things, but if you can access joy you know you'll be okay no matter what.

- If you can fuel your mindfulness practice with joy, it can give you pure energy and motivation that doesn't depend on future outcomes.

Working Toward Greater Happiness

Mindfulness as presented in this book takes place within a context of aspiration for greater happiness for self and other. The idea is you naturally want to be happy, so if you see clearly that some change leads to greater happiness, you'll be motivated to make it. The mindful awareness discussed in Part 2 helps you pay attention to what's actually going on in your life so you can perceive the effects of your thoughts and actions. The receptive attitude discussed in Part 3 helps open the doors of perception wider and lets you see things clearly.

In this part of the book I talk about how to apply the fruits of mindfulness to different areas of your life in order to work toward greater happiness. It always comes back to cultivating receptive awareness of the present and seeing things clearly, but I walk you through how this process unfolds when you're working with strong negative emotions, dealing with stress in a busy life, struggling to balance goals and acceptance, and trying to become more authentic and flexible. I also discuss how mindfulness can increase harmony and intimacy in your relationships. I start off this part, however, with a chapter on how compassion for self and other is essential for effective change.

Compassionate Change

Once you've cultivated some mindfulness, you'll be more aware of what's going on in your life. You'll be able to see more clearly what leads to greater happiness and what doesn't. As proposed in the mindfulness principles from Chapter 3, you'll naturally want to move toward greater happiness, even if that means making changes in your life. However, it's also natural to be resistant to change—for many reasons.

In this chapter I explain how compassion is a prerequisite for lasting change. Sheer willpower may be enough to bring about temporary change, or it may let you enforce a change over time, but only with continuous effort that can lead to tension or exhaustion. Change with compassion means you mindfully acknowledge the reasons you resist change, and avoid getting into a fruitless or harmful struggle with yourself. You try to be firm and clear about the need for change, but also forgiving and gentle when you need to be. Mindfulness can help you know which approach will be most effective at any given moment. It takes patience, but you can end up making meaningful changes in your life based on the insights you achieve through mindfulness.

In This Chapter

- Using the model of self-parenting to approach change with compassion
- Identifying different strategies for change and their results
- How to investigate and overcome resistance to change
- Using mindfulness to know the best way to apply self-discipline
- Learning to do without inner violence but still fulfill your aspirations

The Model of Self-Parenting

When you're working on change, it's extremely useful to think of parenting yourself. This may seem demeaning, but only in comparison to the expectation that as an adult you should be perfectly capable and well-adjusted, which is probably not the case. Instead, think of human development as occurring over the course of an entire lifetime. A huge amount of learning and training happens during childhood, but you continue to learn and grow as long as you're willing to do so. There's always some way in which you can become more responsible, reasonable, effective, kind, or at peace. After childhood you usually have to "parent" yourself through your challenges and changes, because no one else is going to do it for you.

Identifying Your Wiser Voice

Just as a parent generally has more perspective and wisdom than a child, there is a wiser part of you that understands what leads to greater happiness (thanks to your mindfulness practice). There are other parts of you that are more selfish, immature, and wary of anything new. The wise voice may set an agenda for change, but then the more childish parts of you find ways to tune the wise voice out, passively resist its wishes, or even stage an outright rebellion.

 KEEP IN MIND

Think of all the things people do even though they "know better." They continue to smoke, overeat, lose their tempers, stress out over small things, and spend too much money. Clearly the kind of "knowing" they have about what's best isn't the kind that results in change. Mindfulness asks you to investigate the things you know more deeply. You try to maintain receptive awareness of what's happening before, during, and after your decisions and actions. You pay careful attention to how one thing leads to another, instead of forgetting or distracting yourself.

I don't recommend you use the paradigm of Freudian psychology and view this wise voice in yourself as a conscientious "superego" in constant struggle with a base, instinctual "id." This will tend to encourage the kind of violent struggle Western culture is infamous for, even if it only occurs internally. Instead, you can view this inner wisdom as a parent. We all know—whether we're parents or we've only been parented—that children have a will of their own. Parenting is the art of guiding and forming a living being, not the task of crafting inanimate material into a predetermined shape. It's an ongoing interaction between two ultimately autonomous individuals that happens best when it involves cooperation, respect, and clear communication.

Formulating Responses to Discipline

When you were a child, how did you respond to your parents? When they were trying to get you to do something, you were likely to choose one of three responses. One, you could rebel and take the consequences—either because you disagreed, or because you resisted taking orders from anyone else on principle. Two, you could *seem* to obey, but then find ways to undermine the authority figures in your life, acting out in more passive-aggressive ways. Three, you could do your best to adopt the stance of your parents and believe they were right, but if you didn't eventually come to understand and agree with their reasoning, at some point this adoption of a view or a standard of conduct was revealed to be inauthentic for you. Such a realization may have been rather traumatic to your sense of self, or may have resulted in a troubled relationship with your parents.

You probably end up responding to your efforts at self-discipline in similar ways. It's just human nature. You have conflicting interests and desires within you, and different ones will take precedence at different times. One way of looking at this is that various "selves" arise in you depending on the situation. For example, the self who sets your alarm to go off extra early so you can meditate before work has a certain set of aspirations and ideas. The self who hits the snooze button over and over when the alarm goes off has a very different perspective—perhaps one that realizes you'll be exhausted all day if you don't get more sleep. Overall you may feel more identified with your aspiration to get up early than you are with your need for sleep, but both of these things are part of you and will continue to try to get their own way unless you introduce some compassionate self-parenting.

The Art of Parenting

The most challenging thing about parenting is that there are no fixed rules; you have to keep responding in the best way you can, given the current circumstances. Things are constantly changing, and the most effective response to a child is something that has to be decided anew with every encounter. Sometimes it's time to demand more from a child because they're capable, and also because it communicates that you respect them. Sometimes it's time to make deals with a child, rewarding them for good behavior and hoping the good behavior will reinforce itself— or at least keep them healthy and safe. Sometimes it's best to explain to the child why a certain behavior is preferable (in which case you'd better know why). Sometimes it's just time to hold a child and give them unconditional support and love.

Default Approaches to Discipline

Just as some parents favor a certain approach—strictness, reward, argument, or unconditional approval—over others, you probably tend to favor a particular kind of approach to dealing with yourself. Instead of maintaining mindful awareness of the present moment, seeing what's needed, and accessing a whole range of responses, you default to one or two. Perhaps you easily let go of any expectations you've set for yourself and make up for any disappointment by being extra gentle and indulgent with yourself. Perhaps you carry on prolonged arguments with yourself, constantly questioning your own decisions.

 MINDFUL EXERCISE

Call to mind something you would really like to change about yourself. If you like, write it down, along with your responses to the following questions. Make your responses as honest as possible (what you really tend to think and do, not what you think you should). Why is this change a good idea? What weaknesses or shortcomings do you have that make this change necessary, or difficult? How would you describe yourself when you're resisting change or acting out a negative pattern? Why do you think you act like this? Now look back over your responses. What kind of self-parenting approach are you taking? Is there judgment or harshness in any of your answers?

The most harmful default parenting approach is to rely on harsh judgments, verbal abuse, and overly punitive actions to induce change. This is true whether you're applying the approach to someone else or to yourself, but even if you would never treat another human being this way, you may feel justified in taking this approach with yourself. You may beat yourself up inside for not acting in certain ways. You may repeat your internal demand over and over as if you've just been too stupid and lazy to understand it up until now. You may even hurl abusive comments at yourself internally, such as, "You're hopeless and disgusting. No wonder you're depressed." (Or fat, broke, anxious, or lonely.)

Imagine taking this same harsh approach with someone else. This probably allows to you to recognize how mean and harmful it is, and how it's very unlikely to produce any positive change in someone. The most likely outcome is the subject of the harsh approach is either going to tune out any feedback, or internalize all the judgments and figure it's hopeless trying to change. In fact, she may figure the best response would be to act out even more, seeing as she's already worthless. If you take this uncompassionate approach with yourself, the effect is the same. You'll find part of yourself getting righteous and frustrated while another part resists or sinks into lethargy or neurosis and makes change impossible.

Compassionate Parenting

A compassionate parent does his best to take care of his child's long-term well-being and happiness. No parent is perfect all the time, but he aspires to be motivated primarily by his child's best interests and not just his own. When a child fails to fulfill expectations, fights back, or acts out, a parent may feel temporarily frustrated, judgmental, or discouraged—but then he considers carefully how to respond. What is the best way to engage this child? What response is most likely to encourage the positive behavior that is desired? Even more important, what will lead to the best outcome for the child overall? Perhaps a short-term goal needs to be adapted or even dropped to support the child's confidence, or the health of the parent-child relationship.

The basic assumption in compassionate parenting is that the child is good, lovable, and has potential. Starting from this foundation, the parent can be firm or even unyielding without her attitude degenerating into disrespect or dislike toward the child. Children will often respond with their best effort despite their internal resistance because they sense how much their parent loves them and believes in them.

 TAKE CARE

Responding compassionately when you experience a setback in your efforts to change doesn't mean you give up your desire to do things differently. Sometimes it may seem like the only options are to keep on failing to change, or to forget about your goals and make your peace with the way things are. There's certainly a time to do the latter, but it's also possible keep your aspirations in mind and just take a long-term view. You may not have figured out a way to make the change yet, but it's worth it to keep trying.

Fortunately, the same kind of compassionate approach is effective in self-parenting. When you want to change, you start out with reasonable expectations that aren't going to result in discouraging failure right off the bat. You maintain dignity and self-respect throughout the process, cultivating faith that you can, eventually, become more mindful, self-disciplined, generous, healthy—whatever it is you want. You don't have to dream up some optimistic view of yourself; you just make your aspirations open-ended: it's always possible to improve to *some* extent. You observe "failures" realistically, and contemplate the best response to them with a constant willingness to change your approach or try something completely new.

Working with Resistance to Change

Sometimes you realize there's something you'd really like to change in your life—particularly in your patterns of thought, speech, or behavior—but *change just isn't happening*. At such times, it's important to examine carefully what's getting in the way of change. You can use mindfulness to do this. As you move through a decision point in your life, you stay present and receptively aware of exactly what's going on. You reserve judgment because you don't want to limit or censor your perceptions. When you go ahead and make a choice that runs counter to your aspiration, what's happening? What are you thinking and feeling? What is it you want?

Identifying Your Childish Viewpoints

What you're usually going to find is a childish part of yourself opting for some kind of short-term happiness over the longer-term happiness that's the goal of your aspiration for change. The characteristic feature of a childish viewpoint is its limited perspective. In cases where a real child needs guidance from an adult, it's generally not because the adult is a better a person than a child in terms of morals or values; it's just that the adult has a much larger perspective in terms of space, time, and causation. For example, a child may whine for a second ice cream sundae because they aren't able to conceive of the very real connection between a second sundae and feeling sick and miserable later. When the adult refuses to buy the second sundae, it's because of her greater knowledge of cause and effect and her ability to follow the chain of causation over a longer period of time.

The childish parts of ourselves are similarly limited in their perspectives. The part of you that gets caught up in social media and procrastinates your work is thinking, "Just one more minute, just one more minute!" The part of you that overindulges in food, drink, or other pleasures at the expense of your health is thinking, in the moment of the indulgence, "Health? What's health? What a boring old fuddy-duddy you are. Enjoying *this* is what matters!" The part of you that flies into a rage even though you're working on anger management is thinking pretty much the same things as a toddler having a temper tantrum: "No! No! No! Me! Me! Me!"

Parenting Yourself

The temptation when you start to identify the childish parts of yourself is to judge or reject them, but the most effective thing is to approach them with mindful and compassionate parenting. When they're really acting out or suffering from the repercussions of "their" choices, you embrace them patiently and gently. Perhaps you sigh inwardly, "Oh dear, what are we going to do about this?" but you don't make things worse with abuse or rejection.

You wait for the right moment and then you try to understand the motivations of your childish part without making judgments. It helps to imagine this part of you really *is* a child as you listen patiently to its concerns. Chances are the concerns will sound small, deluded, and petty to the wiser part of you, but what does that matter? The important thing is that you listen and understand. Not only will that communicate compassion, it will also reveal the best way to deal with the situation.

KEEP IN MIND

Recognizing and acknowledging your selfish, irrational, or mean thoughts and impulses can be difficult and uncomfortable at first. Remember, feelings and thoughts can be observed as they arise in the same way you observe sounds, sights, and other sensations. As discussed in Chapter 5, you can learn to experience them without identifying with them. They're part of the reality of the present moment, but only part.

For example, let's say you often end up snapping at your partner when you feel stressed and irritable. You've looked at the situation with mindfulness and recognized your irritation rarely has anything to do with your partner, but your mean, sarcastic, or impatient verbal interactions with her are undermining your relationship. You form the intention to take a couple of breaths before responding to your partner when you're feeling stressed and then use more gentle and respectful speech. Sometimes this works, but most often you find yourself resenting yet another expectation being placed on you when you're stressed—so you keep letting your speech be marked by irritation.

Now let's say you examine this situation in your life even more carefully, with even more awareness and receptivity, and you notice as you snap at your partner you're resenting the fact that she's *not* stressed. A part of you is thinking, "If she's not stressed and I am, then she can do more to help me!" Perhaps your partner hasn't taken on as many projects as you have, or is more efficient at getting them done. When she's sitting reading a novel while you're still working, you feel resentful. You can probably imagine a child having a similar fit because they have to finish a chore while their sibling is already relaxing in front of the television!

Sometimes simply recognizing that part of you is being childish is enough to let you start changing a habit. At other times, however, some active self-parenting may be required. In the example above, you might offer your resentful self some sincere empathy, "I know, dear, it's no fun to work when other people are relaxing." Then you might ask some questions that gently point to how the situation isn't actually unfair (you've chosen your projects or how you manage your time), or how you might be able to ask your partner for some help. Just as in the case of parenting children, there isn't going to be one magical solution to your problem. Even an effective approach will have to be applied repeatedly and changed when necessary.

Convincing Yourself to Change

Certain deeply ingrained habits can seem nearly impossible to change even after you've spent lots of time, money, and effort trying. What's probably happening is a part of you is *very* attached to a pattern of thought, speech, or behavior you want to change. You may have tried all the parenting approaches you know on this resistant self: abuse, punishment, argument, reward—what more can you do?

The first step is to mindfully recognize what's really going on. No matter how much you identify with your aspirations, a part of you is stronger and continues to ignore or laugh at your noble goals and intentions. Rather than getting angry or discouraged, you can give this willful part of yourself the respect it deserves, as if it's a martial arts partner who has just thrown you to the ground in a match. Acknowledge you have a powerful adversary. This is what people do in Alcoholics Anonymous (AA) when they admit they're powerless when it comes to alcohol.

 TAKE CARE

> Sometimes when you're trying to change something and not having much luck, it's because you've chosen the wrong thing to change, or you're doing it for the wrong reasons. For example, if you're constantly trying to diet because you want to look like a model, the part of you that resists the diet may have a good point. If you're trying to become a better conversationalist so people will like you, the introverted part of you may wish you could just be yourself. When you mindfully examine your resistance to change, stay open-minded about what you might learn.

Despite the challenge, however, if you've identified a change that would really lead to greater happiness for self and others, you don't give up, just as people in AA don't give up. Instead, find out why your "resistant self" acts the way it does. Don't argue with it, and certainly don't tell it that it *shouldn't* feel the way it does. (Again, imagine the effect this would have on another person.) Then appeal to the resistant self's better nature. Find something it cares about and then show it how the change you want will ultimately be in its best interest as well. It's essential that this "showing" not just be intellectual argument, but direct experience of reality through mindfulness.

For example, if you're an alcoholic, there's some kind of reward you get from drinking. Let's say it's release from stress and self-consciousness, resulting in an ability to relax and enjoy your life for a little while. If you cultivate mindful awareness of your life while including and acknowledging the part that wants to drink, that part may come to see clearly how it's choosing short periods of ease and enjoyment that come at great cost. Mindfulness can help *all* parts of you face things you've probably been avoiding. With mindfulness you allow yourself to experience directly the pain your addiction is causing to yourself and others. At some point you can use the very desire that led you to drinking—wanting to relax and enjoy life—to motivate you in your efforts to stop. In a sense, you've convinced yourself to change.

Giving Up Violence

One of the things you'll recognize after spending some time doing mindfulness practice—if you don't already know it—is the use of violence to get what you want always has a cost. Violence includes physical aggression, but more often manifests in other kinds of aggressive actions, rejection, harsh speech, and hateful thoughts. Any of these forms of violence end up causing some harm even if they bring about the desired outcome.

You may end up indulging in thoughts, speech, or behavior that is violent according to this broad definition because you think the ends justify the means. This is especially tempting when it comes to dealing with yourself. You may apply the methods of the harsh, judgmental parenting mode described earlier in this chapter, and figure it's your right to treat yourself however you want.

After mindful observation of your life, however, you're likely to conclude that violence just isn't worth it. It creates negative reactions within you and increases your stress level. It means you walk around feeling as if the present state of your life isn't acceptable, and results in an ongoing struggle that makes you feel divided inside. Also, a tendency to be harsh and judgmental internally usually leads to you being the same way with others. After you've paid close attention to all the effects of using violence, you'll probably feel inspired to forgo all violent methods even when there's something you'd really like to change. This remains the case even when you consider it might mean you'll never achieve what you want.

 MINDFUL EXERCISE

This is a traditional Buddhist exercise for cultivating compassion called *metta*, which literally means "friendliness." Call to mind a person or animal for whom you feel close to unconditional love. Silently recite each of the following statements, allowing yourself to sincerely mean what you're saying: "May you be free from fear and anxiety. May you be at ease. May you be happy." Repeat this as many times as you like. Then do the same thing for other people, and eventually for yourself. Start with beings for whom it's easy to feel metta, and gradually—perhaps over the course of months or years—work up to people toward whom you feel unpleasant emotions. Sometimes the hardest person to feel sincere metta for is yourself.

A nonviolent approach doesn't in any way rule out setting boundaries or challenges for yourself. What matters is whether the intention behind your efforts is compassionate. Are you parenting yourself, letting a wiser part of you set the aspirations and then encouraging the other parts of you to help fulfill them? Is your goal greater happiness for self and others? Are you setting reasonable expectations—neither too demanding, nor insultingly low? When you don't meet an expectation, do you take a deep breath and simply try again?

Mindfulness can help you know when to be tough with yourself, when to be gentle, and when to take an approach that's somewhere in between. The idea is to maintain honest and open awareness of the results of different approaches to self-discipline. If you really want to make changes in your life, you won't always opt for the easy way out, but you also won't keep up harsh and judgmental approaches that simply aren't effective. When you recognize that change just isn't happening, instead of simply repeating the same efforts over and over, you try something new.

The Least You Need to Know

- If you want people to change, including yourself, you first have to have compassion for them.
- A good parent uses different approaches to discipline depending on the situation—strictness, deal-making, explanation, or unconditional support—and it's useful to be able to use these different kinds of approaches with yourself instead of defaulting to one or two.
- It's especially important not to employ harsh, judgmental, or violent methods to achieve change; these always result in harmful effects, even when applied internally.
- If change is difficult, listen carefully to the parts of yourself that are resisting it. Understanding them can help you find compassionate ways to get all parts of yourself "on board" with positive change.
- If you're patient, attentive, creative, flexible, and determined, the insights you gain through mindfulness can translate into lasting changes in your life.

Friends with Afflictive Emotions

Afflictive emotions are those that tend to have a negative effect on your life. Anger and jealousy can make you act out in harmful ways you later regret. Obsessive desire can drive you to compromise your commitments and responsibilities. Fear and doubt can paralyze you. Sometimes it may seem like there are only two options: suppress or avoid strong emotions, or live an emotional life that may be thrown into chaos at any moment depending on how you feel.

In this chapter I discuss how mindfulness can help you acknowledge and experience the full range of human emotions, but also give you more freedom of choice when it comes to responding to them. It can be tricky, but it's possible to feel your emotions fully without identifying with them. What you do is try to stay mindfully present through your experience of them and refrain from judging, resisting, or entirely believing them. Keeping simultaneous awareness of the body, breath, or your surroundings can keep your perspective wide enough that even an afflictive emotion can seem like a *part* of your reality instead of an absolute truth that must be acted on. When you have a little separation from your feelings, you can question the stories behind them.

In This Chapter

- The nature of afflictive emotions
- Using mindfulness to gain more freedom of choice when you're feeling emotional
- Learning to question the stories behind emotions
- Dealing mindfully with obsessive emotions
- What it means to make friends with emotions

Afflictive Emotions

Afflictive emotions are generally negative, self-perpetuating, and compelling. Some of the major ones are anger, fear, obsessive desire, self-doubt, and jealousy. An afflictive emotion is negative because of how it affects your body, mind state, and life. It may or may not be unpleasant to feel; for example, anger or obsessive desire may actually feel exciting or satisfying in a certain way. The problem is these emotions motivate you to neglect mindfulness. They inspire you to cling to certain views of reality instead of trying to see things more clearly, and drive you to choose courses of action that obstruct greater happiness for self and other.

The second principle of mindfulness, explained in Chapter 3, is: *the greatest happiness is that which applies in the longest term and at the largest scale—which includes the happiness of others.* Much of human suffering is caused when people choose lesser happiness at the expense of greater happiness. This choice often happens because of ignorance (people just don't see what leads to greater happiness), but when afflictive emotions are involved, this ignorance becomes willfully enforced. Under the sway of an afflictive emotion, you don't even *want* to see things clearly. Your receptivity to anything that might run counter to your emotion is shut down. Actions that express or relieve your emotion seem so attractive it's pretty much impossible to consider the negative impacts they might have on you or others.

Self-Perpetuating

There are other strong emotions that may feel compelling and painful, such as grief, shame, remorse, or intense concern due to difficult circumstances. However, these are not usually *afflictive* emotions because they don't tend to self-perpetuate, so they're not the same kind of problem. They tend to have a natural life expectancy; if you endure them, they will eventually work themselves out and you'll move on. Your life circumstances will change and so will your emotions. Sometimes you'll even have learned something from dealing with the strong emotions, or felt your life was somehow enriched by the experience.

 **KEEP IN MIND**

Sometimes nonafflictive emotions can become negative, self-perpetuating, and compelling. This usually means there's an afflictive emotion mixed in somewhere. For example, grief over a loss may be combined with anger at the people you think are to blame for the loss. Natural remorse over an action that had harmful consequences can trigger self-doubt. If you find an emotion sticking around and occupying most of your mental space, look for the presence of an underlying afflictive emotion.

The afflictive emotions, on the other hand, have an agenda. It tends to feel as if they're busy arguing their point, finding reasons not just for you to continue feeling them, but for you to feel them even more intensely. The classic example of this is fear. When someone suggests there's something to be afraid of and you believe them at all, a seed of fear sprouts in you. It grows and you start to interpret more things as evidence there are reasons to be afraid: suddenly it seems there are movements in the shadows, and you hear the creaking of footsteps that weren't audible before. Afflictive emotions catch you in their grasp and don't want to let go until you've done what they think is essential for you to do, whether that's fly into a rage, have an affair, or shrink back from a challenge.

Compelling Stories

Afflictive emotions are compelling, in part, because of the stories they're telling you. Most emotions are complicated experiences that include feelings, memories, agendas, stories, and views of the way things are. As discussed in Chapter 5, emotions differ from feelings, which are your initial, in-the-moment responses to things as you quickly evaluate their relevance to your well-being. Feelings are very simple and come in only three flavors: like, dislike, or neutrality. Unless you fixate on them or believe they reflect reality, feelings can pass quickly. Emotions, on the other hand, tend to last longer and take on a certain life of their own. An emotion may explain some of your feelings, or an emotional state can be triggered by feelings, but emotions are intimately tied up with stories about your life.

For example, let's say over time you've built up a strong dislike for a friend's partner that borders on hatred. Your emotion is based on things this person has done and the negative impact he is having on your friend's life. When you encounter the subject of your hatred face-to-face, you experience a strong *feeling* of dislike, but your emotions extend far beyond that immediate, visceral negative reaction. You know you can have a feeling of dislike for someone arise for relatively unimportant reasons—such as his manner of speech, or resemblance to someone else you have known. The feeling isn't such a big deal, but your emotion about your friend's partner *is*. You have *reasons* for your emotions!

 TAKE CARE

You may actually be attracted to being completely caught up in your powerful emotions. There's a certain thrill that can come from being "out of control"—when the cautious, responsible, self-conscious aspects of yourself get pushed aside so you can do something new, exhilarating, or risky. Part of the attraction here is the joy of feeling alive and directly engaged with your life—which is also what mindfulness practice can help you access, without the usual costs associated with acting out afflictive emotions like anger or obsessive desire.

Emotions are more compelling than momentary feelings not only because of the stories associated with them, but also because those stories end up being part of your self-identity. Even if they're sad or unpleasant stories, they seem to reflect your best estimation of reality, so you come to rely on them. When you feel an afflictive emotion, as far as you can tell, there's something going on in your life that requires immediate and dramatic action. It may seem something or someone is threatening you or the people and things you care about, or that you have a fleeting opportunity to obtain something without which you'll never be truly happy. It may appear that if you don't stand firm or assert your view, your dignity or autonomy will be forever compromised, or your life is in peril of completely falling apart unless you figure out a solution *right now*.

Mindfulness and Afflictive Emotions

When it comes to afflictive emotions, mindfulness can be difficult. Mindfulness requires a willingness to suspend judgment and let go of thinking about the past and future, and making this kind of effort can be the last thing you want to do when you're feeling a powerful, compelling emotion like anger or obsessive desire. However, anything you can do to ground yourself in the present and slow things down a little bit can help. You might take a couple of deep breaths, go for a walk, or have a pleasant conversation with someone. Any amount of time you're able to keep your awareness on what's going on right here, right now, is time you're *not* acting out the afflictive emotion and letting it self-perpetuate.

Greater Tolerance, Less Reactivity

It may not seem like a big deal to practice mindfulness for 30 seconds instead of losing your temper, but it's actually a huge accomplishment. (Even if you end up losing your temper anyway, even a short delay gives you something to work with.) It's difficult to step back from our strong emotions because most of us are highly identified with them, even if we don't think of ourselves as particularly emotional people. For example, you probably say "I *am* scared" when you're feeling that emotional state. At the moment you're speaking, the emotion defines you, at least in part. It's certainly the defining aspect of your present moment.

A more accurate description, of course, would be, "I'm feeling some fear right now." This thought acknowledges that the fear is an emotion. It also acknowledges that you're not synonymous with or defined by the fear, and that emotions come and go. There was a time before you felt the fear, and there will be a later time without fear—so fear is conditional. If there are other times and places without fear, it's also possible fear could subside right here, right now. Chances are it won't—at least not instantly—but this raises the question of what's keeping the fear alive. Is it all due to external factors, or is there something in your body-mind contributing to the experience?

Mindfulness practice helps you realize that, in fact, it isn't that you *are* fearful (or angry, miserable, depressed, obsessed, etc.); it's simply that you're feeling a particular emotion right now. This shift in the way you understand an emotion becomes a difference you experience in your body, not just in your use of language. As you center your awareness on your breath and notice your desire to hide, fight, or say something you'll later regret, you remember you're bigger than the emotion and its associated urges. The blinders of an afflictive emotion are momentarily taken off, and you receive some input from the universe outside of your emotional concern.

 MINDFUL EXERCISE

> Next time you feel a powerful surge of afflictive emotion (anger, fear, obsessive desire, self-doubt, or jealousy), see if there's an action you feel compelled to do. Perhaps you want to yell, throw something, or say something negative. Perhaps you want to check your email for the twentieth time today for the message from that special someone. Identify the action, and then *don't do it*—at all, or for the next hour. Don't fight the emotion, and go ahead and do something else. Just don't do the *one* thing you identified. Let the urge arise and pass away. (In the case of self-doubt, you might need to take a positive action that's the opposite of an urge to withdraw.)

If you can manage to endure the emotional storm to the point that you see it start to subside, you'll be well on your way to being able to live a full emotional life without being controlled by your emotions. Psychologists have many names for this process of learning to relate differently to your emotions, including affect tolerance, urge surfing, and decentering. Mindfulness can help you with all of them. In each case, essentially, you'll be calling the bluff of powerful emotions, which can be summarized as, "If I tell you to do something, don't question me. My observations reflect the true state of reality, and you'd be a fool to ignore me."

The Stories Behind the Emotions

After you've employed mindfulness to gain some space around afflictive emotions, you can cultivate awareness of the stories behind them. You do this in the same way you cultivate mindfulness of anything else: pay attention as closely as you can, and stay receptive by suspending judgment. You don't set out to either justify or argue with the stories; you simply want to see them as clearly as possible. Once you do, you gently question them—not to prove them wrong, but to open up just enough space of doubt that you aren't *absolutely* compelled to act in the way the emotion is telling you to.

Just recognizing the stories *as stories* increases your freedom of choice. A story may be more or less true, but it's an interpretation of reality, not synonymous with reality itself. When you acknowledge something as a story, you admit just a little possibility that it reflects a limited viewpoint, or that there may be different interpretations of the same events. Even if you're still convinced your story is valid and worth acting on, there's at least a part of you that has admitted it isn't utterly infallible. Maybe, just maybe, you've made some error in perception or judgment. Maybe, just maybe, you shouldn't bet the bank on your story quite yet.

Below I cover the major afflictive emotions, the typical stories that go along with them, and ways to examine those stories more carefully. As you use these approaches in your own life, try to avoid attaching too strongly to an agenda to change or get rid of the emotion, or to an idea that you shouldn't be feeling it. This response will sometimes just intensify the emotion, as part of you worries you're going to miss its crucial message to you. It may also add a layer of guilt to the situation that isn't helpful.

Anger

Anger arises when you think you need to protect something. Most often this is yourself, something of yours, or something you're identified with, but you may also feel the need to protect others. Sometimes the perceived need to protect is obvious and you also feel a sense of righteousness or aggression. Sometimes it's more subtle and you just end up feeling resentful or irritated. When anger is nurtured and sustained over time, it hardens into hatred. This is assigning someone or something the permanent status of enemy.

When Is Anger Useful?

The ancient Buddhist view of anger is that it can be useful information at the moment it arises. All it's really telling you is you *think* you need to protect something. Maybe you do and maybe you don't, but you should pay attention to what's going on. After the momentary experience of anger informs you, however, its usefulness is at an end. What it does is narrow your perspective until it's focused almost entirely on the object of your anger and the things that are fueling the emotion. This is obviously the opposite of mindful receptivity, which would open up the doors of your perception, let you see more clearly and objectively, and let you make wise choices.

 TAKE CARE

When you're angry with someone, you may think it's valuable to express it so they understand how you feel. However, speaking out of anger generally makes you state things more strongly and harshly than you would otherwise. You're more likely to make absolute statements, like "You never listen" or "You're disrespectful." It's possible to convey that you're upset—even that you're feeling anger—without actually letting anger color and bias your speech. Most people will get the point, and you won't have said hurtful or silly things you can't take back.

The one situation in which anger might continue to be useful is if you need to physically protect someone, which is probably why it evolved to affect us the way it does. In modern life, the vast majority of cases where you experience anger aren't going to benefit from the single-minded, furious energy it can provide. Instead, holding on to it simply limits your perspective and makes it likely you'll say or do things you'll later regret. In addition, nurturing anger over time negatively affects your mind state and health. Buddhists have likened it to taking poison or grasping a hot coal with the intention of harming someone else; ultimately you hurt yourself more than you hurt the other person.

Questioning Anger's Story

When you're angry, there's a compelling story about your situation that you believe with deep conviction. Perhaps you think you *know* your partner is being deliberately disrespectful, or that your boss is trying to undermine your position at work by humiliating you in meetings. Maybe you *know* the opposing political party is plotting the downfall of the nation, or your neighbor gets great satisfaction out of letting you clean up his dog's messes in your yard. The story doesn't have to be rational for it to fuel anger. At some point I realized whenever I encountered red lights or slow-moving traffic, I would get angry and think, "The universe is trying to get in my way!"

Although the stories behind anger seem obviously true, there are two questions you can ask yourself about them that may help you feel slightly less obligated to hold on to them. The first is, "What else is going on here?" Anger narrows your perspective, so you're bound to be missing something. If you look even briefly for what that might be, you're inclined to relax your grip on your anger for a moment and open up—at least a little bit—to mindful awareness. The existence of other factors or points of view don't necessarily invalidate your story, but acknowledging them helps you take off the blinders of anger.

The second question to ask yourself when you're angry is this: "Is this an emergency?" Of course, most of the time it's not, but anger tends to include a sense of imperative. Even if you're not inclined to actually say or do something out of your anger, you probably want to. If you don't act out, your motivation is sublimated into stewing over what you might do in the future, or what the course of justice would look like if you only had the means to bring it about. If any part of you can admit this isn't an emergency, you have a chance to postpone judgment as well as action. You can acknowledge that your anger is telling you there *may* be something that needs protecting. Then you can relax back into mindfulness and try to maintain awareness of everything that's going on instead of just your story about it.

Fear

Fear is similar to anger in that a feeling of fear is information: you're thinking there *may* be something to be afraid of. Anger is the "fight" part of your instinctive "fight, flight, or freeze" response, and fear is the "flight or freeze" part. Fear is also similar to anger in that it narrows your perspective down to the object of your fear and draws your energy and attention into identifying more evidence of danger. In terms of evolution, fear is about getting you ready—physically as well as mentally—to forget about everything else and flee as quickly as possible.

Anxiety and Worry

In modern life you're more likely to experience fear in its less dramatic forms. You're rarely going to fear for your immediate physical safety or survival, but you're likely to fear for your well-being in a more general sense, and perhaps also for your long-term survival in terms of health, social status, or financial security. This will most often be experienced as compulsive worry or anxiety. The element of fear is what differentiates worry and anxiety from rational consideration of how to take care of your life.

 KEEP IN MIND

Mindfulness can help you notice your anxiety. Pay attention when you're thinking a lot about something you need to take care of. If you aren't mindful of your mental activity, you're likely to continue mulling something over and over, without realizing it's causing you stress. In anxiety you tend to dwell on something because you think it's important, but without actually making much headway in terms of solving your problem or coming up with a workable plan. You may want to devote some time to conscious and mindful analysis and planning, instead of letting anxious thoughts buzz around in the background.

The story of fear, anxiety, and worry is that you aren't up to facing whatever challenge is in front of you. You'd be better off fleeing, and if you can't or won't flee the only option is to freeze. This leads to paralysis or ineffectiveness that makes your worry and anxiety generate stress without producing substantial results. Fear convinces you doom is imminent and keeps you in a state of stress or panic. This impedes your ability to think clearly and, over time, compromises your health.

Questioning Fear's Story

The first question to ask about your story of fear is this: "What am I really afraid of?" Sometimes fear keeps you captive because the imminent danger remains vague and unspecified. What's dreaded is a situation that's generically terrible and unacceptable. When you turn your mindful awareness toward the object of your fear, you may find it loses some of its power. Perhaps you notice it's not so much that you fear poverty but that you fear what people will think of you if you're not financially solvent. This means that resolving your fear depends in part on letting go of your concern about other people's opinions, not just making more money. Perhaps you realize your compulsive worry about your health is due to your fear of being helpless, having watched others go through illness and old age. While you can't entirely escape these physical eventualities, you can work on your ability to graciously accept help without feeling your dignity is compromised. Seeing the nature of your fear may not make it disappear, but it may make it seem more manageable.

The second question to ask is, "What if I just do my best?" Remember, the story of fear is that you aren't up to facing the challenge in front of you. Your mind can generate an infinite number of scenarios where your best efforts fall short or you make the wrong decisions. If you question this story, an unconditional kind of confidence can arise because you observe your fear with mindfulness and recognize that it's not doing anyone any good. It's only going to interfere with your best efforts; so what if you let go of the worry and fear, and stayed centered in meeting challenges with everything you've got to offer? If things fall apart anyway, there's nothing more you could have done. This kind of conviction can be the result of seeing things more clearly with mindfulness. It's not that you adopt an optimistic view that everything will work out for the best no matter what. Instead, you lose your willingness to suffer fear because you see how stressful and useless it is.

Obsessive Desire

Obsessive desire is when you become fixated on something you want to obtain or experience. You go beyond identifying something as desirable and working toward it; the object of your desire starts to seem more important than anything else in your life. You can't stop thinking about it, and all other activities and responsibilities seem like onerous obligations that get in the way of enjoying, working to obtain, or even just fantasizing about the object of your desire.

 TAKE CARE

The attraction of novelty is often an important part of obsessive desire. Things you already have—relationships, jobs, homes, possessions—can become more and more difficult to appreciate, so you need something new to give you access to that sense of vitality and pleasure that makes life worth living. Unfortunately, this obligates you to a constant quest for novelty. The alternative is to cultivate mindfulness so you can directly experience and appreciate the things you have, instead of relating to them only through the filter of your ideas about them (see Chapter 9).

The forms that obsessive desire can take are many, but several common ones are greed, envy, and infatuation. When you're feeling greed, you desperately want more of whatever it is you desire. For some reason, the money, power, sex, excitement, or pleasure you've been enjoying isn't quite enough. When you're feeling envy, you're convinced that you're lacking something important or especially wonderful that someone else has. The comparison can make you bitter and unable to enjoy your life as it is. The most classic form of obsessive desire is infatuation, particularly the romantic or sexual kind felt for another person. Infatuation can be so powerful and intoxicating that you find yourself willing to risk destroying other important things in your life in order to satisfy your appetite for contact with the object of your desire.

When You *Must* Have It

Whatever the flavor of an obsessive desire, chances are it compromises your mindfulness. Like the afflictive emotions discussed so far, desire seriously shuts down your receptivity to anything other than the object of your emotion. You probably won't even notice the harm you cause as you do anything to obtain what you want. You won't be able to appreciate what's going on around you if it isn't directly related to your desire. When the obsession is particularly strong, you're very unlikely to center your awareness on the breath, create some space around your feelings, or meditate—so gaining perspective on your desire will be difficult.

The story of obsessive desire is that the thing you want will let you become who you're really meant to be, or taste what life is really about. There is an intensity and promise that seems to be inherent in the object of your desire. It makes mundane life pale in comparison. Perhaps the pleasure of a beautiful new house would let you relax and let your creative juices flow in a way they never have before, so you spend hours fantasizing about it. Perhaps you know driving that amazing new car would bring a new level of satisfaction to your life on a daily basis, so you're willing to go deeply into debt for the privilege. Perhaps the intimacy you experience with your new lover seems to be the key to truly feeling alive, in contrast to the boring relationship you have with your partner.

Questioning Desire's Story

When you're experiencing obsessive desire, you're often convinced you've never felt this way before. "*This* relationship (or object, or opportunity) is different," you think. "This isn't just a momentary intoxication; this is the key to true happiness." It can be incredibly difficult to make yourself question this conviction, but it can be very helpful if you do so—even for a moment. Ask yourself, "Have I felt this way before?" Or, "What about a year or two from now, when the novelty has inevitably worn off and the costs of my choices become more evident?" You don't have to dwell at length on past emotional states or potential future ones. It's enough to recall that, indeed, you have been very excited about things in the past that you later came to see as mundane or inadequate. It's enough to recognize that you have, indeed, made some choices based on desire that you later came to see as being less than perfectly wise. These realizations suggest that *just maybe* your current point of view is biased.

KEEP IN MIND

According to the Buddhists, desire is one of the primary causes of suffering, and the stronger the desire, the worse the suffering. Basically, it's painful not to get what you really want, or to be forced to endure what you really don't want. It's not that it's wrong to want anything; it's just that a measure of perspective and acceptance can prevent your desires from becoming sources of stress and misery.

Another question to ask yourself is this: "Who else might be affected here?" Obsessive desire is pretty much always very selfish. Maybe there will be some side benefits for others, but it's primarily about *your* comfort, ease, pleasure, excitement, status, etc. When you stop to think about others, the part of you that sincerely cares about their well-being might inspire you to tread more softly in your efforts to get what you want. Perhaps it's your right to spend your money how you want, but if you fall on hard times and appeal to others for help it will be a financial strain on them. Perhaps it's time to take care of yourself and spend lots of time and energy on a new hobby or lover, but your children are feeling neglected. Is there a way you can enjoy your life without requiring others to pay the cost? Examining your story in this way isn't meant to make you feel guilty; it's just meant to widen your perspective beyond the object of your desire.

Self-Doubt

It can feel like there's no end to self-doubt when you're in the midst of it. Once you start to doubt yourself, why should you trust any of your judgments? The odds seem to be stacked against you; sometimes you achieve the outcome you desire, but there's always a significant risk of disaster. You may avoid taking bold actions in order to avoid such disasters. Alternatively, you may act despite your doubts, but then be consumed by worry and remorse afterward. In either case, the dread of being wrong—and being seen as wrong—is one of your primary concerns. You may spend a fair amount of time feeling stressed, worried, and unhappy as you replay scenarios over and over in your head to understand where you screwed up, and how you might avoid doing so in the future.

Undeserving of Confidence

When you're mired in self-doubt, it's the lens through which you view everything. Compliments and successes are viewed as suspect, subjective, or just lucky. Criticisms and failures, on the other hand, are viewed as strong evidence you were right to doubt yourself all along. This biased view helps keep self-doubt alive. Even when things are going fairly well, you're likely to feel that, at some level, you're fooling people. If they really knew you, they'd worry. Extreme self-doubt can leave you socially isolated, afraid to explore your potential, or depressed.

The story of self-doubt is this: you're flawed and limited, and are therefore very likely to be wrong, make mistakes, cause harm, or suffer embarrassment despite your best efforts. Mistakes point out your flawed nature, which is a cause for deep shame. This shame is painful and should be hidden as much as possible. Also, another of your limitations is that you lack the capacity for change. You're permanently banned from the ranks of people who feel bold, confident, and sure of themselves.

Questioning Self-Doubt's Story

The first question to ask your story of self-doubt may seem counterintuitive: "Why do you think you're more special than anyone else?" Ironically, self-doubt can arise from holding higher standards for yourself than for others. Even when you're in the depths of your low self-estimation, you'll probably have to admit at least some other people screw up as much or more than you do. When you think of those people, however, this is probably what goes through your mind: "Yeah, but I don't want to be like *them*." Why not join the human race? We're all flawed, goofy, selfish, short-sighted, and limited. Cultivating acceptance of your imperfections can go a long way toward freeing yourself from self-doubt.

 MINDFUL EXERCISE

If you ever struggle with self-doubt, take some time to vividly imagine what it would take to banish that doubt and give you plenty of boldness and confidence. You may want to write your answers down. In any case, don't censor or edit your thoughts at all. Some of them may be unreasonable (such as being able to tell ahead of time exactly what will work in a given situation) or impossible (such as wanting to be taller, or an extrovert instead of introvert). It's helpful just to become more aware of the standards and expectations you're holding for yourself. Consider whether you want to keep doubting yourself until you meet them.

The second question for self-doubt is, "Where do you think confidence comes from?" Those of us who struggle with self-doubt generally hold an idea that confidence arises when you've evaluated your likelihood of success at 95 to 99 percent. However, although confident people may feel certain they're going to succeed, this isn't all there is to it. Confidence can also come from building awareness of the following things over time: nothing ever qualifies as a *complete* success, and mistakes are part of the learning process. Can you have confidence you'll take responsibility for the repercussions of your actions? Can you have confidence in your ability to apologize and learn? Try engaging life as if it's a series of challenges meant to test and train you, and see what happens.

Jealousy

Jealousy twists you up inside by targeting what you care about most and convincing you that you're in danger of losing it to someone who has outcompeted you for it. Few emotions can feel more miserable than jealousy, which starts with fear of loss but then partakes of other afflictive emotions as well: anger, obsessive desire, and self-doubt. Jealousy dramatically distorts your ability to see things clearly. You start to interpret everything as evidence your jealousy is warranted. You may start to feel paranoid, as if you can't trust your usual means of determining that everything's okay. You vividly imagine all kinds of terrible, painful scenarios that could be happening now or might happen in the near future.

The story of jealousy is cruel and personal. Not only do you face the loss of relationship or position, the important people involved believe you're no longer worthy of it. They see someone else as better, smarter, more attractive, or more powerful than you. If you don't do something to take control of the situation, loss is pretty much inevitable. Perhaps you need to monitor a loved one and restrict their freedom to keep them from going astray. Perhaps you need to get more devious than your potential adversaries and work to undermine them. In any case, you may be aware that jealousy alienates people and makes you petty and mean but, heck, you've got to do what you've got to do.

Questioning Jealousy's Story

The first question to ask about jealousy is, "Is it worth it?" Trying to monitor and control other people is exhausting, and it generally backfires. Jealousy in romantic relationships and friendships usually just leads to more lack of trust, as you become convinced your jealous behavior keeps the other person in line. The other person tends to feel trapped and disrespected, and may be inclined to lie just to avoid a confrontation. In other situations jealousy reveals you to be insecure, and efforts to get people on your side can make them feel manipulated even if they indulge you. Do you want to hang on to who or what you want through jealousy indefinitely? Perhaps the alternative of loss seems unbearable, but this question may make you wonder just enough to loosen jealousy's grip.

 **TAKE CARE**

Sometimes jealousy is compelling and painful because your pride is hurt. In this case it's not so much that you care about a particular relationship, role, or opportunity; it's that you feel angry that someone might be disloyal, or might choose someone else over you. If you want to get free of this kind of jealousy, you'll have to work on letting go of your pride—but after that, you may feel there's not a whole lot of motivation for feeling jealous.

The second question is, "Whose loss?" Often, jealousy goes along with (or triggers) self-doubt. When it seems a significant person in your life might be choosing someone else over you, it can feel devastating. However, if you're at all inclined to fight the loss you're worried about, you must have some self-esteem left. Look at yourself instead of at the person you're feeling jealous about. Are you a decent person? Have you done your best? Have you worked hard, tried to be supportive, and been honest and faithful? Have you kept your promises, even if the other person might be thinking of compromising theirs? If a partner leaves you or a boss passes you over for promotion, then, whose loss is it? It's possible to be your own fan despite the conclusions of others.

Making Friends

As you start to question your afflictive emotions and resist acting out their imperatives, it can be easy to turn this effort into a struggle with yourself. It helps to think of dealing with your strong negative emotions as if you were working out a compromise with a friend with whom you have a disagreement. This is consistent with the compassionate approach to change I discussed in Chapter 13. In the case of working with afflictive emotions, you want to make sure you avoid taking an oppositional stance against what you feel. Afflictive emotions are powerful enough that the part of you trying to get free of them is usually going to lose—unless that part makes friends with the afflictive emotions first.

It may seem unwise to befriend a potentially harmful emotion, but this doesn't in any way mean you have to believe or act out the emotion, just as you aren't bound to do something just because a friend tells you to. What it does mean is that you try to understand the afflictive emotion and the concerns or desires behind it. Instead of deciding the emotion is bad and needs to be eliminated as quickly as possible, you see if there's some way you can work with it and convert it—or at least calm it enough to let you practice mindfulness. You'll generally find the emotion is arising because of a desire to protect and take care of yourself or those you care about. Even if it's partly deluded, in a sense it means well.

The Least You Need to Know

- Not all emotions are afflictive.
- Afflictive emotions have a negative impact on your life because they encourage you to neglect mindfulness. They're self-perpetuating, compelling, and associated with stories about the way things are and what you should do.
- Some of the major afflictive emotions are anger, fear, obsessive desire, self-doubt, and jealousy.

- Mindfulness can help you see your afflictive emotions as *part* of your overall experience, instead of the definition of it. It can also help you stay grounded in the present through strong compulsions to act out an emotion.

- You can create more space around afflictive emotions by mindfully questioning the stories behind them.

Getting Things Done with Less Stress

You probably spend most of your time and energy taking care of your life—maintaining your health, taking care of your responsibilities, making a living, and nurturing relationships. Fortunately, mindfulness isn't something special you add to your long list of activities, and it isn't a stress-relieving technique that requires you to put aside everything else in order to practice it (although there's a value to doing that at times).

Mindfulness is something you can cultivate every moment *as* you take care of your life and get things done. When you're mindful, you're more attentive, present, and available. You get out of your own way and are better able to respond quickly and appropriately. You tend to experience less stress, and feel less discouraged by challenges. In this chapter I discuss how to practice mindfulness as you go about taking care of the practical aspects of your life. I also talk about some of the main sources of stress when you're trying to get things done, and what to do about them.

In This Chapter

- How to bring mindfulness to your daily activities
- The relationship between mindfulness and taking care of your life
- Dealing with a sense of imperative or time pressure
- Gaining some freedom from work-related concerns
- Learning to see whatever you do as an expression of generosity

The Basic Approach

If you want to extend the benefits of mindfulness into the more active areas of your life, you start by taking a new perspective on things: it's worth being present for *everything* you do, because you can *always* see things more clearly and learn to take better care of your life. In Part 2 I walked you through a series of classic objects for mindfulness you can use to develop your awareness, including your body, feelings, states of mind, and psychophysical factors like ill will, lethargy, energy, or concentration. Not only can you practice awareness of all of these things as you go about your daily life, you can also make the very objects and concerns of your life the focus of your mindfulness. Anything—the manner in which you wake up in the morning, the breakfast you eat, the clothes you wear, the drive to work, etc.—can become an object of your mindfulness. You can see things more clearly and understand them better.

Watchful, Curious, and Awake

Becoming mindful of your life doesn't mean you continually analyze it or second-guess your choices. Mindful awareness is more like watching than analyzing. Although that sounds simple, your inclination to watch the day-to-day unfolding of your life tends to be severely compromised by your assumptions that you've seen it all before and you already understand it sufficiently, as discussed in Chapter 9. You figure you don't need to question things or pay attention to them unless they're new or causing serious problems. When you focus the lens of mindfulness onto your life, you try to stop making these assumptions. Maybe you know what happens next, maybe you don't. Maybe you understand your own motivations, maybe you don't. Instead of assuming, you try to develop the kind of curiosity discussed in Chapter 10 about your own, apparently mundane, everyday life.

 KEEP IN MIND

It's much easier to be mindful when you're doing something you enjoy, or something you consider interesting or worthwhile. Go ahead and practice cultivating mindful awareness during those kinds of activities—they're a good place to start. However, you'll only experience the full benefits of mindfulness if you also start paying more attention during activities you don't enjoy, or that you view as boring or merely necessary.

Talking about mindfulness as a way to help you get things done more effectively may imply that it's a special, newfangled solution to life's problems. In fact, mindfulness is so basic to being human it's amazing that it even needs to be identified or discussed. It simply amounts to being awake for your life—attentive, receptive, open, and willing to adapt. For the reasons discussed in Chapter 2, however, mindfulness *does* need to be talked about and deliberately cultivated. Still, it's always good to remember it's essentially something very basic and natural, and it can come to describe the way you operate moment by moment.

Awareness of the Body

Cultivating mindfulness as you go about your activities generally involves taking a moment to become aware of your body or physical sensations. (Chapter 4 explains in detail how to do this.) Mindfulness of your physical experience expands your receptivity and grounds you in the present moment. You still remain aware of what other things are going on, but your perspective changes slightly.

For example, you may be working on the computer. If you go about this task in a habitual way, chances are your attention is completely focused on the task itself. This may seem like the best or only way to get something done, but if you expand your awareness to include your body, you'll notice it doesn't interfere with your ability to do the task. Instead, you also become aware of yourself doing the task. You notice your posture and whether you're tense. You notice your mental and emotional state—whether you're anxious, tired, or resistant. You become aware of the whole context of the task, including how you're progressing on it in terms of time, and its priority level in the overall list of things you need to accomplish.

 MINDFUL EXERCISE

> While you're going about your daily tasks, pay attention to your hands whenever you remember to do it. Notice their position and movements. Be aware of any sensations you feel in or on your hands. Pay attention to whether they're resting on a table or a steering wheel, holding a cup or toothbrush, gripping something with force, or gently and skillfully manipulating an object. You don't have to change what your hands are doing at all. Simply bringing them into your awareness will bring you back to the present moment. When you do this, what else do you notice? Can you taste a moment of "just being" in the midst of your activity?

You might say mindfulness is less about paying attention in any special or intense way, and more about making sure your awareness stays open. When you're thinking about the future or the past, or absorbed in thoughts or projects, your field of awareness narrows. There may be a time when doing this is fruitful, but generally speaking even intense thinking sessions benefit from periodic grounding in mindfulness. The longer you go without checking in with what's going on in the present moment, the more likely you are to miss important information. Your back may get sore because you're hunched over your project. You may entirely miss the emotional reactions of someone you're dealing with. You may become so intent on a task you can't put it down, even though other things need your attention. Your efforts may be stressing you out to the point that you're frustrated and irritable and no longer working efficiently. Cultivating mindfulness in all settings helps you make decisions more in harmony with the state of your body, mind, and circumstances.

Effective Means Mindful

It takes a moment to shift into mindfulness gear while you're doing something. It doesn't have to take long, but it can be beneficial to pause for at least a few seconds. The longer you can give yourself to attend to physical sensations and settle into the present moment, the calmer you'll tend to feel, and the more perspective you'll have. Generally speaking, when you resist taking a moment to be mindful, you're probably quite stressed and a moment of mindfulness will be all the more useful. Still, don't require too much of yourself, or you're likely to forgo mindfulness altogether in your efforts to get things done!

After you pause and expand your awareness to include the body and sensations, you're able to perceive more of what's going on within and around you. You're much more likely to recognize when an urge to think, speak, or act arises in you—before you go ahead and follow that urge. Often, the first thing that arises in you when you're actively engaged in the world is a *reaction*. Stimulation from your environment interacts with your conditioning, and your body-mind spits out an answer (even if you keep that answer to yourself, it's still present in your mind). When you introduce mindfulness into the picture, you have a chance to consciously reflect on your reaction and take other aspects of the situation into consideration. What results from this is your best *response* to things. This response is usually wiser and more effective than your reaction would have been.

 **DEFINITION**

> A **reaction** is an impulse to think, speak, or act that arises more or less spontane-
> ously in your body-mind after you experience something. It's likely to be habitual and
> highly conditioned. A **response** is conscious and deliberate thought, speech, or action
> you choose as being your best way to answer or deal with the situation in front of you.

For example, let's say you're fixated on straightening up your apartment before company comes over. They're due to arrive in an hour and you have lots to do. You feel anxious about being able to finish everything in time (and avoid your visitors realizing you usually live in a pigsty), so you try to move quickly. When you need to open a drawer and it sticks, you react by yanking on it harder. When it still won't open, you react further by getting angry and pulling on it with all your strength. As it flies open, you see something was wedged in the drawer that you've now broken.

A mindful response to the same scenario would be to acknowledge your frustration when the drawer first gets stuck, but then would involve a pause to take stock of the whole situation before reacting. You might take a deep breath and sigh, but you'd probably open the drawer gently, part way, and see if you could ascertain what's keeping it closed and remove it. In the case where you indulge your reactivity, it's not that you lack the intelligence to know an object might be blocking the drawer and yanking on it might break it. You are simply so focused on your immediate agenda that you don't let other information and possibilities enter your awareness. Generally speaking, mindfulness doesn't make you a smarter, nicer, more patient person; it just lets you access the smarts, kindness, and patience you already have.

Things You *Must* Do

It's very tempting to use your responsibilities as excuses not to be mindful. Essentially, you figure you've *got* to take care of something, so you don't have spare time and energy for niceties like mindfulness. There are commitments to be kept, deadlines to be met, dependents to take care of, clothes to be washed, bills to be paid, exercise to keep up with, and social connections to maintain. For many people, modern life involves a "to-do" list that never shrinks no matter how hard they work. Most of the things on such lists do not seem optional. Almost everything comes along with a sense of imperative, which means you're pretty much always neglecting something you *need* to get done. This can lead to an enormous amount of stress.

Experiment: Everything Is Optional

One of the great things mindfulness allows you to do is experiment with the way you approach things and then observe the results. As discussed in earlier chapters, mindfulness helps you become less identified with your thoughts, judgments, and emotions. You begin to recognize them as being *part* of your overall experience, and not necessarily reflections of absolute truth. You don't have to believe them, or act the way they're telling you to. This opens up other possibilities, and when you try a different approach, mindfulness lets you monitor the outcome so you can learn what works best.

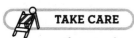 **TAKE CARE**

If you tend to procrastinate or take things too lightly, your life probably won't benefit much from doing the attitude experiments discussed in this chapter. Stress probably isn't your problem. Still, cultivating mindfulness as you go about your work can help you stop procrastinating so much because you'll be more aware of when you're doing it, and more aware of the consequences later. Mindfulness can also help you take more responsibility for things by letting you see where you're underemphasizing the importance of something just because you don't want to do it.

Here's the attitude experiment to try if you want to get things done with less stress: *look at all of the tasks on your to-do list as optional.* Your first reaction to this suggestion is probably to think of all the things on your list that can't possibly be viewed as optional. You *have* to make dinner for your kids and pay your bills! However, despite your conviction, try looking more closely at your reasoning. For each task that isn't optional, there's an "or else." If you don't feed your kids, they'll starve (or complain loudly). If you don't pay your bills, your utilities will get shut off. These likely outcomes are probably completely unacceptable to you—thus the sense of imperative associated with the tasks.

However, even in these cases you're making a choice. Because you don't want such-and-such to happen, you're going to complete a particular task. Ultimately, you don't *have* to do anything. You do things because you want to take care of your life. Sometimes it can make a big difference to make this slight change in attitude from thinking of yourself as laboring under a bunch of imperatives to thinking of yourself as voluntarily doing your best to take care of things. You might not even need to intellectualize about it—just "try on" the attitude that whatever you're doing is optional. How does this feel different in your body and mind? Does it make you less resistant or overwhelmed? Does it make you feel more relaxed and enthusiastic? And, most important: are you able to get things done just as efficiently, or even more efficiently? You may find mindfulness makes tasks inexplicably easier and more enjoyable.

Experiment: Worst-Case Scenario

A closely related attitude experiment is to make peace with the worst-case scenario you can imagine if you fail to complete the important tasks on your list on time. Sometimes, of course, this worst-case scenario really will be unacceptable because it threatens someone's health and safety. Most of the time, however, if you really think about the worst-case scenario, you have to admit that although it sounds like the end of the world to you, it really isn't. Maybe your visitors will arrive before you're done cleaning and get a low opinion of your housekeeping. Maybe you'll arrive at a meeting 10 minutes late and people will think you're flaky. Maybe you won't finish painting before the weekend is over and you'll have to walk around your ladders and paint cans until the next time you have a chance to work on your project.

Can you make your peace with the worst-case scenario? Imagine it happening and then observe the reactions in your body and mind in the present moment. You may tense up somewhere in the body, or you might start thinking about all the reasons the scenario would be a disaster. What is the essence of your determination to avoid it? Chances are good it has to do with other people's opinions of you, or with your own convenience, comfort, or pleasure. If you notice this is the case, don't argue with yourself or judge your concerns. Just gently point out to yourself that if you accepted the possibility that just maybe your worst-case scenario will happen and you'll have to deal with it, you could go about your business with much less stress.

MINDFUL EXERCISE

Think of a task you *really* need to do, or else terrible things will happen. Don't pick something that might result in physically endangering someone, but short of that, let the issue be something serious that's causing you stress. Let yourself imagine all of the likely negative repercussions of *not* taking care of things in a timely manner. Be specific; it may be good to write them down. If necessary, consider the further repercussions of direct results. How would you deal with each thing on your list? Although you're going to try to avoid them, can you imagine still finding ways to appreciate your life even if they happened?

Remember, chances are very good that if you do a task mindfully and let go of the sense that it absolutely must get done, you will, nonetheless, get it done. In fact, chances are even better you'll get it done, and get it done well! If you have a hard time letting go of your sense of imperative, try doing it in small steps. Let go of it a little bit, or just for a while, and then observe what happens. This can build your confidence in letting go of your habitual ways of engaging tasks in favor of mindfulness.

It Has to Get Done *Now*

Stress often arises from a sense of time pressure—something needs to get done now, or very soon. Alternatively, it isn't that a given task needs to get done quickly, it's that you feel the need to keep checking items off your to-do list to keep from getting completely overwhelmed by the number of tasks you have to do. This leads to two typical reactions. One, you work with a sense of impatience and hurry, anticipating the task being over even while you're still doing it. You may push too hard on things physically and mentally, trying to get everything to move a little bit faster. Even when it's clear they're not going to, you may find it hard to relax—as if everything will slow down unless you keep your mind and body tense. Two, you keep working until you've used up your energy, patience, and ability to think clearly. You know you're compromising your health and you aren't working as efficiently or well as you could, but you figure you have no choice.

Experiment: Just This Moment

Nothing counters a sense of time pressure like the very basic practice of mindfulness of your breath, or of the movements of your hands. You're unlikely to be able to argue yourself into letting go of the effort to hurry things along. If you can win that argument and slow down, that's great. If you're like many people, willfully trying to slow down meets with huge resistance. Instead, just try shifting your attention to something physical that's happening in the present moment. This turns your attention away from the near future, so you're less likely to be preoccupied with it.

Mindfulness of the breath or the hands is a very basic practice, but it's also very effective. However, you'll probably have to bring your awareness back to these simple things over and over. Your mind will repeatedly wander, or leap to the future. To encourage yourself to keep up the effort of staying in the present moment, you might remind yourself that mindfulness will actually help you be more efficient. You might also invite your hands to move as quickly as "they" would like, as long as you can maintain awareness of them. If you do this, you may find your hands seem to have a mind of their own as they go about complicated tasks with amazing skill.

Experiment: Gentleness

An attitude experiment you can try when you're stressed about not having enough time is to imagine everything you're handling is very delicate and expensive, so you have to be very careful and gentle. In this case you can still move quickly, but instead of pushing too hard, throwing things around, or slamming things down, you have to be mindful about how you treat them lest they break. If you think about this when you're hurrying to get something done, you'll probably notice you treat things like tools, doors, and supplies as if they're unbreakable, unimportant, and easily replaced. Maybe they *are* sturdy and cheap, but treating them like this encourages you to manipulate your environment as if everything is there only to further your agenda.

KEEP IN MIND

There's a classic Zen essay about bringing mindfulness to your work called "Instructions to the Zen Cook," written in 1237. The author, Zen master Dogen, advises the cook to treat the rice, vegetables, and other ingredients "as carefully as if they were his own eyes." Can you imagine treating everything with that level of care? (Translation by Thomas Wright in *From the Zen Kitchen to Enlightenment: Refining Your Life* by Kosho Uchiyama)

Here's an example of how trying to be more careful and gentle with things can change the whole flavor of your work experience. A friend of mine was a cook in a kitchen that served three gourmet meals a day to guests. It was a small kitchen operating under almost constant time pressure, and the temptation to hurry and get stressed was very strong. To encourage his own mindfulness in the kitchen, my friend adopted the policy of "no noise." Instead of banging pots and implements around, he tried to move them with a minimum of noise. Rather than just telling himself he *shouldn't* hurry, or feeling bad because he did, he adopted one simple rule and it affected everything he did.

It Needs to Be Done *This* Way

You may examine your sources of stress and realize much of it comes from a determination to do things a particular way. Of course, you're likely to think of this as the *right* way. You may not even be perfectionistic, or at least not about most things, but about certain tasks you have standards you can't let go of. Maybe you need to proofread all copy twice. Maybe you need to make sure your team has practiced to the point that you know they'll operate smoothly when they get to the tournament. Maybe every corner of your house needs to be vacuumed weekly.

Mindfulness doesn't require you to lower your standards; it simply requires you to recognize when your standards are the primary source of your stress. When you do this, you may end up finding small places you can compromise to reduce your stress. You may end up realizing that *this time* you're not going to pull things off quite the way you'd like to. When you're completely focused on a standard, you're not being mindful. You're likely to miss some of the impacts of your choices on your own body and mind, or on others. When you cultivate receptive awareness of what's going on, you may notice trying to meet one of your standards is simply having too high a cost. This realization that the cost is "too high" isn't a moral judgment, and it doesn't come from outside. It's something you may or may not conclude for yourself. Seeing more clearly, you may find greater happiness leads in a different direction than meeting your standard.

Experiment: Leaving Things (a Little) Shabby

There's a rather fun experiment you can do if you tend to stress out about doing things a particular way. For the most part, go ahead and do a task according to your usual standards. Then, stop a little short. Leave things just a little bit shabby or go just a little unprepared. There doesn't have to be a dramatic difference from the way you usually do things; other people don't even have to notice. In fact, they probably won't, but *you* will. Let your photographs get printed with the red-eye still unfixed. Let dust build up on the top shelf where no one looks. Let the agenda for the meeting remain somewhat vague.

 **TAKE CARE**

Sometimes the desire to do a task in a careless or incomplete way is a subtle way of rejecting the activity. Perhaps you think it's beneath you, or you resent having to do it. When this is the case, you might improve your state of mind by taking extra care with a task instead of taking shortcuts. Just as you "believe" your own mind when it judges something as unpleasant, your mind is likely to "believe" your body when it starts acting as if a task is rewarding and worth doing well.

Of course, if you habitually let these kinds of things slide, this may not be the exercise for you. Still, there are probably certain things you *don't* let slide, so try this experiment with those tasks. Notice how you feel when you "finish" the task, but not up to your usual standards. Does it feel like you're getting away with something? Is any part of you relieved you didn't have to bother with every detail? What happens over time? Does anyone notice the difference? You may decide to keep up your standards in the future, but it's possible to pick them back up consciously and deliberately so they don't carry quite the imperative they used to.

You Are the One Who Has to Do It

Sometimes, of course, you really are the only person that's going to get a particular thing done. No one's likely to show up to clean your house when you live alone (unless you pay them), and it's probably not a great idea to have someone else send your mom a card for her birthday. Still, there can be tasks that involve taking care of things for which a number of people share some responsibility. This often happens in communal households, at work, or in other kinds of organizations.

When you see something that needs to be taken care of but no one else is doing it, you not only face the burden of doing it yourself, you also face the possibility of resentment. You have enough to do as it is, and now there's a task on your list because others are too oblivious or lazy to do it. Alternatively, they recognize the need but take it for granted that you'll have it covered. You do the work because you want things to be cared for, but probably do so with a sense of dread that people will take advantage of you even further because of your willingness to pick up their slack.

Experiment: Picking Your Thing

There's no denying people will sometimes slack off and let others take responsibility in communal situations. It's not necessarily that your resentment is unfounded. However, taking stock of your circumstances with mindfulness will allow you to see which responses will be useful, and which will simply increase your own misery and have little or no effect on others. If you stay receptive instead of getting too caught up in your own opinions and reactions, you can identify what *you* can change about the situation.

 KEEP IN MIND

Most of the time, in households, communities, and organizations, people either feel they're already doing more than their share, or they resist doing things because they don't want to end up doing more than their share. Ironically, communities and organizations function best when everyone feels like they're doing more than their equitable portion of the work—so you might want to try it and figure, despite how it feels, it really is just your share.

One experiment you can try is to pick one or two tasks you can think of as yours to do. These are generally things only you seem to notice need to be done, or things you take care of better or more conscientiously than anyone else. You choose these things while keeping in mind your own stress level and other responsibilities. Ideally, you quietly pick one or two things you can handle and then make a vow to yourself to take care of them without worrying about any of the other tasks, or about what anyone else is or isn't doing. If you can manage this, you might even be able to be cheerful about the responsibilities you've chosen.

Experiment: Letting Others Step Up

At times the sense that you're the one who has to do something is related to your standards, as discussed in the previous section. Others may be willing to tend to a particular task, but it pains you to watch them do it because of their lack of ability, conscientiousness, or timeliness. Depending on your stress level and number of responsibilities, you may opt to delegate instead of doing something yourself because the cost of doing it is just too high. This can lead to an ongoing sense of stress anyway, however, as you still feel some responsibility for the task that's now being done in a way you don't approve of.

A useful experiment is to invite others to do a task, even though you know it won't get done in a way that meets your standards, and then just watch. Without mindfulness, your attention is going to be on the flaws in their work and the repercussions of things being done to lower standards. With mindfulness, you can be aware of these things as well as the benefits of getting others to participate. Not only do you have less to do, it can be extremely valuable to get other people more engaged in taking care of communal responsibilities. It can improve relationships and increase people's sense of ownership in a household or organization. It doesn't always work, but sometimes you might find the compromise in terms of standards has been more than made up for by the benefits of not trying to do everything yourself.

Activity as Generosity

Finally, it can help your stress levels a great deal if you can recognize in what way your work is an act of generosity. When you're doing something out of sincere generosity, you usually feel inspired and enthusiastic. What you're doing seems worthwhile and positive, even if it will only provide a small benefit to one person. However, it can be hard to see an activity this way if you're doing something you don't enjoy, you're getting paid to do it, or you feel like you have to do it. Yet pretty much everything you do contributes in some way to taking care of the world. Even if you're only looking after yourself, that's something no one else has to do.

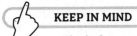

KEEP IN MIND

Think about your encounters with the generosity of other people as they simply go about their daily lives. A cheerful checkout clerk can brighten your day. A careful receptionist may call you when there's a cancellation and give you the opportunity of an appointment much sooner than you anticipated. Someone who lives near you may cultivate a lovely flower garden that inspires you whenever you walk by. An attentive driver may help you avoid an accident. In all of these cases, people are just doing the best they can and benefiting others.

You may be able to adopt a sense that your activities at home and out in the world express generosity, but it may not be so easy. Still, part of mindfulness practice is recognizing you have influence and choice when it comes to the way you use your body and mind. You're not doomed to simply react to your circumstances. A different perspective may transform the nature of your experience, so it may be worth adopting it for its own sake instead of waiting to be convinced. You may need to adopt the attitude that your work is of benefit to the world over and over, moment after moment, but each time you do, it can lend a sense of joy and enthusiasm to your efforts—natural stress reducers!

The Least You Need to Know

- Mindfulness is something you can practice every moment—even in the midst of taking care of your responsibilities.
- Being mindful not only reduces your stress, it makes you more attentive, responsive, and effective.
- No matter what you're doing, expanding your awareness to include your body or physical sensations increases your mindfulness.
- When you're able to gain some perspective on your own attitudes, you can experiment with them to find creative ways to get things done with less stress.
- Looking at everything you do as a beneficial contribution to the world, no matter how small, can help you feel more positive about your activities.

Changing Your Mind, Not Your Life

In this chapter I talk about how to change your mind so you can feel sincerely satisfied and at peace about your life. The name of the chapter suggests you should do this *instead* of trying to change your behavior or conditions, but I really mean something slightly different. When there are things you'd really like to change about yourself or your life but it's very difficult, you have the option of working with your mind instead. This may sound like lowering your standards for yourself, but it's not. The Buddhist analogy is this: if you want to avoid hurting your feet, don't cover the earth in leather—cover your *feet* in leather. Make the change that's practical and doable, and has the most profound and far-reaching effects.

It would be wonderful to be able to make this chapter about all the ways mindfulness can solve your problems. I would love to be able to recommend mindfulness exercises that will help you to eat better, shake off depression, get more physical exercise, stay within your budget, and bring about justice in the world. Unfortunately, that's not what mindfulness is about. While the practice definitely has psychological and physical health benefits (see Chapter 1), you don't necessarily get to decide ahead of time what benefits you're going to get, or how they'll manifest.

In This Chapter

- How mindfulness helps even though it doesn't solve your problems
- Changing things for the better without getting too caught up in goals
- How to tell when to try harder, and when to accept the way things are
- Not making happiness and joy contingent on certain outcomes
- How what you do with your mind actually changes reality

Instead, mindfulness is about learning to be present with your life just as it is. Sometimes when you do this you'll realize something new and it will lead to change in your life. At other times it will simply give you the freedom to accept the way things are. This doesn't mean you stop trying to take care of your life, because that's your responsibility as a human being. It does mean you practice mindfulness in a very open-minded, open-handed way. You try to hold agendas more lightly, and cultivate a sense of unconditional satisfaction with your life.

The Trouble with Goals

Without even realizing it, you may be postponing true happiness and satisfaction with your life until you achieve a certain set of changes and improvements. Before allowing yourself deep contentment, you may have a list of questions you ask yourself: do you floss, exercise, and meditate on a daily basis? Do you regularly see your doctor, keep your house clean, file your paperwork, pay your bills, and stay informed about the things you're going to vote on? Do you research the environmental impacts of all of the things you buy, and find ways to make earth-friendly choices? Do you eat well and limit your use of intoxicants? Do you keep in contact with relatives, support your friends, and spend enough time with the children in your life? Do you maintain a positive attitude, save money, and think deeply and critically about things instead of letting yourself be influenced by the media? If you manage to do all of these things, are you also able to be patient with people who can't?

 KEEP IN MIND

You might find "aspirations" more compatible with mindfulness than "goals." A goal is an end point or outcome toward which you direct your efforts. By definition the goal isn't here and now, and your efforts are about the future. An aspiration, on the other hand, is a desire to achieve something high or great. Even if greater achievement lies in the future, you experience the aspiration here and now. It guides your efforts in a particular direction, but if you fail to achieve quite what you hope to, this failure doesn't invalidate your efforts along the way.

None of the things listed above describe shallow aims. They're all activities or ways of being that result in better mental and physical health, and involve taking good care of people and things. We should probably all work at doing them better for the rest of our lives. It is perfectly natural to want to change, to improve yourself and the world around you. There is nothing wrong with preferring clarity over confusion, equanimity over fear, connection over loneliness, success over failure, and comfort over poverty. Actually, if you don't feel such preferences there might be something wrong. In any case, whatever you prefer, it is essential that you keep taking care of your life and working on yourself lest you fall into arrogance or complacency.

Ideas and Duality

Unfortunately, goals tend to set up a duality. A separation is created between two ideas: one, your imperfect and unacceptable life as it is; and two, the great, healthy, balanced life you would lead if only you were able to make certain changes. The sense of separation between these two things can sometimes come to feel very, very large. So large, in fact, you may feel despair and sadness. Your current life can seem inadequate or even pathetic—hardly a source of deep satisfaction, gratitude, and joy.

It's very tempting to think if only such-and-such changed, you would be happy. You postpone feeling deeply satisfied with your life until your character flaws are fixed and you operate with skill and flair in all areas of your life from the personal to the professional. The thing is, this is never going to happen. There will always be something else to improve. The almost-perfect "you" that you're waiting to achieve is just an idea.

Avoiding Remorse

Another problem with goals is that they invite you to neglect mindfulness. As long as you're thinking about your goal, you're not entirely present with your life as it is. This can be a way of avoiding discomfort or shame when you don't live up to your own ideals; you distract yourself with the thought that you'll improve or change. This distraction not only keeps you from perceiving what's going on fully and clearly, it deprives you of the valuable experience of sincere remorse.

Sincere remorse arises when you let the full negative ramifications of your choices and behaviors sink in. This may be as simple as acknowledging the pain of the stomachache you got after yet again indulging in too rich a meal. It may be as complicated and challenging as facing squarely the high degree of alienation that has developed between you and a loved one because of the way you've treated them for many years.

 KEEP IN MIND

Sincere remorse is just something you feel, not a confession you need to make to others about your mistakes or inadequacies. The word evolved from a Latin word that literally meant "bite back." This refers to the experience of feeling actual distress or pain because of the harm done by a past action (the action bites back). Because of your empathy and compassion, you feel such distress even when the harm was experienced by others.

The kind of remorse that arises in these situations has nothing to do with guilt, or with meeting standards—your own, or anyone else's. It's a completely natural response because, as explained in Chapter 3, you're wired to recognize happiness and prefer it over suffering. It's essential to recognize the pain and harm in a situation and experience remorse for any part of it you're responsible for. This is part of the "seeing clearly" described in mindfulness principle #3: *change occurs naturally when you see clearly what leads to greater happiness* (Chapter 3). Ironically, then, clinging to a goal can end up impeding change to the extent it interferes with your mindfulness.

Change or Acceptance?

Whether or not you are involved in a 12-step program, you're probably familiar with the Serenity Prayer, usually attributed to Reinhold Niebuhr:

> God grant me the serenity
>
> To accept the things I cannot change,
>
> Courage to change the things I can,
>
> And wisdom to know the difference.

This prayer is a good summation of the benefits of mindfulness with respect to your own behavior and to the practical aspects of your life. You study your life carefully and start to recognize patterns in your personal life as well as in the world around you, and learn to dance with vitality and grace between acceptance and aspiration.

Freedom Despite Conditioning

It's important to remember in any given moment your choices are constrained, but not determined, by your conditioning. What course you choose to take is affected by your point of view, your understanding, your tendencies, your culture, your desires, and myriad other things. All of these causes, in turn, have been affected by your own past behavior and choices, as well as the behavior and choices of others. There is no way to be utterly free of who and what you are. There's no way to step outside of your experience to achieve some kind of ideal objectivity.

Still, in a moment of action of body, speech, or mind, there is an opportunity to make a new choice. There is a space within which you can operate freely, acting from a place of awareness that to some extent is free of your conditioning. Your view and your repertoire are limited by your conditioning, but you're not synonymous with them. There is a part of you that can greet each moment as new and fresh, as if you have never greeted such a moment before. Change is possible! The experience of this can mean the difference between despair and a sincere enthusiasm for this adventure you call a human life.

When you taste some of this freedom—when you are actually able to make some real changes in your behavior and your life—your aspiration can start to get in the way of your acceptance. After all, there is no clear boundary between the things you cannot change and the things you can.

What is acceptance, and what is just laziness or fear? Once you find some change is possible, why accept anything the way it is?

Knowing When to Accept

I remember being disappointed as a child when I heard adults confess their limitations with an air of resignation. "I don't have enough patience for that," or, "There goes my temper again." I wondered why they had given up trying to change. As an adult I find myself saying similar things. "I could never do such-and-such kind of job; I would find it too stressful," or "I don't have the self-discipline to do such-and-such." Now I understand, however, that it's not that I've given up trying to change. I'd ideally like these things to be different, but I have chosen my battles.

 MINDFUL EXERCISE

Mindfulness requires you to be honest with yourself. Think of something you'd really like to change about your behavior. This can be a way you think, speak, or act (or a combination of these). How long have you been trying to change? How often have you mentioned to others that you intend to change? How many different approaches have you tried? Have you spent money, time, and energy on your efforts? Has anything improved? This exercise isn't meant to make you feel inadequate or discouraged—it's meant to encourage you to be honest. Sometimes it's easy to become preoccupied with your intentions and forget to face the truth of your life as it is.

Some things just end up being extremely difficult to change. Unless something is a life-or-death matter, or causing serious harm, it can be a waste of time and energy to spend your life beating your head against it. The graceful acceptance of your limitations becomes a source of humility and compassion. You can learn to give others the benefit of the doubt, and be grateful for the ways in which your strengths and weaknesses are complementary to those of other people. What you can't do, someone else can. What you can do well is yours to do.

How do you know the difference between what you can change, and what you can't? It isn't easy, and things change over time, so you have to keep asking the question, over and over: "Can I change this, or should I accept it?" Basically, if something can be changed, an opening occurs. This is a new direction you can go when you apply yourself to the problem, and you should take advantage of it! The problem usually doesn't shift very far, but some progress is made fairly easily through a change in approach. On the other hand, when something cannot be changed—at least not yet—you get the sensation of pushing against a many-ton boulder: despite your grueling efforts, frustration, and determination, nothing budges. When this is the case, it's best to put the issue on the "back burner." You can keep an eye out for how to change it, but avoid letting the struggle to do so take over your life.

Not Resisting Difficulty

Mindfulness doesn't get you out of experiencing and feeling the pain of old age, disease, death, change, loss, trauma, and things being different than how you would like them to be. It also does not relieve you of being a limited being who needs to work hard to overcome harmful habits of body and mind. In short, mindfulness does not help you avoid times when things are difficult. And sometimes they're very, very difficult. What mindfulness can give you is the ability to stop resisting the difficulty. This may not sound like much, but in reality it is extremely valuable. The ability to stop resisting things can mean the difference between utter despair and a profound, gracious dignity in the midst of it all.

The ways in which things can be difficult are infinite. Eventually everyone understands the ways your life gets touched by the "big" sufferings like death, physical pain, illness, loss, and trauma. Less obvious but often just as challenging is suffering like depression, anxiety, boredom, fear, guilt, and doubt. You also suffer from being trapped in patterns you can't seem to change, being unable to find harmony in your relationships, and being unable to fulfill your aspirations. Human life is difficult. This is so fundamentally true that it's the first teaching of Buddhism.

 **KEEP IN MIND**

Just to get one thing clear: when you stop resisting suffering it does not mean you stop trying to resolve difficulties in any way you can. The basic activities of a good human life include efforts to free yourself and others from suffering, make positive changes in your life and in the world, and bring about ease and lasting happiness.

What does it mean to stop resisting difficulty? You let go of any idea that it *shouldn't be like this*. Or, alternatively, I/he/she/they/we shouldn't be like this. As long as you hold on to that kind of idea it's like your small self is digging its heels in to stop the earth from turning, screaming, "Nooo!"

You think, "This is not how I want to be. I should not be experiencing anxiety/anger/fear/judgment/etc. This is not the life I was meant to be living. This isn't fair. This isn't right. This person should not be obstructing me. That person should not have misunderstood/judged/betrayed/abandoned me. Evil should not prevail in the world the way it does. Bad things should not happen to innocent people. I am stuck in this dysfunctional relationship. It seems like I will never be financially secure/loved/able to …."

As you lodge your protest against the challenges in obvious and subtle ways, it takes its toll on your mind and body. Your efforts to make changes become colored by a desperate imperative—things *must* change, or else! You carry around a ball of tenseness in your gut or heart where you push against the difficulty whenever you remember it.

What is the good of dropping your resistance to the things you wish were different? Instantly your life feels whole again; it is no longer about "me" over here resisting the difficulty and pain over there. It's just your life, which can be embraced with tenderness and acceptance despite all of its shortcomings. Instantly you feel relief as you drop the intense effort to stop things from being as they are, which in any case is utterly fruitless. Instantly you—and others—are transformed from beings to be scorned, judged, or pitied into beings who gain great dignity in enduring this difficult human life. Ironically, dropping your resistance to things "being as they are" frees you up to take much more effective action than you could otherwise.

Radical Acceptance

In Chapter 9 I talked about cultivating enough acceptance to be able to settle into mindfulness and see things clearly. The acceptance I'm talking about here takes this one step further. What you're trying to do is stop making your complete contentment and satisfaction contingent on achieving anything in the future. This doesn't mean you stop taking care of your life; it means you embrace the gratitude and joy described in Chapter 12 *now*. There will always be things that need changing, and there will always be things that resist your best efforts to change them. Are you going to wait until you've gotten through your to-do list to feel a deep sense of peace about your life, and about life in general?

Experience That's Free of Ideas

Mindfulness allows you to experience life directly, without the duality of ideas. You don't even have to fight ideas; you just have to return to awareness of the present moment. Life is real. Ideas and words are just creations to describe it so we can communicate with one another. The things you see, hear, smell, taste, and touch are the truth of your life. Where are your ideals and goals when you're completely present in this moment? When you're being completely mindful— receptively aware of the present, without judgment or evaluation, without ruminating on the past or anticipating the future—where are your goals?

To settle into radical acceptance in this moment, you have to give up all hope of things being different. You have to accept all things, including yourself, just as they are. The good thing is you don't have to *like* any of it. Your dislike is just part of your experience, and doesn't have to obstruct you from releasing yourself into utter, complete, unconditional, radical acceptance. Only then will you be still enough to experience the clear, unconditional peace that is accessible to you at any moment.

TAKE CARE

On the other side of the coin, giving up any effort to change things does not mean you decide you're perfect just as you are, or nothing around you could benefit from change. That is simply the opposite of rejecting things, and is just as antithetical to mindfulness. You don't latch onto the thought that everything's fine; you try to experience your life directly without getting caught in judgments about bad or good.

If you are anything like me, you resist this kind of acceptance. What does it mean? What about effort? If you become content, won't that mean you'll stop trying to change things? Fortunately, you don't have to worry about effort. Not if you really practice mindfulness. Radical acceptance involves looking straight at what you are accepting. When you look, you'll see your busy mind, along with all kinds of other things—like your greed, your fear, your weakness for distraction. You will also see your desire for things to be different. All things will be present, and everything will enter the equation. The motivation for change arises naturally out of mindfulness, independent of abstract goals or ideals.

What if Nothing Ever Changed?

To test your level of acceptance, contemplate for a moment the possibility that in your lifetime, however much time remains to you, you will never be substantially different from the way you are now. You will never get rid of those flare-ups of anger. You will never be able to improve your self-discipline or concentration. Your relationships with friends and family will never blossom into the heart-warming stuff of movies. You will never lose any weight, or be any more attractive or charming. Your intellectual, spiritual, or creative attainments will never amount to much more than they already have. You will never tap into the energy, passion, equanimity, and joy within you much more than you already have. Can you accept that? Can you regard yourself as you would another being, and accept yourself as worthy and sufficient?

 KEEP IN MIND

This kind of radical acceptance may sound dramatic, but it doesn't have to come all at once. You enact it in small moments throughout every day, throughout every session of mindfulness practice. And each time you enact this acceptance, the shift can be significant, calming, and healing. In the instant you move from resistance to acceptance, you move from being someone who isn't practicing to someone who is. And with your practice, no matter what is going on, comes a greater sense of stability, purpose, spaciousness, and freedom.

The sense of completeness that is available to each of us has nothing to do with comparisons—to others, or to ideals. In fact, it only becomes obvious when you drop all comparison and experience life directly. This process is beautifully conveyed in a story told by Zen master Uchiyama Roshi, in his 1990 book *The Zen Teaching of Homeless Kodo*. Uchiyama explains how he chose to practice Zen with his teacher, Sawaki Roshi, because he hoped to become more like him. Uchiyama felt himself to be rather incompetent, but saw Sawaki as strong. He asked his teacher if by practicing Zen—which includes meditation and mindfulness—he could become strong. Sawaki said no, practice doesn't change a person. Despite what his teacher said, Uchiyama believed that eventually he could improve.

Eventually, many years later, Uchiyama appreciated that even though he had attained a measure of peace from his practice, it wasn't because he had changed in any fundamental way. Instead, he had found deep acceptance for who he was. He expresses it this way: "I realized that I hadn't really changed at all. In that moment it was natural for me to say to myself, 'A violet blossoms as a violet, a rose blossoms as a rose.' There are people like Sawaki Roshi who resemble huge rose blossoms. There are other people, like me, who resemble tiny, pretty violet blossoms. Which is better? It's not a relevant question. I should blossom wholeheartedly, just as I am."

Despite the fact the mindfulness is unlikely to change you, there is a big difference between a violet that is trying to become a rose, and violet blossoming wholeheartedly just as it is. You can tell when someone is at peace with who they are, because whatever kind of person they happen to be, they are radiant.

A Real, Complete, and Elegant Life

Most of us, most days, would not describe our lives as complete and elegant—elegant meaning of high grade or quality, beautiful without ostentation. There may be many parts of your life that are satisfying and beautiful—parts you choose and enjoy, and think of as your "real" life. However, there's a lot of stuff in between those parts. Your "real" life may feel like a thread you often lose touch with, then pick up again, and occasionally lose altogether.

In contrast, you may find that when you view the lives of others, especially in the context of a book or movie, you are able to see how all the disparate parts can come together as a whole. Even when someone's life includes tragedy, difficulty, mistakes, boredom, depression, or oppression, you can see it all as being part of the arc of a whole life. The whole thing is "real," and if any part was missing, it would be a different life. Even if someone doesn't end up obviously "redeemed" or happy in the end, their existence contributes somehow to the poignancy of life in general.

> **MINDFUL EXERCISE**
>
> Imagine you are a filmmaker and want to make a film about you (pretend you aren't you). As the filmmaker you intend to portray your life as being rich, well-balanced, rewarding, and elegant. What real scenes and interactions from your life would appear in the film? A good-bye kiss with your partner or children in the mornings? Laughter with a friend? Being very engrossed in your work, and gratified by the result? Picture all of the positive film clips from your life that you can. What if you saw a film that showed these, and de-emphasized the parts of your life you feel dissatisfied with? Chances are you'd feel inspired, despite yourself.

This view of the completeness of other's lives is not limited to dramatic tales. It can also be experienced when you watch a video or hear a description of someone in another culture going about their everyday mundane tasks. From your removed vantage point you can see the beauty in their simple, repetitive motions. You can see the noble fortitude they display as they go about their work—cleaning, farming, or raising children. The women walk a mile through the desert to get water and then carry it home on their heads, hips swaying in their colorful garments as they calmly walk back home. The old farmer works in the soil with his bare hands, pulling out roots and placing them in an old basket. So simple, yet so strangely elegant.

Yes, *Your* Life

But then, as you go about your mundane daily tasks, you fail to see the completeness and elegance of *your* life. The life you think has a chance of being complete, coherent, and elegant is somewhere else, and involves doing something else and perhaps even being someone else. It can't be this. "Just little ol' me?" you may think. "Just drinking coffee, eating cereal, driving, doing my job that has pretty minimal impact on the grand scheme of things, going to a restaurant, watching TV? Me, with my scattered mind, uncharitable thoughts, bad habits, unrealized ambitions, and piles of unsorted junk? What's complete, coherent, and elegant about all this, unless I set my standards very, very low?"

Mindfulness involves settling into the exact life you have, wholeheartedly, without comparing yourself to others, or even to any ideals. The result of this is an ability to see your life as complete and elegant—at least some of the time. And even when you can't see it that way, you know it's possible to do so. This is not to say you begin carrying around a neat narrative that could be portrayed in a 90-minute movie; the story is not the point, and actually only gets in the way. The point is that you can view your own life with interest and respect, and inhabit it completely because you aren't looking for a life somewhere else.

It is difficult to stress this point enough: really, it's about you, just as you are, in your life, just as it is. Even though in the end the details don't matter, you are nowhere else but in the details. You might say this is about "accepting yourself for who you are," but such acceptance might still stay at a superficial level: telling stories about who you are and talking yourself into the idea you're really not that bad after all. Completely inhabiting your life is more immediate, gritty, and neutral than this. It's not about you being okay in the final analysis; it's about *this* being your chance to be alive, so what are you going to do with it?

 **TAKE CARE**

> You have to be careful about sharing this kind of radical acceptance approach with someone who is depressed or in despair, in case they misunderstand it. They may think you are saying, "It's never going to get any better than this awful experience you are having. You just need to give up hoping for anything better." Fortunately, that is not true; they do not have to give up hope for anything better, because their experience of their life just as it is could be radically different.

Embracing Things as They Are

When you deeply settle into your life, no matter what your life looks like, there is satisfaction, relief, strength, and dignity that come from recognizing your life as complete and elegant. Frankly, it feels better to be fully present—no matter what's going on—than to be casting about here, there, and everywhere for your "real life." You are better able to appreciate each moment and recognize it as significant. Just as you appreciated the simple beauty and dignity in the actions of the women calmly carrying water back to their families on their heads, or the old man fingering the roots in the soil, you watch *yourself* loading the dishwasher, reading the back of a macaroni and cheese box, and meeting a customer's eyes. You see real life unfolding in the shape of *your* moment-by-moment experience.

Contrary to some romantic ideas, the simple elegance and dignity of human life is not limited to the distant past or to nonindustrial cultures. It has just taken different forms, and you may find it difficult to recognize certain forms as elegant and beautiful because they are so familiar. They are too close to you. When you finally recognize the elegant forms of your life, it comes as a surprise how close they've been all the while. There is nothing you encounter that doesn't count as "real life." There is no moment that is wasting your time. There are no interruptions in your "real life" as you live out your limited amount of time on this earth. Isn't it nice to know the time waiting in traffic, even if you're feeling agitated because of it, is not actually stolen from your real life?

Positive Thinking

When someone suggests the "power of positive thinking," you may think it's just something you do in your mind to make yourself feel better. You may think it involves choosing to put a positive spin on things rather than listening to your discriminating wisdom when it says something is amiss. You probably also figure that drawing positive conclusions instead of negative ones doesn't change the reality outside of you. Sure, positive thinking changes your subjective experience. It's more pleasant and less stressful, for example, to feel relaxed than it is to feel angry. When you feel grateful, your chest feels warm and energy flows through you, but when you feel suspicious and stingy your chest feels tight and your body feels tense. So there's a good argument for cultivating positive feelings over negative ones if you can.

Changing Reality with Your Mind

However, feeling good isn't all there is to it. When you are able to consciously transform the way you relate to an experience, you can change the very nature of that experience. This is because reality doesn't have the hard edges you usually think it does. There is no reality "out there," separate from your mind; you will never be able to perceive a thing without the involvement of your mind. And what is the use of any reality "out there" that can never be perceived? In a sense, reality is born as you perceive it. Don't get me wrong, this doesn't mean nothing exists except what sentient beings have perceived, as if only the subjective is real. Rather, it is that your reality arises in the encounter between subject and object.

 KEEP IN MIND

All experience is preceded by mind,

Led by mind,

Made by mind.

Speak or act with a corrupted mind,

And suffering follows

As the wagon wheel follows the hoof of the ox.

All experience is preceded by mind,

Led by mind,

Made by mind.

Speak or act with a peaceful mind,

And happiness follows

Like a never-departing shadow.

-Words of Shakyamuni Buddha, from *The Dhammapada: A New Translation of the Buddhist Classic with Annotations,* (translated by Gil Fronsdal)

This may seem overly philosophical, so here is a concrete example. Say a woman butts in front of you in line at the grocery store. She's busy talking on her cell phone and clearly in a big hurry, and takes the opportunity of a few extra, ambiguous feet of space to nudge her cart into the line in front of you. It is possible she just didn't notice, but that hardly seems like a good excuse. Your first reaction is probably to get angry and defensive, and to curse the woman's selfishness and self-absorption. Your self-concern arises, and perhaps you press your cart in a little closer, to guard against any other people who might want to get ahead of you.

Then let's say you try some positive thinking by engaging the Buddhist exercise of imagining that each person you encounter has, in a previous life, been a kind, nurturing mother to you. You recall all beings just want to be happy and avoid suffering (even if they go about seeking what they want in ignorant or destructive ways). Now you notice how anxious and tense the woman in the grocery line is. You know what it feels like to be in a hurry and overwhelmed, and have no difficulty imagining that in certain circumstances you would at least be tempted to act like she just has. You feel a certain connection with her, and certainly some compassion for her. After all, is it likely she would be so pushy if she was spiritually at peace? Some of your anger and tension dissipate.

Now, what is "reality" in this example? A selfish, pushy woman butted in front of you? A suffering sentient being, just like you, acted out the age-old drama of seeking happiness and avoiding suffering? Is reality only the objective observation that a woman pushed her cart into a few feet of space in front of you in a line? Or all of the above? Reality turns out to be fairly flexible, or at least full of possibilities. Which perspective you choose will influence your view of the world, your mood, and how you respond to the people and situations you encounter.

Freedom of Choice

Choosing a more positive relationship to reality through mindfulness does not involve denying or suppressing experiences or reactions you might categorize as negative. In the example from above, you don't have to pretend it isn't rude to butt in front of someone at a grocery store. You don't even have to pretend you don't care about someone butting in front of *you*. Without turning away from any aspect of your experience (internal or external), you have some options about how to relate to that experience.

You can follow trains of thought that take you deeper into emotions like anger or despair, or you can get creative and apply some other techniques and tools. Mindfulness helps you recognize and learn to use those techniques and tools—ways to calm yourself, gain perspective, appreciate your life more, and see things more positively. Then, in any given set of circumstances, it's up to you whether you apply what you've learned and *choose* the state of your body-mind regardless of what goals you've manage to achieve, and regardless of what is going on around you.

The Least You Need to Know

- It's perfectly natural and useful to want more happiness and less suffering, but getting too caught up in goals can be problematic.

- Change is definitely possible, and mindfulness can help you see how to best go about it. However, the real power of mindfulness lies in the fact that it lets you access contentment and joy in your life as it is.

- Difficulties can become much more manageable when you're able to let go of the thought, "Things shouldn't be this way."

- Direct, mindful experience of life is free of comparisons to others and to ideals. It lets you appreciate the beauty and elegance of your life.

- Reality as you experience it occurs at the meeting between your mind and the world. In a certain way, changing your mind actually changes your reality.

Becoming Who You Really Are

Who are you, really, and why does it matter? These questions might conjure up ideas about learning more about your personality, figuring out what livelihood would best suit you, or finding what unique things you might be able to express in the world. However, the mindful discovery of who you really are is different from this kind of self-study. It may indirectly help you find ways to celebrate and work with your unique body-mind, but that's not the main point.

In this chapter I discuss making your "self" the object of mindfulness, and how it is really more about learning what you're *not* than what you *are*. Think of it this way: you've developed lots of ideas over the course of your life about who you are and how you relate to the world, and these ideas mostly obscure or obstruct who you *really* are. Basically, your "self" is part of an ever-changing flow of causes and conditions—more of a process than a thing. Mindfulness can help you experience yourself this way, and consequently help you to take things less personally. It also helps you respond more authentically and creatively to life because it lets you break free of your stories about yourself and how you relate to the world.

In This Chapter

- Benefits of making your "self" an object of mindfulness
- Why you get caught up with concern for "I, Me, and Mine"
- Different aspects of self and how to relate to them
- Real self as experienced just this moment
- Getting free of the stories you tell about yourself and your life

Why Study Your "Self"?

Your sense of self is one of the most fundamental aspects of your experience as a human being. It figures centrally in the "fight, flee, or freeze" response discussed in Chapter 2. *You* want to avoid suffering and move toward happiness, as explained in Chapter 3. Behind all of the objects of mindfulness discussed in Part 2 of the book—physical sensations, feelings, mind states, and psychophysical factors—is a sense that *you* are experiencing them. You form judgments about things based on your evaluation of whether they're beneficial, threatening, or irrelevant to *your* well-being (Chapter 9). *You* are the one trying to approach change compassionately (Chapter 13), deal with afflictive emotions (Chapter 14), and get things done with less stress (Chapter 15).

How you think about your "self" has profound effects on all aspects of your mindfulness practice, and on your life. There are unhelpful ways to view the nature of the self that lead to stress, selfishness, and suffering. Fortunately, these views are based on misunderstandings about self that you can start to see clearly if you make the self an object of your mindful awareness.

Understanding the Misery of "I, Me, and Mine"

Ironically, most of us think that the way to happiness is taking care of "I, Me, and Mine." Almost all of your activities can be categorized as looking out for your own physical, mental, and emotional well-being and the well-being of the things you identify with—ideas, opinions, plans, possessions, people, relationships, etc. (that is, those things that you see as being intimately tied to your well-being). You could almost say that you hold the truth that you need to look out for yourself as being "self-evident." Even an amoeba enacts this truth, right? However, although basic self-preservation and taking care of your life is a natural and healthy activity, the irony is that your very obsession with this kind of activity leads to misery.

Your obsession with "I, Me, and Mine" occurs at least in part because, as a human, you're too smart for your own good. You're able to create elaborate concepts about self and other, past and future, desirable and undesirable. Your basic, natural, functional drive to take care of yourself becomes blown way out of proportion as you brood over the past, analyze the present for threats and opportunities, and try to anticipate future ones. While a simpler animal is devoted to preserving its own well-being and that of its family, humans devote themselves to the maintenance of an infinite number of complex and amorphous things like reputations, roles, ideas, estates, plans, and pride. Your "I, Me, and Mine" develops into an elaborate universe that exists mostly in your own head.

There is a time and place for useful analysis and planning, and you can't function in society without concepts. However, the more obsessed you are with "I, Me, and Mine," the more stress and misery you will experience. That elaborate universe in your head takes an enormous amount of work to maintain, even just mentally, and it is under constant threat. The number of ways things might go wrong are infinite, and if nothing else you have to stay on your toes because everything is constantly changing.

 **KEEP IN MIND**

> You can also gain great joy and pleasure from things you consider to be "I, Me, and Mine." This isn't a problem, except when you try to grasp after or hold on to such happiness. Then the misery manifests as longing for happiness you don't have, or as concern that your happiness isn't going to last. As long as you enjoy things open-handedly, you can enjoy them without triggering the misery of "I, Me, and Mine."

Putting Down the Burden

The fact that obsession with "I, Me, and Mine" leads to misery is one that probably can only be verified experientially. A philosophical argument isn't likely to convince you, because in some ways it doesn't make any sense. You are able to test and verify this teaching if you experiment with your subjective experience of your life. When you put down the burden of worrying about "I, Me, and Mine" for a moment, you feel grounded and relieved. You can deal with what is right in front of you—and even if that is a dire emergency, it will be easier to handle than a dire emergency plus the myriad fears and reactions you can add to it by evaluating it in terms of "I, Me, and Mine."

The ability to drop the concern about self—at least for a moment at a time—is something you develop with your mindfulness practice. It's a little like you're behind the wheel of a car for the first time, and it takes you a while to figure out how to turn the windshield wipers off; there's an internal switch for your concern for "I, Me, and Mine" you can toggle at will. It's not always easy to do, but it's well worth learning how.

Studying the Nature of Self

If you want to learn to let go of self-concern, it can be very useful to examine your concepts about self. What is the self? How do you study it, and how do you forget it? Is there something in your experience which is not the self? You are not meant to read this section of the book and conclude, "Oh, I get it, that's what self is." I hope, instead, you gain an increased appreciation for how profound and expansive this subject is. The word *self* is used to refer to who and what you are, and this can be considered at many different levels. It is not selfish to want to understand who and what you are; it's natural, and greater understanding actually ends up being of benefit to both self and other.

The Conventional Self

To begin with, you have what I am going to call a Conventional Self. This is the sum total of your parts assembled in such a way that your body functions, along with all of the phenomena that emerge because of it. These phenomena include sensations, perceptions, emotions, thoughts, consciousness, characteristics, and tendencies. Because of the way life evolved on our planet, almost all living things manifest as individuals—distinguishable from one another and indivisible into more than one living unit—so the nature of your Conventional Self is separateness and independence.

 TAKE CARE

> Mindfulness can help you get perspective on the different aspects of self, and take refuge from self-concern by centering yourself in the present moment. However, this doesn't mean your Conventional Self is irrelevant! The path toward greater happiness includes getting to understand your Conventional Self better and taking good care of it.

The Conventional Self is a very practical concept. It lets you take responsibility for yourself and interact appropriately with others. In a sense, you could say that the Conventional Self isn't a concept—or, at least, it's not *just* a concept. No matter how intimate you feel with someone, you still have to put food into your own mouth in order to be nourished. No matter how interconnected we all are in an ultimate sense, there's still no way I can see things out of your eyes. Our individuality is an undeniable part of who we are.

Self-Consciousness

This brings me to the next aspect of self: Self-Consciousness. Given your human intelligence, you are conscious of your Conventional Self as a separate existence over time. This Self-Consciousness leads to an illusion and the beginning of your problems. Of course, it is not an illusion that your Conventional Self persists over time, and an awareness that it persists over time is necessary for survival. The problem arises because the utilitarian phenomenon of Self-Consciousness results in an attributive error: you assume because you have a sensation of being a "self" moving through time, there *is* an inherently existing, enduring self which moves through time.

You come to believe you have some kind of self-essence or soul that retains its identity through changing conditions. This can be a very tricky and subtle belief that persists even if you intellectually reject it. Even if you imagine every cell in your body being gradually replaced over time, your personality radically shifting, and all of your opinions changing, you still imagine *you* will be there to reflect on all the changes.

Self-Concept

Once you conclude you have an inherently existing, enduring self, you are, of course, supremely interested in this self's survival and well-being. You try to make it as substantial as possible, which leads you to your Self-Concept. This is everything—all of the sensations, emotions, thoughts, opinions, plans, relationships, roles, possessions, talents, etc.—with which you identify yourself and label "I, Me, and Mine." It overlaps with your Conventional Self but includes many things beyond it; for example, I may include my husband in my Self-Concept even though he is not part of my Conventional Self. In this respect you might compare human beings to the hermit crabs that find bits of debris on the ocean floor to glue to their shells for camouflage. You incorporate more and more things into your Self-Concept until—hopefully—you feel your self is protected, substantial, and real.

> **MINDFUL EXERCISE**
>
> When you find yourself getting agitated or upset about something, stop and observe what's going on with mindful awareness. Ask yourself why you're feeling upset, and see what answers arise without editing or censoring them. Keep following reasons deeper, asking, "Okay, well why does *that* upset me?" See if you can find the point where the issue at hand connects to your Self-Concept, and your concern for "I, Me, and Mine." Is there an apparent challenge or threat to *your* reputation, *your* significant other, *your* possessions, or *your* views? Don't judge this connection as selfish, just acknowledge where your reactions are connected to your sense of self.

Mindfulness practice invites you to challenge your Self-Concept, which is actually quite fragile. The things you identify with are terrifyingly subject to change and loss, and when pieces of your Self-Concept get stripped away, your self feels smaller and more vulnerable. This can cause anxiety, depression, angst, denial, or a desperate scramble to find new stuff to identify with self. Life events will often shake or damage your Self-Concept and cause you to turn to things like mindfulness practice for relief from the resulting stress. However, when you are ready, challenges to your Self-Concept can inspire you to start studying self—its real nature, and how to relate to it differently.

Getting Free of Self

Throughout this book I've discussed how you can cultivate mindful awareness of things in order to see them more clearly. You can also end up seeing the nature of self more clearly when you turn your awareness toward your preoccupation with "I, Me, and Mine," your Conventional Self, your Self-Consciousness, and your Self-Concept. Seeing self more clearly allows you to see what ways of thinking about and relating to it lead to greater happiness, and which do not (see mindfulness principle #4, Chapter 3).

Can You Find It?

The fascinating thing you discover if you stay mindfully present with your experience of self is that, if you try to locate it, you can't. Which part of your body does it reside in? What parts of your Conventional Self or Self-Concept could change or be lost, and yet *you* would still exist? All parts? If your inherently existing, enduring self is the same thing as your Self-Consciousness, who are you when you're asleep? Would you not really be *you* if you were in a coma? If not, once you woke up from the coma, how would *you* come back?

If these kinds of questions seem too philosophical or intellectual, examine your experience of self in a moment of mindfulness. When you're simply resting in awareness of the present, past and future are just abstract concepts; your aliveness at this moment doesn't depend on anything enduring over time. Your awareness doesn't depend on any of the details of your Self-Concept. If you let go completely of keeping track of those details and looking out in a conscious way for "I, Me, and Mine," what happens? You realize you're still perfectly alive. You realize you don't *have* to locate the self.

Empty of Inherent, Enduring Nature

In reality there is no inherently existing, enduring self. What you experience is a flow of causation over time operating in and around your Conventional Self. While your Conventional Self is, in one sense, separate and independent, it is also without fixed boundaries, constantly changing, and completely interdependent with the rest of the universe. Self-Consciousness is an amazing *emergent* phenomenon of an incredibly complex living system, not proof of a soul.

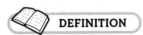 **DEFINITION**

An **emergent** property or phenomenon arises out of the functioning of a complex physical system, and would not arise from the functioning of any of the parts taken in isolation, nor from all of the parts taken together unless they are configured and functioning in a particular way.

If you maintain mindfulness over time, you end up watching your Conventional Self, Self-Consciousness, and Self-Concept change over time and morph according to conditions. You learn not to rely on them so much. Essentially, you're experiencing what the Buddhists call "emptiness," which isn't about things being empty of meaning or value; it's about things, including the self, being empty of an inherently existing, enduring essence. When you're able to experience the three aspects of self as empty, you are liberated from the bondage of fear and greed felt on behalf of your inherently existing self. You still feel plenty of concern about the well-being of your Conventional Self, but the fear and greed are not nearly as powerful as when you are worried about the survival of some kind of self-essence.

Real Self: Direct Experience of Flow

Basically, here's the scenario. You've worked hard at mindfulness of self and have some direct experience of the fact that there is no inherently existing, enduring essence inside you. So what the heck are you? The experience of emptiness can be rather unnerving. It's a bit like walking on air, moving forward as you usually do but without any of the usual (apparent) support. Once you've gotten used to the sensation, however, you become more confident you aren't going to fall into the void.

MINDFUL EXERCISE

Sit still and turn your attention to your physical sensations. Concentrate on your breathing, sound, or sense of body position, or expand your receptivity to include any sensations that come your way. When you have a moment or two when you feel completely present, look for your sense of self. Note how your aliveness and awareness at this very moment don't depend in any way on your past or future, or any of the details of your life such as your education, job, interests, or possessions. Can you settle so completely into the present that you experience yourself as being nothing more than awareness itself?

In fact, you wonder why, despite everything, you feel so … alive. You feel more *you* than you ever have, or like you have come home at last, or like you are so stable nothing in the universe could knock you over. And yet when you try to find what defines *you*, you can't find anything. The truth of this self does not rely on any details of your Conventional Self, Self-Consciousness, or Self-Concept. So in a sense it's not *you* or *yours* at all! Your real self is just what you are when you're *without* the delusion of inherent, enduring self-existence. When you become "who you really are," you're just an aware, living being who is part of a flow of causes and conditions. Your "real self" exists only in this moment.

Freedom from Stories

Being able to experience your "self" as flow frees you up in many ways, but one of the most important things it does is give you the confidence to drop the stories you tell yourself about your life. Before applying mindfulness to your sense of self, you probably believed such stories were true. Even if you were able to acknowledge some of the ways your narratives were biased, incomplete, or unreasonable, this acknowledgment was most likely intellectual and not grounded in your real body-mind experience. Mindfulness practice gives you a way to tap into the moment-by-moment sense of self as flow, which operates more or less free of your stories and ideas.

When you get more used to living without your favorite stories, it calls the validity and necessity of those stories into serious question. In the remainder of this chapter I cover two of the most common stories people tend to tell themselves, and the results of letting these stories go.

The Story "I'm Okay"

Most people are proud of being okay. It's only natural; as a child you were fragile and dependent, but as you grew up you learned how to take care of yourself. You've learned to look after your own physical needs, and you've found your niche in the world where, for the most part, you feel valued, satisfied, and safe. Sometimes life presents you with challenges, but you've also gained confidence in your ability to respond to challenges effectively and creatively. Being competent, stable, and okay seems synonymous with being an adult—at least one worthy of respect.

But then, sometimes, you aren't okay. Just admitting this to yourself, let alone to others, can be very difficult. The story of being okay has become part of your identity, so to consider you're *not* okay can be extremely disorienting. It's also terrifying to contemplate the possibility you don't have things under control, or your ability to successfully navigate any challenge is in question. Your concern that other people will judge you for feeling overwhelmed by your problems can keep you in denial, or at least quiet.

 TAKE CARE

> Sometimes, if you think of yourself as having a mindfulness practice or religious faith, or as being a "spiritual" person, there is an extra strong motivation for convincing yourself and others that—despite your actual experience—you're doing great. You think you shouldn't feel the way you do, or that it's a sign that your practice or faith isn't sufficient. Of course, by denying how you're really doing, you're not giving that practice or faith a chance to work!

It takes immense courage to admit, even to yourself, that you don't feel fundamentally okay. That you're questioning the stories you tell about yourself and the world. That you are full of confusion, doubt, or fear. That you may need help, or new ways of thinking, being, and doing. That you have realized how much you don't know, or how you were wrong, or how, sooner or later, you are going to die and lose everything. This kind of experience is the essence of both teenage angst and what's often called a "midlife crisis," although it certainly isn't limited to any particular life stage.

It is very sad and unfortunate when you can't let go of your story of being okay. Holding on to the idea of your "okayness" results in the suppression of thoughts and feelings, which then affect your behavior and health. Because there are truths you need to avoid to maintain your story, you end up divorced from parts of your experience and living less wholeheartedly and authentically. A charade of "okayness" can make you rigid and defensive. You often end up avoiding people who are suffering because their difficulties remind you of your own. Perhaps the saddest part about not admitting when you're not okay is that you consequently don't seek answers to your questions. You fail to explore new ways of thinking and being that might resolve your inner conflicts. You neglect to face your fears, so they control you.

Actually, none of us are completely okay. Ever. If you look carefully at your life, you can always find a limit to your sense of comfort, understanding, and control. The universe is infinite, as are the ways you can relate to it. It takes a great deal of effort and deep self-examination to truly feel okay when you face the stark reality that your life and everything you value can be radically altered or lost in an instant. Or that you will inevitably lose everything, including your body and consciousness. Or that despite your best efforts to construct a positive (or at least acceptable) world view, the amount of injustice and suffering in the world is inconceivable.

The good thing is you can learn to embrace and even value periods when you don't feel okay. It's possible to face and practice with them, survive, learn from them, and consequently improve your life. It's always uncomfortable when you first recognize you're not okay. Well, actually, it continues to be uncomfortable because you're being present with your confusion or distress. But after a while, when you have gone into and come out of such periods a number of times, you gain confidence in your ability to keep on living as deeply and authentically as you can. You gain faith that periods of inner struggle come and go, and don't invalidate your independence and worthiness as an adult. Who you really are isn't dependent on a story about being okay.

The Story "I'm Not Okay"

Of course, you may have ended up incorporating the story of *not being okay* into your identity instead. When you experience pain or difficulty in your life and don't feel like you can do something that will change things, it's natural to start getting identified with an unpleasant state of being that seems like it's going to go on and on. You may consequently dwell on your difficulties and pain, and how there's nothing you can do to fix things. If this is your story about your life, it can lead to great despair and depression if you blame yourself, and great anger and bitterness if you blame others. Chances are you do some of both.

 **KEEP IN MIND**

The flavor of your "I'm not okay" story depends on where you think the primary problems are coming from. What are the biggest things that obstruct your happiness? They may seem internal or external. Internal reasons not to be okay include mental and emotional states like depression, anxiety, or forms of mental illness. They may include character flaws like laziness, addiction, or a quick temper. External factors can be financial and relationship challenges, or living in troubling conditions. Physical difficulties like illness or disability may seem internal or external depending on how you look at them.

Based on your challenges, you end up telling yourself one of two versions of the story about not being okay. First, because of internal problems or your inability to cope with external ones, you blame yourself. It's not just that your circumstances aren't okay, *you* aren't okay. You have some fundamental flaws and limitations that mean "okayness" is beyond your reach. Second, if you see most of your problems as external, you figure your happiness is dependent on external conditions, at least to some extent. In this story you don't blame yourself for not being up to the task of coping with or changing things, but in your story you play the role of victim, or at least someone who has no option for happiness.

The first "I'm not okay" story, in which you blame yourself, is challenged by your mindful experience of self. When you experience self as flow, you realize there are always causes that came before the current conditions—including your internal and physical characteristics and states. If you suffer from depression, how did that come about? Genetics, upbringing, past experiences? If people in the past or present have contributed to your misery, how did they end up with the suffering that motivated them to act in harmful ways? If you tend to have a temper, did you learn it from someone? If it's just a matter of personality, an amazing amount of this is due to genetics. And who's to blame for that? If you trace causes back through time, you can't find any place for the blame to stick. Even if you could, in the case of any individual, which part of them bears the blame if they have no inherently existing, enduring self?

Even more important, when you're mindful and manifesting your "real self," your reality doesn't depend on past or future. Blame is about the past, and your story of not being okay is about the future, or about evaluations of the present. Just this moment isn't "okay" *or* "not okay." It just is what it is. It's free of stories, and rewarding in and of itself.

Fortunately, you can maintain mindfulness and still take responsibility for your life as it is, but you do so by facing reality here and now and responding as best you can. It isn't necessary to dwell on blame in order to change. As stated in mindfulness principle #3, *change occurs naturally when you see clearly what leads to greater happiness* (Chapter 3). If you stay present and receptive, engaged and responsive, you'll take care of your life. The important thing is what you do right now, not the stories about whether you and your life are okay or not in some abstract sense.

 TAKE CARE

It doesn't work if you only maintain mindfulness as long as you see positive results. If you make your mindfulness contingent on change, you'll just be setting yourself up for more disappointment and more self-blame. The freedom offered by mindfulness is stepping out of the story of blame entirely, recognizing that your ability to appreciate your life right now doesn't depend on the past or future. You won't really be able to settle into mindfulness as long as you hold on to an agenda for change—you just have to do it, or do it for its own sake.

As for the second story, the one in which you decide your happiness depends on your conditions, see Chapter 12. Simply being present in your life with mindful awareness can help you access an unconditional appreciation for your life just as it is. This doesn't mean you have to like the way things are, but cultivating the ability to enjoy the simple fact of being alive and aware means you can be okay no matter what's going on. This isn't easy, but it's well worth finding a way to be happy that isn't dependent on your circumstances.

The Least You Need to Know

- It's very stressful looking out for "I, Me, and Mine" all the time.
- Life is much less stressful if you can relate to your sense of self in a more mindful way.
- If you look very carefully, your self isn't the inherently existing, enduring thing you think it is.
- Real self is part of a flow of causes and conditions, and is essentially just awareness.
- Getting more in touch with the real nature of the self decreases your self-concern and frees you from stories about self.

Mindful in Relationship

As stated in the mindfulness principles in Chapter 3, any real, lasting happiness you experience includes the well-being of others. Taking care of beings and things other than yourself isn't something you do because you want to be generous and noble; it's something you do because you stop differentiating so much between what's good for you and what benefits the world around you. Still, it's useful to think specifically about how mindfulness in your relationships and activities helps the world. It may increase your sense of motivation!

In this chapter I discuss how mindfulness can be applied in your relationships and activities. You can be more present and attentive with intimate partners, children, and other family members. You can cultivate more receptive awareness when you're interacting with co-workers and friends, and be less biased and affected by your preconceived notions about them. You can see more clearly how you feel about your work, and how you might experiment with some of your attitudes in order to relate to it in a more positive and effective way. In your roles as a member of society, a citizen of your state and country, and a resident of this planet, you can find ways to be

In This Chapter

- Mindfully working on yourself in order to improve relationships
- Cultivating awareness of expectations, narratives, and assumptions in relationships
- Exploring your relationship to work and people you encounter there
- Using mindfulness to help you see your relationship to the larger world

engaged and responsible without succumbing to burnout, despair, anger, or feeling overwhelmed. Mindfulness doesn't just reduce your stress or make you feel better—it also allows you to be more effective and helpful in the world.

Taking Responsibility

The most important thing to keep in mind when practicing mindfulness for the benefit of others is this: it's all about taking responsibility for *yourself*, and has little or nothing to do with the actions of others. This runs contrary to most advice you'll get about helping the world, which tends to focus on communication and leadership skills, and other ways to get people to change. Such approaches may be very useful, and mindfulness can help you learn and apply them more effectively. However, even if you want to actively encourage others to change, it's essential that you start with yourself.

What you want to do is see things more clearly, so you can choose the path that leads to greater happiness for both self and others (see mindfulness principle #4, Chapter 3). When you do this, you'll notice the many ways you either fail to recognize what would result in greater happiness, or choose alternative ways of behaving because you're clinging to ideas or judgments, or opting for short-term, small-scale happiness instead. For example, you might notice you didn't really listen to someone, and then you disappointed them because you made assumptions about what they needed. You might see how you discourage the creativity of your work team by immediately pointing out how a new idea would be impractical.

 **TAKE CARE**

> Noticing all of your own shortcomings isn't meant to turn into a negative habit of self-criticism. As discussed in Chapter 17, you're not defined by these shortcomings or mistakes, they're simply part of the flow of causes and conditions that make up your life. At the same time, this means you can take some responsibility for them, and make choices that will encourage change.

The greatest advantage of mindfully working on *yourself* instead of trying to change others is that an enormous amount of change can happen without it depending on their participation. Typically, when you're dissatisfied with a relationship, your work, or the state of the world, you're likely to complain about the behavior of others and bemoan the fact that they seem unwilling or unable to change. Perhaps you lodge your complaints with the people in question, but how often does this produce any positive results? Instead, you can focus on what *you* can change about your own behavior and choices, and you don't have to worry about convincing anyone else something's wrong and needs attention.

The amazing thing is that your change will influence others. It's not that you're the only one who should be responsible, or that you should give up on other people improving or contributing in a positive way. It's simply that you leave their behavior more or less up to them. Usually, as you shift your behavior, the people around will respond. Practitioners of mindfulness can tell you many stories of how relationships and situations changed dramatically around them, at least partly in response to their effort to take mindful responsibility for themselves. Parents become less critical as you stop looking for their approval, and when you're able to be less reactive to any criticism. Partners step forward to help more when they aren't being accused of laziness. Political opponents are more receptive when you speak from your own heart and refrain from vilifying them. This kind of positive response is never guaranteed—and it generally doesn't work to have it on a hidden agenda—but you'll probably be surprised at how often it happens.

Personal Relationships

Few things in life reveal your limitations to the extent that personal relationships do. It's relatively easy to feel enlightened all by yourself on a mountaintop, but feeling wise, compassionate, and patient when interacting with people is much more challenging. Someone else's ideas and desires may run counter to yours. You may find yourself unable to communicate clearly what you mean, or feel resistant to someone's expectations. The ways people can "push your buttons" are pretty much limitless. That's why relationships are such a wonderful opportunity for mindfulness practice—they show you what you still need to work on. Below I'll talk about some of the ways to use mindfulness to improve your relationships. For each particular kind of relationship I chose one or two examples of mindfulness practice that will tend to be most useful, but most of the practices offered can actually be applied to any relationship.

Intimate Partners

If you're in an intimate partnership, you'll probably have found it's very difficult to hide anything from the other person. With time and proximity they're going to see you when you're at your worst. They're going to know your habits of body, speech, and mind. They're going to be familiar with what makes you angry, discouraged, impatient, insecure, and resistant. Your partner will eventually know what you're good at (such as paying the bills, or being supportive of the kids) and what you're not so good at (such as clear communication, or cleaning up your messes).

If your relationship is more than a few months old, chances are you'll have started to construct stories about each other. These stories are full of expectations, scripts, and judgments. You start to assume you know what your partner is thinking, how they'll react to something, and what they're capable of. To some extent you'll be right, but if you let these stories dictate how you interact with your partner, you'll actually just be interacting with your ideas and will be completely missing real, intimate engagement with the other person.

MINDFUL EXERCISE

Call to mind any relationship problems you have. Do any of these people misunder-stand you? Do they seem disinterested in things you care about? Do they make unfair assumptions, or fail to take their share of responsibility? Now, without arguing in your mind about who's right or who's wrong, can you imagine giving up *any* expectations of others? What if you took care of yourself within reason by making choices about what *you* do, but not by making demands or by expressing anger or judgment? What if you looked at each act of generosity, kindness, or responsibility by others as a voluntary gift? You may want to apply this exercise in real interactions and watch how things shift.

Mindfulness with intimate partners involves trying to experience your interactions with them in a fresh way. In Chapter 9 I talked about how to use mindfulness to let go of your ideas and judg-ments in favor of experiencing your life directly. This means letting go of thoughts and reactions in order to be receptively aware of the present moment.

For example, let's say your partner starts the same old discussion that always makes you upset. All kinds of things will arise in your body-mind because of this. To start off, you'll have already made the assumption this will be the same old discussion. You may feel upset because your part-ner keeps bringing this issue up despite your reaction. You may wonder if they care about you at all, or are just determined to get their own way. This thought may make you angry, and cause your blood pressure to rise and your body to become tense. In retaliation you may say something deliberately hurtful, which then causes your partner to get upset and the whole situation esca-lates emotionally. This cascade of events may be something that happens over and over in your relationship, and runs the risk of becoming a dysfunctional trap.

Staying mindful throughout an interaction like this requires you to stay as focused as possible on the present by grounding your awareness in your physical sensations or breathing. You try to rec-ognize your thoughts as thoughts, and feelings as feelings. Instead of immediately believing they reflect reality, you reserve judgment for the time being. You refrain from acting out your afflic-tive emotions until you have more clarity and perspective about what's going on (see Chapter 14), which might mean you have to wait until later to offer a response! If you can maintain mindful-ness throughout such an encounter, you can notice you're not ready to respond. Maybe you say nothing, or maybe you ask to talk later. In any case, your mindful response will probably be off-script, and will prevent typical chain of reactions from getting started.

Children

Children of all ages—infants to teenagers—are acutely aware of whether you're being mindful. They won't consciously think of it as being "mindful," but they'll know when you're fully present with them and when you're not. A baby will often cry when put in the arms of someone who is busy talking or doing something else, and therefore who doesn't stop to pay at least some direct attention to them. A toddler will be mischievous or throw a tantrum when they become aware their caretaker is distracted. Young children will know when you're not actually listening to them, or pick up when you're preoccupied with something, and they may either act out or withdraw. Teenagers will definitely stop talking to you unless you're fully present with them—instead of being caught up in your thoughts and judgments about what they should or shouldn't be doing.

Mindfulness practice helps you get better at slowing down and realizing when you're not being present with a child. The ongoing practice of letting go of stimulus-independent thinking will allow you to tune into the present moment with a child even though you have lots of activities and interests competing for your time and attention. Mindfulness makes you much more aware of the contents of your own mind, so you'll be conscious of the thoughts, feelings, and judgments that come up in reaction to a child's behavior. Having noticed these reactions you can make more compassionate and skillful choices about what to do next. Best of all, mindfulness can help you to simply enjoy the company of children. When you let go of thoughts about the past and future and engage the present moment without comparisons, you can get on a child's wavelength and share some of the wonder with which they experience the world.

Family

You most likely share a long history with your family members. Without mindfulness this history tends to harden into narratives about your family as a whole and the people in it. In this narrative people aren't autonomous individuals as much as they're *your* mother, sibling, aunt, uncle, niece, nephew, or cousin. When you see or interact with family members, it can be very difficult not to be preoccupied with memories of past interactions and injuries and assumptions about other people's motives. It's also difficult not to fall into typical roles with respect to other family members, and expect them to fill their expected roles with respect to you.

 KEEP IN MIND

As well as being of benefit to harmony and interpersonal interactions, practicing mindfulness with family can be very informative. You can observe patterns of behavior and speech that are typical for your family, or that influenced you as you were growing up. With the nonjudgmental receptivity of mindfulness, you may notice new things about the dynamics of your family relationships. They may help you understand a great deal about yourself.

Mindfulness can revolutionize your familial relationships in that it can help you start with a clean slate. You start by practicing mindful awareness when you're with family members—paying more attention to what's going on in the present moment than to thoughts about the past, or worries about the future. Whenever your mind wanders away from the present, you simply bring it back by turning your awareness to a physical sensation. Instead of interacting with someone through a fog of resentment or assumption, you relate to them in a fresh way, as you would with anyone else.

The most important part of this "clean slate" is being able to relax and trust your mindfulness to alert you to any need to protect yourself from family members who have hurt you in the past. You don't have to ruminate on past events in order to stop family patterns of disrespect or violence. When you're mindful, you're even more aware and able to respond in the moment—so if something happens that is unacceptable to you, you'll recognize it and be able to do something about it.

However, you may find you'll be able to graciously live with many of the actions of family members that previously would have pushed your buttons and made you react defensively. Most likely, many of the things they say or do that you find irritating or offensive aren't really that bad unless you interpret them in the context of past interactions. For example, the tone of your mother's voice when she asks about your date may trigger you because of past criticisms she's made about your romantic life. However, in the present she hasn't actually said anything critical. If you're able to ignore what you *think* you read in her tone and not react, you're managing to interact in a fresh way instead of falling into an old narrative. She may even give up trying to comment on your dates because she sees it makes no difference to you. In any case, you can start interacting with family in a real, intimate way through mindfulness.

Friends

Friendships are a wonderful opportunity for practicing generosity. If you're able to examine your friendships with mindfulness, you may find your motivation for maintaining relationships is often based on self-centeredness. It is worth investing time and energy into a friendship if it's fun, exciting, or beneficial to you. If someone isn't very entertaining or physically attractive, or they don't have anything to offer you, they aren't worth seeking out. If someone who was previously worthwhile gets boring, it's time to let that friendship fade away. Maybe the person has hit hard times, gotten depressed, or stopped drinking and partying. Maybe they're no longer connected socially in a way that gives you an advantage. It can be humbling to notice your own motivations in friendship and how rarely they have to do with selfless devotion to maintaining relationships. It requires a suspension of judgment and a measure of courage to examine your life with mindfulness (see Chapters 9 and 10).

This isn't to say, of course, that certain friendships shouldn't be important to you because you have a natural rapport with someone, or share interests. You also don't have to take on a helper's mentality and feel responsible for the well-being of everyone you come in contact with. All that's required to bring greater generosity to your friendships is mindful awareness of your motivations and actions—and the repercussions of those actions. If you make a habit of dismissing possible friendships or discarding relationships for selfish reasons, you'll most likely find your life filled with superficial relationships with people who are also willing to dismiss or discard you. In order to maintain social connections, you'll probably feel the need to stay attractive, entertaining, financially stable, well-connected, or any of the other things you consider essential to captivating friends. It's also likely part of you will be worried about being left all alone if you ever fall apart or need support.

KEEP IN MIND

The next time you're deciding whether or not to seek out the company of a particular friend or acquaintance, be mindful of what criteria you're using. Be honest with yourself. Do you think about how fun it was the last time you spent time with this person? Do you think about how you need this person to do something for you? Do you think more about the activities or other social connections you'll experience through this person than you do about them? Do you have any friendships in your life that you maintain simply because you care about those friends? You may want to make those friendships a priority in your life!

What happens when you take a different approach to friendship? What if you decided to maintain the friendships you have the best you can, even if they change or are becoming less interesting to you? What if you made the oldest friendships you have a priority? What if you made an effort to stay loyal and present for a friend who is going through a hard time? What you'll find if you can observe everything with mindful awareness is that there are many valuable rewards of friendship that are only tasted over a long period of time, after the relationship has lasted through many changes in your lives. You'll also find, as stated in mindfulness principle #2 (Chapter 3), the happiness of others isn't separate from your happiness. When you support a friend, it can be a source of immediate, great joy.

Work

Whatever you do, work is a significant part of your life. Most likely, you spend the largest single chunk of your waking hours working. You may spend more of that time in a workplace than you do at home, and more time surrounded by co-workers than by family or friends. Unless you love your job or feel very identified with it, your work may not be your first choice of venue for mindfulness practice—simply being present and aware, not anticipating what you'll be doing when work is over. However, if you're able to bring more mindfulness to your work and how you relate to it, it can have a huge impact on your life—if only because of the amount of time and energy you spend on work.

Are You What You Do?

If you honestly examine your attitudes around work with mindfulness, you'll probably find you're heavily identified with what you do. It may be that you're fortunate enough to earn a living doing something you love, or something you think is very important. In this case you've probably invested a great deal in your work, or derive personal satisfaction and a sense of identity from it. You may feel ambivalent about exactly what you do for a living, but nonetheless it may be extremely important to you to provide for yourself and others. This is part of why unemployment can be so devastating. Finally, even if you dislike what you do for work, you may also feel you're defined largely in part by your job—even if it's in a negative way. You might think, "I'm just a _____." After all, telling one another what we "do" is often the very first thing we share when we first meet. This can encourage the conclusion that you are what you do.

 TAKE CARE

It's also important to notice your judgments and assumptions about other people based on what they do for a living. Not only does this interfere with your relationships with others, you'll end up applying those same judgments to yourself whether you realize it or not. Even if you're proud of your job right now, life can change and you might end up doing something you think is menial, unworthy of respect, or a sign that you aren't a capable or valuable person. If you can start seeing people clearly, without the filter of assumptions based on what they do, you'll be doing yourself a favor.

Mindfulness is very helpful if you want to identify and challenge your attitudes about your work, and work in general. You can pay close attention and observe when and why you feel excited and motivated about work versus when and why you feel resistant, embarrassed, or even miserable about it. You can notice beliefs and assumptions you hold about what kinds of work is valuable, or what kinds of working conditions are tolerable. You'll be aware of how you feel when someone asks you about what you do.

As you become aware of your reactions, thoughts, feelings, and beliefs around work, you'll start to become freer of them. As in all mindfulness practice, when you realize these are all just thoughts and feelings, not necessarily reflections of reality, you can consider other possibilities. What if you identified less with work? What if you gave up caring what others think about what you do? What if you embraced whatever you do as an opportunity for generosity? (See Chapter 15.) Are you identified with meaningful things in your life besides work? Generally speaking, asking yourself such questions will lead to a more conscious and well-considered relationship with what you do.

Bosses and Institutions

Unless you work for yourself or own your own business, you have a relationship with superiors and with the company or institution that employs you. Depending on the boss or institution, these may be fruitful, pleasant relationships or stressful and problematic ones. Most people do not enjoy being told what to do, particularly if they don't agree with *what* they're being told to do. If you think what you're being asked to do, or the direction the organization is taking, is inefficient, pointless, dishonest, or even harmful, it can be very difficult to have a positive attitude about your work, let alone your bosses and overall employer.

One of the eight essential aspects of the Buddhist Eightfold Path is right (meaning correct, true, or appropriate) livelihood. This points out how valuable it can be to feel a resonance with your livelihood—to believe it's *not* harmful, and that you can do it with a clear conscience. This is something to take into consideration if you find yourself at odds with your work situation. However, you may not have the option of changing livelihoods, or perhaps it wouldn't actually improve the situation much for you to switch jobs (perhaps you're likely to encounter similar challenges at any job you'd be able to get). In this case, it may be useful to take up the mindful practice of forbearance discussed at length in Chapter 22.

To practice forbearance in the workplace, you honestly acknowledge your thoughts and feelings about the situation. You don't try to tell yourself to just get over them, or ignore them. On the other hand, you're also making the choice to stay with your job—so what can you do? You forbear—which means to endure, put up with, and be patient. This is more effective than it might sound. Essentially, you accept the situation isn't ideal and will probably continue to cause you stress as long as you're in it. That's okay. If the stress becomes unbearable, then you'll have to do something—but it can help a great deal to give up the struggle against how things are. You can recognize feeling rather ill-at-ease with your work is likely to continue, and give up the idea things should be different, or that somehow you'll be able to make them different. Instead, you embrace the ambiguity and return to being mindfully aware of your life, moment by moment. You'll see it's not all bad.

Co-Workers, Clients, and Others

You probably end up encountering all kinds of people throughout your day, at least most days—co-workers, clients, customers, salespeople, and strangers. Many of these people you have only a limited amount of interaction with, wouldn't choose to interact with on a personal basis, and many of them don't matter a great deal to your life in a literal sense. In fact, if you live in a big city, a whole bunch of the people you see every day you'll never encounter again in your life. It may not seem as important to use mindfulness to improve your "relationships" with these relatively peripheral people as it does to work on your relationships with intimates, family, friends, and people who have influence over your life.

MINDFUL EXERCISE

The next time you're at work or out in public, make an effort to be more aware of the people around you. Choose one person at a time. Become aware of everything you can about the person without alerting her to the fact you're paying special attention to her. Be conscious of her physical proximity, posture, and movements. Can you get a sense of her mood? Does she seem to be preoccupied, or in the present moment? Does anything about her clothing or personal possessions give you a sense of her personality? If you speak to her, what kind of response does she give? Is there anything you can do for her? People provide fascinating subjects for mindfulness.

However, this is exactly the point. Interactions with the "peripheral" people in your life provide a wonderful opportunity to practice mindfulness because paying special attention to them usually isn't going to be something that benefits you in an obvious way. It's easier for your interactions to be free of the subtle agendas that are present in many of your other relationships. It's also more likely you can engage with co-workers, clients, and others without the filters of expectations and assumptions you place on people you know well, or are deeply invested in.

When you use mindfulness in such interactions, you're setting aside your usual self-concern to be more aware of the people around you. You meet the eyes of the grocery store clerk, take a moment to notice a customer's body language, or find out how a co-worker is doing. At the very least, you'll probably notice how often your interactions with relative strangers are guarded and stingy—that is, how you approach them while trying to minimize engagement. This attitude may account for some of your stress as you go about your day. You don't have to judge yourself for this, but being aware of it can give you a way to relieve a little stress and feel more connected when you need to. All you have to do is slow down a little and be more mindful of the interactions you're having with people.

The World

What good can mindfulness do the world in a larger sense? Is it all about making your life happier, or perhaps the life of those immediately around you? What about bigger issues of societal and cultural problems, politics, or the environment? These questions lead us back to mindfulness principle #2: *the greatest happiness is that which applies in the longest term and at the largest scale—which includes the happiness of others* (see Chapter 3). "The world" is the largest scale you can consider (at least at this point in human history), and includes the happiness of all the people on the planet. Just as mindfulness helps you see clearly what does and doesn't lead toward greater happiness in your own life, it can help you see more clearly how your behavior and decisions impact the larger world.

Mindfulness can help you become more aware of the patterns and problems in the culture around you. Through practice you'll have gotten better at identifying thoughts, feelings, and judgments, and not necessarily believing they reflect reality. Some of the content of your mind will be the result of influences from society, and with mindfulness you can start to question some of it. You may notice you hold opinions that aren't even the result of your own thinking. You may find reactions arising in you that aren't even based on your own personal experience, but were simply learned from others. If any of these thoughts, feelings, and judgments are false or harmful, mindful awareness of them will help motivate you to change.

 TAKE CARE

Of course, you can only count on the effects mindfulness will have on you. As discussed earlier in this chapter, your choices and actions are likely to influence others, but this isn't something you can expect. If you practice mindfulness with the intention of changing others, you're liable to be disappointed—in part because your agenda will interfere with your mindfulness. It takes a certain faith to concentrate on what you can influence, and let others do their part. If you look at some of the most successful leaders of change throughout history—such as Gandhi, Martin Luther King, Jr., or Mother Teresa—this is what they did. They led by example and appealed to the better nature of those around them.

Engaging with political and environmental issues, for many of us, can be overwhelming and discouraging. The sheer number of problems, competing ideologies, and possible responses can result in numbness or paralysis. It can seem like the only viable way to live is to avoid thinking too much about the problems of the world—to enjoy your life as best you can, contribute to a few charities, and vote, but otherwise figure there's nothing you can do.

It becomes possible to remain more open and receptive to the political, economic, and environmental problems in the world when you can use mindfulness to recognize your reactions, and set the problems aside when you need to. One of the primary reactions that it's useful to notice is a sense of guilt or responsibility for world problems, coupled with a subtle (or obvious) belief you should be able to fix them. While all of us bear some responsibility in this interdependent world, a great sense of perspective and freedom can come from recognizing how much is beyond your control. If you can center your awareness in your sphere of influence, you can let go of the sense of responsibility for everything else. At the same time, you can let yourself acknowledge the pain and suffering in the world in a more open-hearted way, because it doesn't cause the cognitive dissonance it did when you carried a sense that you *should* be able to fix things.

The Least You Need to Know

- The mindful approach to working with relationships is primarily about taking responsibility for your own thoughts, speech, and actions.

- Changing your behavior often positively influences the people around you, but you can't count on it.

- One of the most valuable mindful approaches to relationships is being able to engage the people close to you with a clean slate—letting go of assumptions based in the past, and expectations for the future.

- If you want to increase your sense of intimacy and connection with others, it's important to pay more attention to people regardless of how the relationship serves or interests you.

- Simply becoming more aware of your thoughts, feelings, and judgments around your work, your working relationships, and the larger world can bring about positive change.

A Mindful Life

If you want to, you can continue to strengthen your mindfulness over the course of your entire life. You can also adopt it as a practice that affects everything you do. You may or may not be inclined to get formal about your mindfulness, but if it makes a difference in your life you'll probably start to feel some dedication to it.

In this part of the book I explain how you can develop your mindfulness further. I start out by offering suggestions for how to incorporate mindfulness into your daily routine and develop it into an ongoing, sustainable practice. Then I explain the importance of mindful ethics. Basically, if you keep on making a mess of your life, it will be difficult to settle the mind into receptive awareness, and you'll be working against your own greater happiness. Ethical guidelines can help keep your life on track and simplify decision-making. Finally, I discuss how living a mindful life can help you find meaning and purpose no matter your circumstances.

Mindful Things to Do Every Day

The more you practice mindfulness, the better you get at it, so it's worth finding ways to do it throughout your day. Also, the more mindful you can be in all areas of your life, the better off you're going to be. You can cultivate receptive awareness of the present all day long, from the time you wake up until the time you go to bed. You can be mindful at home, at work, while commuting, with family, and with friends.

In this chapter I describe ways you can help yourself remember to be mindful more often, which is often the biggest challenge. I also suggest various things you can do throughout your day to help you pay more attention to what is going on around you. Some of the approaches to mindfulness covered in this chapter involve actions you do with your body, some involve experimenting with your attitude, and others involve reflecting on your thoughts, speech, and behavior. These suggestions are just meant to get you started; in fact, there are infinite ways to encourage your own mindfulness. It's good to get creative and see what works for you.

In This Chapter

- Tips for remembering to be mindful
- Reading and studying about mindfulness to seed your mind with awareness
- How deliberate patterns of behavior serve as "rituals" to encourage mindfulness
- Mindfulness practices you can do wherever you are
- Bringing more awareness to everyday activities

Remembering More Often

You may find despite your intention to be mindful throughout your day, there are long periods of time where you simply forget to do it. These tend to be times when you're busy and you opt to focus on your agenda instead of cultivating awareness of the present. It's also easy to lapse out of mindfulness when you're doing something routine. At such times your tendency will be to fall into a habitual approach while letting your mind wander.

How can you remember to be mindful more often? Unfortunately there's no magical solution to this problem. For the most part, simply continuing the effort over time, patiently and relentlessly, will increase your sense of mindfulness throughout your life. It can be helpful to strengthen your dedication to mindfulness by carefully noting what you appreciate about mindful moments, and identifying how the practice is benefiting your life. If you allow yourself to relish the times you're mindful, it will provide positive feedback to your body-mind, and you just might find yourself waking up to the present moment more often.

Study and Reading

Although mindfulness is something you actually have to *do,* not just think about, it can help a great deal to read or listen to books, articles, or talks about it. This has the effect of planting seeds in your mind that are directly related to mindfulness. The topic of receptive awareness of the present moment can start to creep into your stimulus-independent thinking (such as daydreams and analysis) and ironically end up reminding you to pay attention to the present moment.

 TAKE CARE

> As you read about how mindfulness can help improve your health and your ability to cope with life, remember not to get too caught up in using mindfulness as another tool to get what you want. There's nothing wrong with aspiring to greater health and happiness, but if you approach mindfulness with the same kind of gaining idea you use when approaching other things, you're liable to get impatient with it. It's essentially a lifestyle change, not a quick remedy.

The study of mindfulness in a more academic sense can also open your mind to the many different aspects of life that can be affected by the practice. For example, there are books about how mindfulness relates to parenting, teaching, eating, creativity, sex, money, and urban life. There are books on using mindfulness to address very specific concerns like anxiety, depression, trauma, obsessive-compulsive disorder, and chronic physical pain. There's even a monthly magazine called *Mindful* with timely articles on the latest research and tips on how to apply mindfulness in practical situations. The more things in your life you come to associate with mindfulness, the more often you'll think to work on it.

The Value of Rituals and Verses

Rituals don't have to be religious. They're just things you make a habit of doing in a particular way, or at a particular time. You can establish rituals that either remind you to be mindful, or encourage the practice of paying attention to what's going on around you. Because they become habits, you get used to doing them and don't have to try so hard to remember them.

Rituals can be very informal, in the sense that if someone watched you doing one they probably wouldn't even notice. Informal rituals might include always putting your shoes straight, holding cups with two hands, or taking a deep breath before you answer the phone. Each time the relevant situation arises (you're putting away your shoes, drinking your coffee, or responding to a phone call), you're reminded to work on mindfulness. Then, as you do the ritual, you practice receptive awareness of what's going on. You *notice* your shoes, the movements of your hands, the fact that you're drinking coffee, or the state of your body-mind before you start a conversation with someone. For a great set of informal rituals you can do throughout your day, read *How to Train a Wild Elephant: And Other Adventures in Mindfulness* by Jan Chozen Bays.

A ritual can also be somewhat formal, such as reciting a thought-provoking poem or quote each morning, or lighting a candle or stick of incense on an altar. Note that ""altars" don't have to be religious either; they can simply be a clean, elevated space where you place pictures or symbols of things that are significant and inspirational to you. Meditation can be approached as a ritual, as can a period of time you're devoting to simple work done with as much awareness as possible.

Another kind of formal mindfulness ritual is reciting a verse as you engage in a particular activity or as you encounter a particular situation. Buddhists have been using such verses for thousands of years, and they have proven to be effective for many people. You can create your own verses, such as "As I turn on the light, I remember gratitude for all of my resources," or "Stopped at a red light, may I remember to appreciate each moment of my life." You can also find verses written for use during all kinds of different activities—including sweeping, greeting someone, washing the dishes, and gardening—in Thich Nhat Hanh's *Present Moment Wonderful Moment: Mindfulness Verses for Daily Living.*

 KEEP IN MIND

If you want to incorporate some mindfulness verses into your day, you might start by writing out the verses on index cards and taping them up where you're likely to see them at the appropriate time. You can put a meal verse on your dining room table, a tooth brushing verse next to your bathroom mirror, and a driving verse on the dashboard of your car.

A Day's Worth of Mindful Practices

When I teach mindfulness, I find people appreciate hearing specific examples of how to practice and apply it in everyday life. What does mindfulness look like when you're at a high-stress job, at a movie with friends, or on the city bus? It's fairly easy to understand what you're supposed to be doing when you're meditating or doing a simple task like washing the dishes (not that it's easy), but what about the rest of your life?

I hope you'll find, as I did, that mindfulness is like a fascinating hobby you never have to put down. You can practice it anytime, anywhere. It makes life more interesting, as well as giving you tools for responding to it more skillfully. In the rest of this chapter I walk you through some mindfulness practices you can do over the course of a day in a fairly typical modern life.

Waking Up

What do you do the moment you wake up? Grit your teeth and turn off the alarm as quickly as possible? Sigh? Smile? Stretch? Become aware of where your partner, child, or pet is? Just noticing how you wake up is a good first step. Then you might consider something you could do to cultivate mindfulness and positivity in your first moment of wakefulness. After all, if your first thoughts and feelings of the day are of resistance and resentment, this is probably going to color how you experience the rest of it.

You might pick a verse to recite right away, such as the old Zen saying, "Every day is a good day." Ideally, you'll be able to mean it, but saying something like this can make a difference even if the recitation becomes rote or half-hearted. Perhaps all it will do is call your attention to how you aren't feeling like today's a good day, but you'll still have increased your awareness of what's going on for you. Instead of a verse you might sit on the edge of the bed and take a few deep breaths, or stand and stretch, becoming aware of a body that is awake and functioning one more day.

Meditation

If you can make meditation part of your daily routine, it can have amazing effects on your life and your ability to be mindful throughout the day. (The instructions for meditation can be found in Chapter 8.) Just as an exercise routine can help you feel more energetic and physically healthy all day long, meditation can help you feel calmer and more mindful even when you're not actually engaged in it.

The length and timing of your meditation sessions should be chosen based on what works best for you. Thirty minutes is an ideal amount of time, but longer is fine, and even 5- to 10-minute sessions are beneficial if that's all you have time for. Many people find early morning is a good time to meditate, before they dive into the activities and social interactions of their day. Others find mornings difficult and prefer to sit in the evening. Whether you do silent meditation, guided meditation, or walking meditation (see Chapters 4 and 8), some time devoted to simply being aware—and nothing else—can be the most effective practice for helping you be more mindful at all times.

Washing Up

Washing your face, showering, and brushing your teeth are activities you do so regularly, your mind probably wanders constantly as you're doing them. These are simple, physical tasks that are perfect for mindfulness practice that is based in awareness of the body and physical sensations (see Chapter 4). You can pay attention to the sensations of water flowing over your skin, perceptions of warmth and cold, and the smells of soap and toothpaste.

MINDFUL EXERCISE

The next time you're looking at yourself in the mirror, notice your thoughts about your appearance. Are you pleased? A little dissatisfied? Harshly critical? As usual, don't edit your thoughts and feelings. In fact, invite them to come out clearly by engaging in a dialogue with them, as if you were commenting on someone else's body. Then become aware of whether your evaluative thoughts about your appearance arise every time you're in front of a mirror (or a reflective surface like a window). Don't judge or try to get rid of your thoughts, just acknowledge how persistent and pervasive they are. Is there any part of you that sees the whole scenario as rather ridiculous?

Simple, repetitive tasks like washing and caring for your body are things you can easily ritualize by always doing them a particular way—deliberately. It's good to choose a way that's just a little bit different from your habitual way, so you'll have to pay attention. You might brush your teeth with your nondominant hand, or carefully let your cupped hands fill with water to wash your face—three times. Maybe you spend an extra 30 seconds massaging the shampoo into your scalp. Each of these deliberate actions will bring your mind back to the present moment.

Mindful Eating

Usually, even if you're enjoying a particular meal, you aren't as mindful of it as you could be. Cultivating more awareness while you're eating can be very rewarding and beneficial. It makes you better able to appreciate the sights, smells, and flavors of the food. It also makes you more aware of when you're full and might be overeating, or eating primarily for emotional reasons.

There are a number of ways to increase mindfulness while you're eating. You can say a verse at the beginning of the meal. Depending on your circumstances, you might choose to eat in silence, or without reading or watching anything. You can slow down your eating process by chewing and swallowing each bite before reaching for the next. Of course, you can also simply return your attention to the flavors and textures of the food whenever you realize your mind has wandered.

There are a number of different online programs available via websites or apps that allow you to track the food you eat in a way that increases your mindfulness of your eating patterns overall. From a mindfulness point of view tracking your food wouldn't be for weight loss purposes, but something you do to cultivate greater awareness of your relationship with food. Many of your eating patterns have become so habitual, you don't even realize how much you're eating, how often, or how much you indulge in foods you know to be overly fatty, sugary, or rich. If you can maintain the nonjudgmental, receptive awareness of mindfulness as you use food or exercise tracking tools, they can be very helpful.

Commuting in Silence

If you have a regular commute by car or mass transit, consider doing it in silence. Rather than turning on the radio or putting in ear buds to listen to something, just drive, or just sit. If you're just sitting, try not reading anything, either. Just cultivate awareness of what's going on within and around you. You'll probably find this ends up being a much more calming and restorative way to spend your commute than listening to something, even if the listening is something you enjoy. If you hate to give up your music or news, try spending one part of your commute in silence.

It helps to choose something to pay special attention to as you drive or ride. One of the best things to become aware of is your own state of mind. Are you tired, excited, worried, or content? What kinds of things are occupying your mind at the moment? You might be surprised how out of touch you can become with what's going on in your own body-mind unless you deliberately "check in" with yourself like this. Another thing you can do while commuting is watch people and try to guess *their* states of mind. You can also practice politeness in traffic, deliberately counteracting your habitual urge to hurry or compete. Let people merge in front you, stop for pedestrians in crosswalks, and refrain from tailgating someone who's driving too slowly. This can be a fascinating exercise in watching your own internal reactions, and folds mindfulness into driving.

Working on One Thing at a Time

Even when you have many things competing for your attention, can you do one thing at a time? Psychologists tell us this is all we're actually capable of, anyway—multitasking is an illusion created by our ability to jump very quickly from one task to another and back again. With mindfulness, it's possible to remain receptive to the various needs arising around you while still maintaining a centered awareness of one task.

KEEP IN MIND

You might find it helpful to actually time yourself as you do a particular task two different ways—once while rushing, and once while practicing mindfulness—and compare the difference. Most of the time, you'll find no increase in efficiency when you rush, or that rushing buys you at most about 30 seconds. On the other hand, rushing probably makes you feel stressed and irritable and often leads to mistakes. Remember, don't judge yourself for hurrying, just try to cultivate awareness of doing so and the results.

It can be a tremendous relief to *just* make copies, take someone's blood pressure, or walk down the hall to a meeting. Even though there may be time pressure on you and a long list of tasks awaiting you when you've completed this one, for a few moments you can let all of that go. You commit yourself to the task that's in front of you and acknowledge to yourself that it's not going to get done any faster (or at least not much faster) if you hurry, or if your attention is leaping forward to the next task. You bring your awareness to something in the present—the feeling of paper in your hands, your patient's face, or the sensations of walking. This not only decreases stress, it can help you enjoy your work much more.

Secret Acts of Kindness

Some of the best mindfulness practices simply get you interested in your life in a positive way. Certain practices can even be approached in the spirit of a game, such as trying to do small acts of kindness or generosity that go unnoticed—or at least, *who* has done the act goes unnoticed. This can be a delightful way to feel more connected to the people around you. It's also a great way to strengthen your generosity "muscles" because whatever you do will be a pure act of generosity; it will have nothing to do with getting credit, paying someone back, or making someone like you.

Secret acts of kindness encourage mindfulness in all kinds of ways. First, you need to pay attention to what is going on so you can recognize opportunities for helping in some small way. Second, you have to watch carefully in order to figure out how to help without being discovered. Third, you often get to watch the reactions of others and notice the pleasure and warmth that arises in you even though you aren't getting credit for the action. Alternatively, you can watch yourself wonder why nobody's noticing the wonderful thing you did, which isn't as pleasant but equally informative.

Labeling Your Reactions

Becoming more aware of your own reactions throughout the day is perhaps the most pervasive mindfulness practice of all. You can do this all the time, in any setting. It's particularly useful at work, where you're likely to be bombarded with all kinds of triggers—people you wouldn't choose to spend time with, demands and criticisms, time pressure, disagreements about how things should be done, and competition for status and recognition, just to name a few!

 TAKE CARE

As you label your reactions, be careful not to add judgment or analysis to the label. It may be valuable to think at length about a particular reaction or situation at some point in the future, but the mindfulness practice is just to label. If you jump too quickly to telling yourself a reaction is wrong, or constructing an argument for why it's right, you're letting the reaction take over. The idea is simply to bring mindfulness to the situation; this leads to more clarity, which will help you know what to do next.

Labeling your reactions not only helps you become more aware of them, it helps you recognize *reactions as reactions*. As discussed in Chapter 5, this is the first step in identifying less with your thoughts and emotions. Identifying less with them doesn't mean you suppress or dismiss them, just that you become aware they're just your reactions to what's going on, and not necessarily a complete and accurate portrayal of reality. Throughout the day you can observe your reactions and label them, such as "I'm feeling irritable" or "I'm thinking that he's being controlling." This helps you get to know your own mind very well, and gives you more freedom of choice when it comes to how (or whether) you act out your reactions.

Listening to Conversations

You probably have many conversations over the course of a day, with family, friends, co-workers, and strangers out in the world. This gives you many opportunities to practice listening. If you're like many people, your habitual way of conversing when you're not very engaged in the situation involves stock phrases or rather automatic responses. If you're interested in the conversation, you may end up spending much more of your time and energy thinking about yourself—what you're going to say next, or how what the other person's saying applies to you—than you do listening to what is actually being said.

If you can bring a sense of curiosity to conversations, you'll find yourself paying more attention to what others are saying, what they're not saying, and what *you're* saying. Do you really understand what someone is trying to communicate, or are you just ready to make assumptions and move on? Does someone have something more to say, but they need some space to say it, or perhaps an invitation to speak? Do you constantly turn the conversation back to yourself, jumping in with your own related experience without actually listening to someone else's? Do you generally refrain from offering your perspective, and why? You'll end up becoming more aware of the incredible depth and complexity of human interactions if you can cultivate mindfulness during conversations.

Really Coming Home

Most of us deeply appreciate coming home. Ideally, home is where you set things up so you feel safe and comfortable. It's where you can find refuge from the demands of the world, and be surrounded by people, animals, or things that support and inspire you. You may think you're already mindful as you come home, but chances are you're concentrating on how you're feeling and what you need as you walk in your door. Maybe you're thinking about how you need to take care of others, but that's still about you in the sense that it's about the tasks you need to do before you relax and take care of yourself. Alternatively, the concerns that arose for you earlier in the day may still be front and foremost in your mind, so you aren't actually paying much attention to coming home.

MINDFUL EXERCISE

The next time you find yourself preoccupied with a worry or plan, bring mindful awareness to the situation and ask yourself some questions. Are you perseverating? Perseveration is when your mind ends up in repetitive loops of thinking that don't produce any positive results. Is this a good time to be working mentally on your concern? Do you have enough time to make any progress on it right now? Take an honest look at your mental processing. If you want to keep thinking about the same issue, go ahead. However, you may feel inspired to let the thinking go for the moment when you see it's not actually going to do you much good.

A great mindfulness practice is to take a few minutes when you first get home to greet any beings you live with, and look around with a sense of gratitude. Really look at your partner or child. Take the time to ask them a question or kiss them. Spend 30 seconds petting your dog or cat without doing anything else. For the moment, overlook the mess or the other things demanding your care, and appreciate that you have such a place to return to. Make a ritual of spending a few minutes to *really* come home.

Balancing Care and Ease

When you're at home or work, it's often a challenge to balance the effort to take care of things with the ability to relax and enjoy them. The balance you end up with affects not only your own stress levels and appreciation for your life, but also the people around you. How much time do you spend fixated on getting things done—cleaning, sorting, fixing, planning, answering emails—compared to the amount of time you sit down to relax, listen to someone, or just spend time with them? On the other end of the spectrum, do you focus so much on enjoyment and spending time with people that your house is a mess, your bills are unpaid, and people don't count on you to follow through on things?

The mindfulness practice of balancing care and ease involves deliberately choosing an activity that's outside your habitual routine, wherever that falls on the spectrum between responsible activity and resting in simple appreciation. Then you watch the results. If you err on the side of active care, you'll notice how much the people and animals around you benefit when you slow down to pay some attention to them with no agenda. If you err on the side of neglecting the practical side of life, you'll notice how it can be easier for everyone to relax when things are properly taken care of. The perfect balance point between taking care and taking it easy differs by person, situation, and even by the day or hour. Mindfulness involves becoming more aware of that balance and how to respond with what is most needed at any given moment.

Deliberate Leisure

It may not sound like mindful leisure would be much fun. At least at first, mindfulness can take work, so it can be tempting to completely opt out of mindfulness when it's time to enjoy yourself. In addition, many of the things people do for pleasure tend to pull them out of the present moment or compromise awareness. Is it possible to be mindful while watching television, attending a loud party, or enjoying some wine? Fortunately, the answer is yes, and the effort to be mindful doesn't have to ruin your leisure time.

Basically, all you have to do is be more aware of your recreational activities while you're doing them. Periodically you check in with your body-mind and notice your breathing and posture. You open your awareness to where you are, who you're with, and what you're doing. You pay attention to some of the sensations coming in from your environment, and there you are—present! This can increase your enjoyment of the activity, and also make you receptive to things you might otherwise miss, such as the late hour, or someone who doesn't look like they're having a good time and may need a friendly gesture.

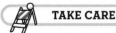 **TAKE CARE**

You may find it difficult to be mindful during your leisure time if you're using that time to escape from your life. If you want your recreational activities to distract you from what's going on in your life, the last thing you want to do is wake up to reality in the midst of them. If you notice this kind of disconnect between your "regular" life and your leisure time, it may be useful to examine what it is you're trying to get away from. Be gentle with yourself; don't try to go cold turkey off your recreational distractions, but invite just a little mindfulness into them. You may discover something in your life that needs care and attention.

Reflecting on Your Day

At some quiet moment before going to sleep for the night, it can be very useful to reflect on the events of the day. Draw the events and activities through your mind in the order they occurred, and notice anything that stands out. Overall, was this a satisfying day, or a frustrating one? Is there anything that happened that has left a residue of worry, regret, anger, resentment, sadness, or confusion? Did anything happen that sparked humor, excitement, or a sense of gratification? Sometimes, without the deliberate "invitation" of reflection, your mind will suppress or dismiss things, so this practice can be like double-checking your mindfulness of the day.

Reflecting on the past, even the recent past, may not seem like mindfulness because it isn't focusing on the present moment. However, as explained in Chapter 5, this reflection isn't actually about the past. It's about your body-mind at the present moment: the memories, experience of residues, and positive feelings are all occurring in the present moment. In a sense, you're turning your awareness not to the past but to how the recent past has affected the state of your body-mind right here, right now.

The Least You Need to Know

- There is nothing you do that is outside the scope of mindfulness. No matter what's going on, you can always try to be more present, receptive, and aware.
- Rituals are established ways of doing certain things, and can be very simple and personal. Adopting or creating small rituals can incorporate mindfulness into many different areas of your life.
- No single mindfulness practice makes as much difference in your day—and to your ability to be mindful the rest of the time—as meditation.
- Anything that encourages you to pay more attention to what's going on in the present moment can be a mindfulness practice, including saying a verse at a particular time, asking yourself certain questions, listening to others, or even creating some kind of game that requires you to pay close attention to your environment.
- Practicing mindfulness throughout the day, every day, helps you get better at doing it. It also means you're more awake for your life.

Developing Your Mindfulness Practice

There are three different ways to define *practice*. It means to do something repeatedly in order to get better at it. It's also a way of behaving or acting that you've chosen to make a habit, or work done according to the guidelines of a particular discipline, such as the practice of medicine or law. All three of these definitions of practice can apply to mindfulness.

When you practice mindfulness in order to get better at it, you patiently and diligently repeat your efforts to be receptive and aware in this moment. When you identify mindfulness as something you would like to make a part of your life, you adopt mindfulness techniques and exercises as part of your daily routine. Finally, if you decide you want to dedicate yourself to becoming more and more receptively aware of your life over the long term, you may want think of yourself as having a "mindfulness practice." You can tend and cultivate such a practice in many different ways.

In this chapter I give you ways to develop your mindfulness practice further, whatever your current level of commitment. I talk about how to stay motivated through your moment-by-moment efforts to pay attention to your present experience. I cover how to find patience and focus, and how to navigate your way through various kinds of challenges to mindfulness.

In This Chapter

- Different ways to think of "practice"
- Keeping up your motivation and interest
- Knowing whether you're on the right track
- Challenging yourself and sustaining practice long term
- Identifying things that deepen and strengthen your mindfulness

Finally, you get guidelines for how to develop and strengthen a lasting practice, including setting a regular schedule for formal mindfulness sessions, attending classes, and participating in a group.

Challenges to Mindfulness

Most people find the effort to be mindful frustrating at some point. Sometimes they find it seems like an insurmountable task and no matter how hard they try, they can't make any headway. If your experience is anything like this, it may feel like mindfulness has simply made you aware of how often you're *not* paying attention. Despite your intention, you may still arrive somewhere after a commute and realize you don't remember the ride. You may still find yourself acting out habits before you realize it, or getting stressed because you can't let go of thoughts about the future.

The primary reason mindfulness can be difficult is that your mind is so used to operating in non-mindful ways. The many reasons people aren't naturally mindful are described in Chapter 2. In addition, you probably weren't raised to be mindful, and even if you were, you probably weren't subjected to the incredible amount of discipline it would take to make a child or young adult learn to control his or her mind. You may have spent many years without making any conscious effort at mindfulness at all—that's 16 hours a day, 7 days a week, 365 days a year. That much thinking has created a lot of habit energy, which you aren't going to change with a few minutes of practice each day.

It's Not as Bad as You Might Think

The great thing is that the benefits of mindfulness aren't limited to people who can keep their minds from wandering. As long as you *try* to keep your mind from wandering, you'll see your life more clearly and learn things. If you practice regularly, you'll find yourself more mindful and less stressed in general—even if your conscious evaluation of your meditation is that it's not very good. If you engage in regular mindfulness practices like the ones in Chapter 19, you'll find yourself more present throughout your day, even if you don't remember to do them as often as you'd like, and even if you only manage to be present for a few seconds at a time.

Mindfulness isn't just about increasing the number of minutes each day you manage to pay attention to what's going on. That's one aspect, but the other aspect is about shifting your whole attitude toward your mind and your life. You decide your life is worth being present for. You start looking at the state of your mind as just one aspect of your present experience. You end up paying less attention to it as a reflection of reality, and more attention to it as a factor that contributes to your happiness or suffering—a factor over which you have at least some influence. You start noticing the content and function of your mind largely determine the flavor of your experiences, not vice versa. All of these things are very significant and beneficial.

KEEP IN MIND

Merely the intention to be more mindful makes you more aware of everything, including the fact that you might have just come out of a lapse in mindfulness. Your intention provides a context for your experience; if you had no ideas whatsoever about how you wanted your mind to be, how would you know whether you were on the right track? Constant, sustained, receptive awareness of the present moment is an ideal—one few people, if any, actually reach. This shouldn't be discouraging, however. Are you going to stop practicing something like kindness because you aren't perfectly kind all the time? Of course not.

The Paradox of Effort and Noneffort

The great irony of mindfulness is that it requires effort, but that effort is primarily about giving up your habitual kind of effort! Any moment you're mindful is due more to what you *aren't* doing—ruminating on the past, anticipating the future, worrying, planning, fantasizing, judging—than to any special mental technique or discipline. In a sense it takes no effort at all to simply be aware; it just takes effort to let go of your habitual activity and self-concern.

In your moment-by-moment practice, it's good to keep in mind this paradox of effort and non-effort. You have to make an effort to change your habitual way of being, but as soon as you remember to be mindful, all you have to do is relax into noneffort. This is a little like someone asking you to physically relax completely—it can actually be very hard to do, even if you're getting a massage or soaking in a spa. The "effort" to let go and trust the present moment completely can be quite a challenge. On the other hand, it may be a relief to know that ultimately mindfulness isn't a special skill; it's just letting go.

The Illusion of Thought-Free Bliss

Another challenge to mindfulness is holding some idea about what it's supposed to feel like. Books and instructions are meant to guide and inspire you, but sometimes they can give you two erroneous impressions: (1) there's a "correct" way to be mindful, and if you succeed at it, you'll experience long periods of unbroken, blissful calm that is free from thoughts and feelings; (2) most people who practice mindfulness have mastered this "correct" way. It's easy to conclude that if sustained mindful bliss eludes you, it's because you don't understand how to practice mindfulness correctly, or you lack the ability to do it.

In reality, everyone struggles with mindfulness. Books, guided meditations, and teachers try to give you an idea of what you're working toward, so naturally they describe what's possible. It is indeed possible to be wholeheartedly engaged in the present moment—calm, at ease, and less caught up in your thoughts and feelings. However, even mindfulness teachers aren't sitting on their cushions enjoying continuous, effortless stillness. They're experiencing thoughts, resistance, and desires just as you are. If they weren't, they wouldn't be able to guide you in mindfulness practice!

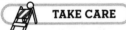 **TAKE CARE**

> It isn't helpful to guess what other people's experience of mindfulness or medita-
> tion is. You might ask them; hearing about the challenges others face can be useful.
> However, ultimately you have to forget about anyone else and just concentrate on
> your own experience. If mindfulness makes your life any better at all, just practice it
> without comparing yourself to others.

True mindfulness is usually *not* thought-free, and it's rarely blissful. On occasion you might experience both of these states, and some people experience them more than others, but they're not the goals of mindfulness practice. The goal is to be receptively aware of your present experience—whatever that is. Sometimes that might include a busy mind, worry, sadness, or sleepiness. The key is to give up resistance to what *is,* not to resist it even more because it doesn't fit with your ideas about what "good" mindfulness should be like. Doing that will only get in the way of your efforts!

Staying on Track Long Term

Sometimes it can be difficult to judge whether your mindfulness practice is on the right track. As described earlier, comparing your experience to others or to an ideal can be problematic. Still, you need some way to know whether you're going about things in a fruitful way, or how to deepen your mindfulness. While ideals can simply get in the way, it *is* possible to become more and more mindful, and to discover new ways of living you didn't even imagine before. If you have a sense that your mindfulness practice is "good enough," that's fine, but you'll also be unlikely to experience the incredible things deep mindfulness practice has to offer. How do you keep "progressing" with your practice without getting stuck in judgment or attached to ideals?

Just Look at the Results

Fortunately, you can trust your own intuition when it comes to guiding your mindfulness. All you have to do is look at the results of any particular technique, effort, or approach in your life. Over time you'll learn to notice whether your mind is wandering, or whether it's open and receptive to your present experience. You'll know whether certain practices result in less stress and more equanimity in your life. You'll notice positive results like feeling more patient with people or experiencing a deeper sense of satisfaction with your life.

If you see any of these results, your mindfulness is on the right track! It doesn't really matter all that much whether your moment-by-moment experience of mindfulness matches what you hear from others or what you read. It doesn't really matter whether it fits your own ideals or hopes. Your conscious evaluation of your practice might inspire you to try to remember mindfulness more often, seek support for your practice, or experiment with new techniques. However, this conscious judgment about your practice is a little like judging a book from its cover—it reflects a guess about the important stuff, based on superficial information.

MINDFUL EXERCISE

If someone you trusted as an authority were to tell you that you were practicing mindfulness *exactly* as it should be practiced—that you were actually quite good at it—how would you feel? Take a moment to recall your recent experiences of mindfulness and meditation, along with your general (perhaps involuntary) judgments about them. If you knew for sure you were practicing correctly, how would that make you feel? Content or disappointed? Is your mindfulness practice based in any way on a subtle hope you can perfect the method and attain the rewards you want? Can you let go even further of evaluations and expectations? If you do, what does that do to your experience of this moment?

On the other hand, you can also trust your own sense of what gets in the way of your mindfulness. You can trust your intuition that a given technique, effort, or approach *isn't* beneficial to your practice. For example, do certain activities or trains of thought encourage you to succumb to old habits instead of being mindfully aware? Do you need to make mindfulness more of a priority in your life? Does a certain technique make you more resistant and agitated instead of letting you relax into the present moment? Whatever you think, you're probably right—no one knows better than you. The question is whether you'll acknowledge what you know and act on it in a way that increases and supports your mindfulness.

Always More to See Clearly

You don't have to worry about progress in your mindfulness practice as long as you keep asking yourself a question like this: "What do I still not see clearly?" There's always *something* you can see more clearly through mindful awareness. There's always something more to understand, and greater intimacy and freedom to experience. Asking yourself a question about what you haven't yet seen or mastered keeps you moving forward, pushing the edges of your practice, and challenging yourself. It also keeps you humble and helps you avoid complacency.

The good thing about continually improving your mindfulness practice this way is that it's not about a goal or an ideal. You aren't setting up a standard and then comparing yourself to it. It's not that you're still inadequate but if you try hard enough you'll achieve what you want and you can stop working. Instead, you're acknowledging there's no end to this process. As long as you sincerely look toward what you haven't yet mastered but would like to, your mindfulness practice will continue to deepen and develop without any need for evaluation, judgment, or impatience.

Effort and Innovation

Essentially, long-term mindfulness practice requires you to keep up diligent effort without expecting to reach any particular goals. This isn't to say you won't experience rewards or benefits, but they won't be the kinds of things you can collect and keep. If you don't keep up your effort, you'll lose the benefits—just as you'll lose your fitness if you stop exercising. Even if you complete a mindfulness course, get a credential, or become a teacher, none of these tangible successes help you be mindful. The moment-by-moment, lifelong practice is something you just keep doing. After a while, it helps if you stop worrying about progress at all and just adopt mindfulness as part of your lifestyle—something you would do even if you didn't experience rewards from it, like being honest or responsible.

 KEEP IN MIND

On the other hand, you may find goals help motivate you. If they do, by all means go ahead and set some. One of my teachers called this a "positive use of greed." If trying to do something like completely letting go of stimulus-independent thinking for longer and longer periods encourages you to practice, then go ahead and try. Just make sure you stay receptive to all of the results, not just the ones you're looking for. Striving for too specific a goal can sometimes make you neglect other important areas of practice.

Over the long term it's also important to be creative and innovative in your practice. Think of it like learning to be an artist, and your medium is your own body-mind. You can learn techniques others have found useful, look for guidance from other "artists," and study the history of the "art." Ultimately, though, you seek to manifest mastery and beauty in your own life, in your own way. Create your own mindfulness techniques, exercises, and practices. If the prescribed methods aren't working for you, experiment and find out what does. For example, if you find it helps your mind to settle if you imagine being in your favorite safe place, go ahead and do that. If you find any mental imagery to be distracting and it helps more to center your awareness in your body, do that. Refer back to the section in this chapter on looking at results; if something helps you be receptively aware of the present moment, don't worry about whether it's correct mindfulness practice. It is!

Strengthening Your Practice

In this section I suggest various options you have for strengthening your mindfulness. The ability to be mindful is similar to other disciplines or skills in that the more time and energy you spend on it, the better you'll get at it. On the other hand, there's no minimum amount of practice you should do, below which mindfulness doesn't do you any good. It's completely up to you. You can try to do a task mindfully once a week, or you can live in a residential practice place where you focus on mindfulness 24/7, or anything in between. You're limited only by your level of interest and commitment and, of course, by your life circumstances.

Regular Formal Sessions

It's been mentioned several times already in this book, but it's worth mentioning again the value of spending time in formal mindfulness practice of some kind. This can be meditation (see Chapter 8), or doing simple tasks where the main point is to be as mindful as you can be for the duration of the activity (see Chapter 4). You can make an effort to be receptively aware all day long (see Chapter 19), but unless you're a master of mindfulness, you're unlikely to notice how present you're actually being in the midst of activity. Being surrounded by distractions or trying to get something done makes mindfulness more challenging. It's extremely useful to set everything else aside for a little while and focus on simply being present.

MINDFUL EXERCISE

If meditation seems like work, it can be hard to make yourself do it—especially if you have lots of other demands on your time and energy. Instead of thinking of meditation as another task, try simply sitting down and doing nothing for a little while. Don't have any agenda at all—except to do *nothing*. Just put your life on pause and try to relax completely. Don't even try to control your mind. Do this for 2 to 5 minutes, longer if you feel like it. If you find yourself eager to jump up and get busy again, or to reach for some distraction, just try to think of these few minutes as a well-deserved break.

The length of formal sessions isn't so important, although the longer the better, generally speaking. Still, regularity is essential. If you have any trouble getting yourself to do formal mindfulness sessions, think of an amount of time to spend in such practice that seems ridiculously easy to you. Five minutes a day, four days a week? Sitting with a group twice a month? Each person will have a different idea about what sounds easy, but all you have to do is find what sounds easy to you. Not "good," virtuous, or ideal—just a little more than you do right now. Then do this amount of formal practice over a set period of time, such as a week or a month, and don't worry about increasing it. Instead, be as mindful as you can about your experience and the effects on your life. Mindfulness tends to inspire more mindfulness.

Take an MBSR Course

The eight-week course called Mindfulness-Based Stress Reduction (MBSR) is highly recommended. It has been taken by more than 20,000 people since it was created in 1979, and its benefits have been the subject of many scientific studies (see Chapter 1). It costs money and requires a significant commitment of time, but it will give you a solid grounding in mindfulness practice. Course instructors undergo extensive training and are certified by the Center for Mindfulness in Medicine, Health Care, and Society, which is part of the University of Massachusetts Medical School. There are qualified teachers offering the course all over the world; simply search online for a class near you.

The class generally meets weekly for around 2 hours, and there's one additional all-day class (or retreat). New practices are introduced in class. Participants engage in practice together, share experiences, and are able to ask lots of questions. In addition, participants commit to at least 45 minutes a day of formal mindfulness practice consisting of a guided meditation, mindful yoga, or silent meditation. There are usually also readings and some other kinds of exercises to do outside of class.

Groups Practicing Mindfulness

Most people find it hard to sustain a mindfulness practice over time, even if they've taken an MBSR course, unless they regularly practice with a group. Humans are social creatures; you may find yourself showing up for a mindfulness session just because other people are showing up. You'll probably find yourself able to meditate longer and stay more still in a group because of what I like to call "positive peer pressure." (If they can do it, so can you!) Sometimes the practice of mindfulness seems more accessible or legitimate because you encounter it in person with other real, living people. It can help you face your own challenges if you hear how other people have dealt with theirs, and the guidance of an experienced teacher can be invaluable. Practicing with a group can also make mindfulness fun, and challenge you to study and try new things.

 KEEP IN MIND

Mindfulness has its roots in Buddhism, and in that tradition practicing with others is considered essential. The Buddhist path is considered to consist of the "three treasures" of buddha, dharma, and sangha. These terms can be interpreted many ways, but one way to look at them is to think of buddha as your ability to wake up and see your life clearly, dharma as the method of waking up, and sangha as the community of people practicing that method together.

If you're resistant to participating in a group, you're not alone. Despite any wariness you might feel, however, it's worth investigating a few groups (assuming you're fortunate enough to live near some). Your local MBSR teacher might be able to refer you to one. Look online for mindfulness or meditation centers, groups, or meet-ups. Most groups are open and inviting, and are used to new people coming and going. They're generally very accepting of different approaches to life and are unlikely to pressure you to commit to theirs. If you encounter anything that makes you uncomfortable or confuses you, either ask about it or find a different group.

You might also try attending a Buddhist center. Sometimes completely secular mindfulness groups can be hard to find. Keep in mind Buddhism is a nontheistic religion, and some people would call it more of a philosophy or way of life than a religion. A Zen or Vipassana center will generally be most compatible with a more secular approach to mindfulness, and these centers will generally be very happy for you to meditate and study with them even if you aren't interested in Buddhism. If you're unable to get to a group, you might want to check out Treeleaf Zendo (treeleaf.org), which has regularly scheduled communal meditation sessions (done by video) as well as a discussion forum and other resources.

The Least You Need to Know

- Mindfulness is like other kinds of skills or disciplines in that the more you practice it, the better you get at it.
- Mindfulness is *unlike* other kinds of skills or disciplines in that it's an effort to *give up* the habitual kind of effort that involves striving after goals and ideals.
- If you experience thought-free or blissful times in your practice, that's great—but mindfulness is about being present for your experience even if it's not thought-free or pleasant.
- You can trust your own intuition about whether you're being mindful and what helps (or hinders) your mindfulness.
- Be innovative and open-minded when it comes to finding ways to strengthen your practice—create new approaches, take a course, or try participating in a group. Whatever works!

Mindful Ethics

Discussions of ethics aren't often included in books on mindfulness, but an effort to live ethically is essential to the aspiration I'm assuming lies behind your interest in being more mindful: greater happiness for self and others. As mentioned in Chapter 3, if you're only interested in attention training in order to improve your performance at various tasks or increase your enjoyment of life, that's fine—you'll still find many useful things in this book. However, if you want to see your life clearly and consequently make wiser choices, you'll need to take your behavior into consideration.

In this chapter I explain how ethical behavior supports your efforts to be mindful, and how giving up self-centeredness and taking the happiness of others into account actually increases your own happiness. I cover how ethics is about taking care of relationships, and explain the usefulness of adopting ethical guidelines for your life. I also present a set of ethical guidelines you might consider working into your life—if you haven't already.

In This Chapter

- Creating a set of ethics based on mindfulness
- How ethics are all about taking care of relationships
- In what ways established guidelines can be useful
- Some classic ethical guidelines to consider
- Ethical questions as reminders to be mindful

Does It Result in Greater Happiness?

Ethics are typically defined as rules of behavior based on judgments of what constitutes morally good versus bad behavior. You may feel a resistance to discussions of ethics because of how often people decide what is good or bad and then try to impose their ideas on others. Any resistance you might feel could also be due to the fact that when ethics come from a religion, a culture, your family of origin, or an institution, they often come along with a sense of duty, obligation, and judgment. On the other side of coin, however, those who champion ethics point out that if everyone picks and chooses which ethical guidelines to follow and when, self-concern can end up winning out over taking responsibility or helping others.

Mindful ethics are different. They aren't imposed from the outside, and individual discernment and responsibility are essential. They also aren't arbitrary. Ethics based in mindfulness are guidelines for behavior based in clearly seeing what does and doesn't lead toward greater happiness. Ethical decisions have to be made with mindfulness in every new situation you encounter because there are many factors to consider. This means making such decisions is never a simple process. Still, there *are* patterns. To ignore them would mean turning a blind eye to some of the truths of your life.

It's All About Relationship

At the center of the patterns of cause and effect in the human sphere are the observations I discussed in Chapter 3: all people just want to be happy, and most human misery is caused by grasping after short-term, small-scale happiness at the cost of long-term, greater-scale happiness (which includes the happiness of others). For example, you may spend too much money, cheat on your partner, or steal something for the sake of short-term pleasure, but then end up suffering from the consequences for a long time. As a society, we're using up irreplaceable resources for our short-term benefit without much concern for the future. It seems human beings are handicapped when it comes to objectively balancing costs and benefits over the short versus the long term, or on an immediate (obvious) versus large scale.

 TAKE CARE

You may find yourself excusing certain actions because you don't care about the relationships they compromise. Perhaps you have no interest in maintaining any connection with that annoying neighbor, any members of that terrible political party, or with that giant, corrupt company. Still, when you feel no need to act ethically with regard to these parties, it just proves the point that ethics are about taking care of relationships. Write off ethics, write off the relationships.

Why should you care about the long term, or the large scale? This brings me to another basic human truth you can personally verify for yourself through mindfulness, if you aren't convinced of it already: your happiness isn't independent of the happiness of others, the happiness of your future self, or the happiness of the planet. If you stay focused only on your own immediate, short-term happiness, you can deny this truth for a while, but eventually you'll pay a high price for ignoring it. This cost will be high enough you'll look back and realize you made some selfish, unnecessary decisions you really wish you hadn't.

What is that cost? Ethics is essentially about nurturing relationships instead of being primarily motivated by self-concern. The cost of operating unethically—that is, based on short-term, small-scale interests—is loss of connection and intimacy. This includes compromised relationships with other people and animals, with yourself, and with your moment-by-moment experience of living.

You don't have to accept this description of ethics; you can simply watch the results of your actions with mindfulness. When you steal, lie, cheat, gossip, or indulge anger, what happens? A typical nonmindful evaluation of the results of such actions focuses on self-justification, or on whether or not you got caught. Alternatively, if you stay present with your experience before, during, and after your actions with receptive, honest awareness, you'll notice other things. There may be people you can't look in the eye anymore, a sense of anxiety about being found out, or a decreasing ability to stop yourself from acting out certain negative behaviors. A classic example of this principle in action is described by the saying "The thief looks behind the door." Your actions affect the state of your body-mind, even if no one else knows about them.

Whether you consciously care about a relationship or not, it's to your benefit to take care of it because scientific research suggests human beings are hardwired for empathy. You actually can't cause someone else stress or misery without feeling some negative effects yourself. In order to cause harm to other living things, you need to override your natural compassion. (Compassion means "suffering with" because you witness the pain of others with empathy.) The more you suppress or ignore empathy, the harder it is to feel emotionally connected to anything.

How Ethics Support Mindfulness

In a very pragmatic way, behaving ethically is a good idea because it generally means you make less of a mess of your life. It's hard enough to calm your mind, maintain receptivity, and focus on the present when things are going smoothly. Imagine trying to do this when people are angry with you, you have to worry about someone discovering your lies, you're deep in debt because of poor choices, or you're in prison. Life throws you enough challenges without making things worse in ways you don't have to.

Honoring your relationships with ethical behavior is very conducive to the receptive attitude necessary for mindfulness. Lack of ethics creates conflict and puts you on the defensive (or offensive). The degree of conflict can be subtle, extreme, or somewhere in between, but it makes you much less likely to be able to relax into the present moment. Instead, you'll be anticipating future interactions, justifying yourself, rehashing old stories, or lamenting past actions or events. Generally speaking, conflict is agitating, even if it's relatively minor. For example, think of snapping in anger at a co-worker. This situation is likely to leap into your mind later, when you're trying to be mindful, because of the low-level anxiety you feel about the next time you're going to see this person.

 **KEEP IN MIND**

The ancient Buddhists identified one of the greatest rewards of ethical behavior as "freedom from remorse." It's very conducive to a calm, receptive state of mind to know you're doing your best, you've come clean about your mistakes, and you've made amends as best you can.

Finally, any use of mindfulness to reduce your stress or make you happier is going to be of limited usefulness if you're just treating symptoms and refusing to address underlying causes. Some of the stressors and problems in your life you won't be able to do much about, but if you want to get your life more in order it helps to have ethical guidelines to rely on. Ethics aren't necessarily going to help you solve issues like illness, unemployment, or loneliness, but when you're facing such challenges it's good to keep your relationships honest and healthy. It's also good to be standing on firm ethical ground so you can be as present and mindful as possible as you address the underlying causes of your stress or unhappiness.

Relating to Rules and Guidelines

Before I get to specific ethical guidelines, I should say something about the value of having a set of rules you commit to following. Ultimately, you can verify the value of ethical behavior and the validity of particular guidelines through mindful observation of your own life. However, before you've developed a deep and honest mindfulness practice, you're likely to succumb to habit energy, shortsightedness, and self-interest in moments where critical ethical decisions need to be made.

It's much more effective to set some rules for yourself, follow them as best you can, and then observe the results. Wise people throughout history—religious and secular—have found certain kinds of behavior tend to lead to suffering, while others tend to lead to greater happiness. You can verify their conclusions for yourself by mindfully following their recommendations, rather than acting with self-interest to prove to yourself it produces negative results.

 **TAKE CARE**

It's just not practical to start from zero every time you're faced, for example, with a question of whether to indulge anger—should you, or shouldn't you? On what criteria do you base such decisions? How angry you feel? How likely you are to make your point or get what you want? Your guess about how much harm will be done? Whether or not you care about the person on whom you'd like to unleash some of your anger? Such considerations invite a focus on self-interest, or at the very least a decision made while you're upset and biased (see Chapter 14).

It's probably best to think of any ethical rules as "guidelines." This isn't because you should consider your ethics to be optional or unimportant, but rather because the most important things are the greater happiness of self and others and taking care of relationships. On occasion you might need to break one of your ethical rules out of compassion. For example, you may make an effort not to kill but decide to euthanize an animal who is suffering without hope of recovery. When you go ahead and act against your own ethical principles, it's important to pay very close attention to make sure you're acting out of compassion, not selfishness or shortsightedness. It's also important to be ready to take responsibility for the consequences of your action; just because it was done out of compassion doesn't mean there won't be some negative results.

Some Ethical Guidelines to Consider

What I offer in the following sections is a set of 10 ethical guidelines adapted from Buddhism. They have been followed by Buddhists for thousands of years, and represent a distillation of many guidelines for human behavior down to what is most essential. All of us, when we are concerned about our own well-being, tend toward certain actions of body, speech, or mind. People have been struggling with the negative repercussions of such actions for millennia, and those who have studied their lives with mindful clarity have decided these actions—however tempting at times—are just not worth it.

At the core of all of these ethical guidelines is the discovery that acting on self-interest at the expense of others always has negative repercussions. Not only does it tend to cause disharmony in your relationships, it feeds the delusion that your happiness is independent from that of others. It denies the truth of greater happiness, which applies in the longest term, at the largest scale, and includes the happiness of others. Essentially, you opt for small-scale (usually selfish), short-term happiness, but in the final analysis this happiness won't compare to the lasting joy and ease of greater happiness (see Chapter 12). Finally, breaking these ethical guidelines in extreme ways can also get you into serious trouble, so even your small-scale, short-term happiness will be compromised.

Don't Kill Carelessly

The Buddhist version of this guideline is "do not kill," but of course, you have to kill some things just to live, even if it's only vegetables. Ironically, organic farmers rely on blood and bone meal, animal by-products, to supplement the soil that produces vegetables. If you look closely, no one is able to live on this planet without some impact on other living things.

The important thing is that you don't kill selfishly or carelessly. When you do this, you cut yourself off from other forms of life by placing your needs above theirs without consideration or apology. You devalue other lives, perhaps to the extent you don't even think about them being sacrificed for your well-being. The more connected you feel to something, the harder it is to kill it. It's also true that if you kill something, it's hard to feel connected to it. In order to do the act of killing, you have to harden your heart or turn a blind eye to the other being's suffering. In summary, then, careless killing cuts you off from the world.

 MINDFUL EXERCISE

Make a habit of paying attention whenever you have the option of taking or saving the life of a living thing, or you benefit from a life that's been taken. Capture a spider in your house and take it outside instead of killing it. When you cut flowers, take note of a life being ended. When you eat fish or meat, take a moment to acknowledge the life that was sacrificed for you. Notice when you put on something made of leather. You don't have to add a judgment about whether what you're doing is right or wrong, just let yourself be aware of the intersection of your life with another living (or formerly living) thing.

What is killing carefully? It's deciding a life needs to be ended for the greater happiness of self and other, but also committing to not turning away from the suffering the killing will cause. It means taking responsibility for any negative results, and respecting the life being taken. You feel gratitude for the other being's sacrifice, and try to minimize the suffering it will experience. The act of killing carefully is epitomized by the hunter who kills an animal in order to feed his family, but who takes a moment to look into the animal's eyes and say a prayer of gratitude over the body.

At a more subtle level, killing is cutting your connection with anything through rejection or lack of respect. You can kill someone's generosity by rejecting their gift, or kill your connection with someone through hatred. You can kill (or try to kill) certain parts of yourself you don't like, or kill someone's idea by ridiculing it. Any careless act of rejection or violence has negative repercussions for self and other.

Don't Steal

You may figure stealing is okay if the thing being stolen is inconsequential or the person (or institution) from whom you're stealing doesn't really need it. However, while it's true certain acts of stealing may result in more harm than others, judging for yourself in any given situation whether stealing is okay opens up a whole can of worms, as discussed earlier. *You* get to decide what to steal and when, and you're likely to make such decisions based on your own self-interest.

Stealing is all about acting on self-interest over consideration for others. You decide you want something and you want it now, and instead of asking for it (probably because you know you won't get it), waiting for it, or earning it, you just take it. In the process you either disrespect someone else by deciding any negative effects on them don't matter, or you decide *for* them the negative effects *shouldn't* matter. If you've ever had something stolen, you know how this feels. Even if what was stolen was small, the sense of being violated or disempowered can be strong.

What harm is done when you're stealing from a person or a company that has more than their share of wealth, or won't even notice? If you examine your actions with mindfulness, you'll notice stealing has an effect on you and others, even if you aren't creating a situation of literal suffering or need. You're essentially saying with your actions that you're willing to break the social contract any time you feel it isn't fair or important. You'll inevitably feel a separation from those from whom you're stealing; to justify yourself you have to believe they deserve it, they're wrong or selfish, or they're not worthy of your respect. You figure you can gain happiness at the expense of others, which violates the principle of greater happiness (see mindfulness principle #2, Chapter 3).

Don't Lie

The guideline to refrain from lying is similar to the guideline about not stealing in that lying, like stealing, is usually based in self-interest. Some lies are more significant and potentially harmful than others, but almost all of them encourage you to jeopardize the harmony in your relationships in favor of your own pleasure, comfort, or convenience. If you find yourself tempted to lie, look at the reasons why. Chances are good you're trying to avoid taking responsibility for something you've done, curry favor with someone so you'll get the benefit of their affection or support, or get out of doing something you don't want to do.

KEEP IN MIND

Sometimes even small lies are a way to avoid letting people see who you really are for fear they might dislike you or get upset with you. Making a habit of this over time can make it harder and harder to be honest, and it can eventually compromise relationships.

What about little "white" lies? On occasion it might be more compassionate to speak falsely than honestly, but it's important to be honest with yourself regarding who is being served by the lie. Are you trying to spare someone's feelings in an instance where the stakes aren't that high? Maybe your co-worker's cookies weren't very good, but you tell her they were because you're grateful she offered them. In this instance, you might even say you're being honest about your gratitude instead of giving your honest critique of the cookies.

Don't Indulge Anger

I discussed working with anger in Chapter 14, where I pointed out anger can be useful information when you *think* something is under threat and needs to be protected. This is why this ethical guideline is phrased "don't *indulge* anger." You probably can't do anything about anger arising, and you don't necessarily need to. The question is what you do in response to the emotion. If you believe your angry view of the world reflects reality, you'll feel justified in acting on it, or even compelled to do so. Unfortunately, anger gives you tunnel vision (the opposite of mindful awareness), so any actions that indulge anger are likely to be only partially informed and potentially destructive.

The more you indulge anger, the easier it is to keep doing so. Depending on how severe and fiery your anger is, you may end up causing serious damage that you later regret deeply. Even small indulgences of anger can make people wary of engaging with you, or encourage them to lie to you. It can be hard to acknowledge anger but not indulge it, but it may be one of the most fruitful mindfulness practices you ever do. If you can simply *stop* instead of acting out or expressing anger, you have a chance of waiting out the emotion. Then, when you're calmer and more mindful, you can determine whether something does indeed need protection, and how best to do it.

Be Careful with Sex

There is an incredible amount of energy and complexity around sex. It can become an obsession. Longing for it can drive people to desperate actions that usually involve breaking other ethical guidelines. It's intimately tied up with matters of love and intimacy, but it also has an animal aspect that can lead to great misunderstanding between individuals with different views of it. Sex helps maintain the bond between couples, but it can also be means of heartbreaking betrayal.

Throughout history, humans have tried to implement damage control on sex by making up all kinds of rules about it—when to do it, with whom, and in what circumstances. The mindful way is different. It's risky because it asks each individual to examine their own behavior carefully instead of suggesting simple rules to follow. What you're asked to do is observe your actions of body, speech, and mind around sex, and to try to act in a way that respects others and considers their happiness as well as yours.

Being careful means to err on the side of caution, despite the fact that it might mean compromising your short-term pleasure. Generally speaking, sex has the least risk of harm when it occurs in a committed relationship—where two people know each other, and want to take care of each other. The lower the level of intimacy between the participants, the greater the risk of misunderstanding, or of one person being left to deal with repercussions without support. Also, if you find yourself tempted to break other ethical guidelines in order to obtain sex, you can take that as a red flag that you're probably placing self-interest over the welfare of others. If you operate without hard-and-fast rules in this area of your life and want to engage it with mindfulness, it will be necessary to be diligently honest with yourself about your motives.

Be Careful with Intoxicants

Like sex, intoxicants can be a source of great pleasure or great misery, depending on how they're used. What's ideal is a balance between the enjoyment or relaxation you might get from intoxicants and your need to stay clearheaded and take care of self and others. While intoxicants usually mess with your mind and make mindfulness more difficult, it's possible to stay as mindful as you can and recognize when you've had enough. This requires you to be present and aware, just as with any other kind of mindfulness practice. Perhaps you know two drinks is enough, and that more than that turns into many drinks, ridiculous behavior, and/or a hangover. If you maintain some mindfulness, you'll recognize when part of you is thinking a third drink would be great fun, and then have some perspective when you make your decision.

 MINDFUL EXERCISE

If you regularly use some kind of intoxicant, try to maintain mindful awareness as you do so. An intoxicant can be any substance or activity that alters your experience of life in a way that's rewarding, but which also encourages you to continue indulging in it. In a safe and typical situation, allow yourself to imbibe or engage in your usual intoxicant, but watch carefully what it does. What are the rewards? What does the intoxicant allow you to access, let go of, or do? Is there anything about your life as experienced sober that you're avoiding, resisting, or rejecting? Just notice, without judging.

The problem, of course, is that intoxicants are intoxicating. Generally speaking, if you indulge in enough of an intoxicant, you'll reach a state where you really can't be responsible or mindful at all, and where you're likely to keep indulging further no matter what's happening. You certainly don't have to be a teetotaler if you want a mindfulness practice, but getting intoxicated to the point of oblivion is definitely the opposite of cultivating receptive awareness of the present moment. Of course, the irony may be that you're drawn to intoxicants *because* they free you from your regrets, worries about the future, and inhibiting fears. The good news is that mindfulness can do this for you, too—and it isn't intoxicating. Of course, it takes more patience and work.

It's good to keep in mind it's not just alcohol and drugs that can be intoxicating. Anything that provides you with a compelling distraction from your everyday life can be an intoxicant, including gambling, video games, shopping, social media, and television. When you notice a tendency for overindulgence, regret, or repeated interference with your responsibilities and commitments (including those to yourself), you're probably dealing with something that serves you as an intoxicant. Then you can use mindfulness in the process of compassionate change described in Chapter 13.

Be Faithful in Relationships

As discussed earlier, ethics are all about taking care of relationships. This guideline makes that explicit, and invites you to consider making faithfulness your default. Exactly what this means will differ greatly in different circumstances, but it generally means honoring your commitments, being thoughtful of—and sensitive to—others, and treating people with respect instead of just using them. It's being nice, but it's also more than that. When you come to a choice about doing something that will serve your self-interest but may hurt, offend, confuse, or otherwise negatively impact another, you err on the side of restraint in order to be faithful in your relationships.

In some non-Western cultures, people are strongly conditioned and pressured to prioritize their relationships over their own self-interest. This can be taken to extremes where the individual isn't allowed to consider himself as part of the "happiness equation," but instead must constantly override his own needs. If someone does this long enough, he ironically jeopardizes his relationships because he hasn't taken care of himself—so there's more than one way to break this ethical guideline. However, although there may be rare examples of people operating too selflessly in Western culture, most of us need to work on decreasing self-concern in favor of taking care of our relationships.

Don't Dwell on Past Mistakes

Most of the time, when people dwell on past mistakes, they're doing so because they have some hope it will prevent future ones. If the mistakes are your own, you may ruminate on them or talk about them in an effort to figure out what went wrong, make a plan for the future free of such mistakes, and perhaps also make yourself feel bad so you'll feel motivated to change. If you're dwelling on someone else's mistakes, at some level—perhaps unconsciously—you probably hope pointing out the mistakes will make the person realize they were wrong. Even if you aren't sharing your wise insights with the person who supposedly made a mistake or displayed a shortcoming, perhaps if you dwell on the issue long enough you'll manage to prepare a good argument—just in case you get the chance present it, and encourage the person to dwell on their mistakes.

Mindful observation of the way things really work reveals a remarkable discovery: it's not necessary to dwell on past mistakes in order to learn or change! As stated in mindfulness principle #3, *change occurs naturally when you see clearly what leads to greater happiness.* As long as you keep trying your best to see things clearly, you'll notice the negative results of some of your choices and behaviors, and you'll be inspired to change.

 **KEEP IN MIND**

> Sometimes the habit of criticizing others in conversation is something people do to connect. As you and another person vehemently agree so-and-so is truly arrogant or incompetent, the two of you can feel united against a foe. You have common ground, support each other, and have something to talk about. Shifting away from this habit of speech can be disorienting in certain friendships. It usually helps to develop curiosity about your friends and ask them more questions about their lives—this creates connection without discussing the faults of others.

In the case of dwelling on the past mistakes of others, not only does this prove to be ineffective most of the time, it can even be counterproductive if you end up angering, alienating, or discouraging someone with your criticism or gossip. It may be necessary, occasionally, to discuss someone's faults, but it takes mindful observation to know whether you're doing it for the benefit of others, or just to satisfy your own anger or indignation. If all you're doing is dwelling on someone's faults in order to get people on your side or discredit someone, it's another example of putting self-interest before concern for others—something that's bound to have negative effects at some point, even if it's just that the people you talk to will worry you're going to criticize *them* someday.

Don't Compare Yourself to Others

This ethical guideline is closely related to the previous one about not dwelling on past mistakes, but it focuses on the temptation to base your sense of self-worth on being better than other people. Conversely, you may suffer from a low sense of self-worth because you compare yourself to others and conclude they're better than you are. The essential point of this ethical guideline is that, either way, comparing yourself to others is indulging in a whole lot more self-concern than is beneficial to you *or* others. When you do this, you tend to stop seeing people clearly, and respecting them for who they are. Instead, you simply evaluate what about them bolsters or threatens your sense of self in comparison.

Breaking this ethical guideline can be subtle. It may come out in speech, but it often manifests only in your thoughts and feelings. When you see someone who is your height but heavier than you, you may think, "Ha, at least I'm not *that* fat." When you see someone struggling with their toddler, you may think with satisfaction that your parenting style is better. If you look closely, you may be shocked to find out how much of your self-identity is based on comparison: being richer, fitter, smarter, kinder, or more responsible, attractive, educated, or empathetic. Again, alternatively, you may constantly compare and find yourself wanting—and consequently feel discouraged or competitive.

Fortunately, it's possible to move in the world with confidence without having to build up a sense of self based on comparison. When you're being mindful, you're centered in your own experience. There's no room for comparison. Instead, there's receptive attention to what's most needed, and what *your* best response can be in the present moment. Ideas like "attractive," "good parent," or "responsible" are just concepts created to categorize your experience so you don't have to deal with the moment-by-moment ambiguity and challenge of life, as discussed in Chapter 9. In reality, sometimes you're responsible, and sometimes you could do better. Your "self" is an ever-changing flow that's not permanently better or worse than others.

Don't Be Stingy, Be Generous

Stinginess is self-concern when it comes to your resources, whether it's time, money, energy, attention, trust, or possessions. When you're presented with an opportunity to be generous but falter, you're typically worrying about yourself, or those with whom you identify. Will you have enough? Will too much be asked? Will someone develop an expectation and then you'll feel trapped and obligated? If someone gets something for free when you had to work for it, doesn't that compromise the system you're relying on?

 TAKE CARE

Sometimes giving your resources isn't the best choice. Someone may need to take more responsibility for themselves, or you may have to make a reasonable decision about how much you can give considering other commitments you have. This is always a matter of balance, but most of us tend to err on the side of stinginess when we don't really have to.

The problem with stinginess is that when someone would benefit from something you have but you withhold it, it affects both of you negatively. The other person has to go without, and they may feel discouraged about living in a world with so little generosity. You're affected by their struggle, whether you realize it or not. As discussed earlier, your happiness isn't independent of theirs. This is why you feel tightness inside when you walk by someone begging on the street without giving them anything. You're experiencing connection with the person in need even if you don't feel obligated to give.

On the other hand, the practice of generosity can be very transformative and enjoyable for all parties involved. You can experiment with this using mindfulness. Choose a time when you're actually feeling some lack. Perhaps you feel lonely, or worried about money. Then do something generous, like taking the time to call someone just to say hi, or buying someone a cup of coffee. Watch the effects on your body-mind. Does your sense of lack increase or decrease? Chances are it will decrease, which proves you have influence over your state of mind, and it's not entirely dependent on the amount of resources you have.

Ethics as a Subject for Mindfulness

One of the great benefits of trying to live according to some kind of ethical code is it gives you lots of subject matter for mindfulness throughout the course of your day. Ethics come up constantly, at least in subtle ways. For example, do you respond with generosity to your partner when they ask for something first thing in the morning? Do you indulge anger when your dog chews up your slipper? Do you join in on the gossip about someone that's happening in the break room at work? All day long you're presented with ethical decisions. These decision points can serve as reminders to be mindful!

While keeping ethical guidelines generally leads to greater happiness, in the context of mindfulness the emphasis is less on judging whether or not a particular action is right or wrong, and more on simply paying attention. Once you acknowledge, even to yourself, that you aspire to certain kinds of behavior, your aspirations will provide a context for your mindful observation of what really happens. It's important to maintain the receptive attitude discussed in Part 3 of this book in order to stay on track with mindfulness. This includes suspending judgment, cultivating acceptance, and approaching things with a sense of curiosity. If you get too caught up in judging yourself for keeping or breaking rules, you'll stop being able to see things clearly.

The Least You Need to Know

- Mindful ethics are based on the observation of what kinds of behaviors tend to result in greater happiness for self and others, and which do not.
- Ethics are all about taking care of relationships, and generally require you to take others into account before indulging your self-interest.
- Through mindfulness you can verify for yourself that happiness gained at the expense of others always has at least some negative consequences.
- Adopting a set of ethical guidelines for yourself can keep you honest, help you make better decisions, and provide you with an objective context for your behavior so you don't have to constantly judge right or wrong.
- Ethical issues arise all day long, every day—so they make great reminders to be mindful.

Meaning and Purpose

The importance of finding meaning and purpose in your life can't be underestimated. When you feel your life has significance and importance, and makes sense in the context of the world, you feel motivated and inspired. You're able to get through very difficult times without succumbing to despair. You find unique and rewarding ways to contribute to the world around you. Unfortunately, sometimes it can be challenging to find meaning and purpose in your life—or at least in a way that's strong and lasting.

In this chapter I discuss the importance of finding a sense of meaning, and the limitations of the ways people usually go about looking for it. Then I present how mindfulness can let you experience your life as deeply significant and valuable by revolutionizing your whole understanding of *meaning* and where it comes from. Meaning accessed through mindfulness is available to you regardless of your life circumstances, so I also talk about how to do this when faced with difficult times. Finally, this chapter includes a discussion of how to take this process one step further, and find a practical, rewarding purpose for your unique life.

In This Chapter

- Why it's important to have a sense of meaning in your life
- Typical ways of finding meaning and their limitations
- Accessing a sense of inherent and absolute value for your life
- Maintaining dignity and meaning through difficult times
- Finding a practical and rewarding purpose for your life

The Importance of Meaning

The question of meaning may or may not seem very important to you. Perhaps you feel fairly satisfied with your life and a search for meaning sounds like an unnecessary effort to explain, justify, or glorify life. However, if you're fairly happy, it may simply be you have ways of finding meaning in your life without even trying to consciously do so—because a life lived without a sense of meaning can be hard to endure. By meaning I'm simply referring to feeling like your life has significance, validity, worth, consequence, usefulness, or substance.

 MINDFUL EXERCISE

Take some time to imagine you're utterly convinced your life is *deeply* significant, and that all of your actions and choices are of the utmost importance to achieving something you unequivocally believe in—something critical, or something incredibly inspiring. If you don't make your unique contribution, people will suffer, or some wonderful thing will never come about. Can you imagine feeling so motivated that you leap out of bed in the morning, work efficiently because you don't want to waste any time, and diligently practice mindfulness so you can be extra perceptive and responsive? How does this imagined state compare with how you usually feel? Can you see in what way you've decided your life is *not* very significant?

There is ample evidence that many of us do *not* have a strong enough sense of meaning in our lives. According to the Centers for Disease Control and Prevention (CDC), in 2010 (the most recent year for which data is available), suicide was the tenth leading cause of death in the United States. In the United States alone there were 38,364 deaths by suicide, and almost 1 million attempts—and according to www.suicide.org, the United States ranks number 43 in terms of suicide rate by country. There may be exceptions, but for the most part each time someone has valued their own life so little as to kill themselves, they have concluded that the pain of living outweighed the benefits to self or other. Their sense of meaning or purpose wasn't sufficient to inspire further endurance of their difficulties.

Viktor Frankl suggested that much—or perhaps most—human despair arises from living without a sufficient sense of meaning. On the other hand, he believed people can triumph over incredible challenges if they have a strong sense of meaning and purpose. Frankl endured three years in a concentration camp in World War II and lost almost his entire family. However, he came out of the experience with an incredible observation. He noticed as long as people in the camps managed to find some sense of meaning in their lives, they were able to maintain dignity and strength despite their terrible conditions. After the war, Frankl wrote a book about this observation, *Man's Search for Meaning,* and created a system of psychotherapy that centers on helping people find meaning in their lives.

Frankl's conclusion is essentially this: being able to view your life in such a way that it appears significant and useful is a source of enormous inspiration and strength, and you have influence over your view of your life. Gordon Allport, in the preface to *Man's Search for Meaning*, writes, "In the concentration camp every circumstance conspires to make the prisoner lose his hold. All the familiar goals in life are snatched away. What alone remains is 'the last of human freedoms'—the ability to 'choose one's attitude in a given set of circumstances ….' The prisoners were only average men, but some, at least, by choosing to be 'worthy of their suffering,' proved man's capacity to rise above his outward fate."

This "ability to choose one's attitude in a given set of circumstances" is an essential aspect of mindfulness. As discussed in Chapter 5, one of the primary benefits of the practice of mindfulness is the ability to see your thoughts and feelings as *part* of your overall experience. You start to see how they affect your entire perception of the world, and how they aren't necessarily determined by your conditions. Thoughts and feelings are certainly *influenced* by conditions, but you have much more choice than you might think when it comes to the state of your own mind.

Limits of Conventional Meaning

I talk more later about the mindful approach to meaning, but first I want to discuss the ways people usually seek meaning in their lives, and the limitations of such typical approaches. The most obvious thing to do is to look for a way to view the world that lets you see your life as significant, special, or useful—at least in some small way. If you do this, you may try to find something you do, or something you are, that contributes to the world. Alternatively, you may think of someone (or something) you love and enjoy so much you want to carry on no matter what in order to continue engaging him or her (or it).

For example, you may look for something you do particularly well—something that results in appreciation from others, or enables you to perform or produce in ways few other people can. You may look for what deeply moves and inspires you—what "lights your fire" and fills you with excitement and energy. Perhaps this is a particular project or endeavor, watching your children grow and succeed, or the continued development of your understanding and skill in something. You may think of what principles, values, or timeless disciplines seem more important than your own life, and that you might be able to serve in some way—such as justice, peace, ecology, or the arts. You might find your sense of purpose in taking care of people, philanthropy, or activism.

 **TAKE CARE**

All of the conventional activities and sources of meaning listed here are wonderful and natural. If you can inspire yourself and feel motivated by such sources of meaning and purpose, by all means—go ahead and engage in them wholeheartedly! Mindfulness isn't in any way about dampening your life energy or enthusiasm, or making you second-guess your happiness, contentment, or service to the world.

The limitation of searching for meaning and purpose in these kinds of things is simply that they're conditional. What this means is that they change, and are dependent on circumstances. This doesn't mean they're bad or shallow in any way, just that if you rely on them for your entire sense of meaning and purpose, at some point you're likely to find yourself without them, or at least struggling to hold on to them. For example, if raising and supporting your children has been the primary source of meaning in your life, you'll face a difficult transition when your children grow up, move away, and become independent. You may be able to revive your sense of purpose when (or if) you have grandchildren, but eventually you'll face the same problem.

I don't mean to be negative here, only realistic. When you're still in the prime of life or in fortunate circumstances, it's very easy to be so caught up in the wonderful or exciting things in your life that you forget about the inexorable passage of time. Think about it: almost every last one of the people currently living in nursing homes, deprived of their health, vitality, independence, and privacy, once enjoyed their good fortune as if they would never lose it. Eventually we will all lose everything. Even if you're unusually fit, attractive, energetic, intelligent, capable, responsible, creative, or useful, at some point none of the standards you're used to using to view your life as meaningful will apply.

KEEP IN MIND

You may also find meaning and purpose through faith in something greater than yourself. This may be faith in God, or in some kind of positive principle such as universal compassion or the idea that life energy is always conserved (even if it gets recycled). If faith provides you with a stable and strong source of meaning and purpose for your life, consider yourself fortunate. If you ever find your faith wavering, it's not necessarily that the subject of your faith is wavering—it may just be you were trying to take refuge in your ideas about it instead of in your direct experience of it. Ideas are conditional, even if the object of your faith isn't.

Another limitation of finding meaning and purpose in conditional things is that the analysis of whether something is worthwhile or pointless is simply a matter of perspective. As long as you can hold on to a positive perspective, that's great, but all it takes is a shift in perspective—often brought on by a change in life circumstances—to deprive you of your sense of meaning. The classic example of this is being deeply identified with your job or a particular institution. Doing your job well or serving an organization may provide you with a good, inspirational reason to live for a long time, but what happens when you lose your job, or the organization kicks you out or completely changes direction? In another example, you might devote yourself wholeheartedly to some kind of activism for many years, but then find yourself burned out because the fight starts to seem hopeless.

You may have already reached a point where your old sources of meaning and purpose have stopped serving you, or at least you did at some point in your life. While it's well worth searching for new ways to enjoy your life and be useful in the world, ultimately it's extremely valuable to find a way to access meaning without relying on standards *or* conditions.

Meaning Through Mindfulness

Usually you try to find a sense of meaning, purpose, or significance by looking outside of yourself. The "meaning" most of us are after is conferred on our lives by a larger context. Based on how your life lines up with a set of external circumstances, you can make a more or less objective assessment about whether it's important, useful, or remarkable. For example, if your life has had a positive impact on many other lives, it can be judged worthwhile. If you've created quality monuments, works of art, or institutions that will outlast you, then your life is significant. If you're devoted to an ideal, discipline, or movement that keeps the lights of beauty and love alive in the world, then your life is meaningful.

A Different Kind of Meaning

There's a different way to access a sense of meaning and purpose in your life. It's not something that runs counter to these kinds of conditional sources of meaning—as mentioned earlier, if you have these kinds of inspirational projects or ideals in your life, that's wonderful. This alternative method of seeing your life as significant is something you might want to cultivate *in addition* to all of the richness and activity in your life. Or, if you've had trouble finding meaning and purpose in conditional things, this is a way for you, too, to see your life as valuable and important.

This alternative way is to experience your life directly, without comparisons, and without concepts. Instead of looking for meaning to be conveyed by something outside your life, you look for meaning within it. This does *not* mean setting up your own standards and disregarding how your actions affect others, or what anyone else thinks. That would simply be adopting a different, contrary set of concepts about what's meaningful, where you figure centrally (and the last chapter talked about what happens when you do that—it doesn't tend to lead to greater happiness).

The Direct Experience of Value

The direct, concept-free experience of life I'm talking about here is something you can only access this very moment. Because it's free of concepts, you can never abstract it or describe it fully. It never becomes a status you can hold on to and take solace in: "My life is meaningful." Instead, the kind of deep meaning and purpose you can access through mindfulness is like a clear, clean water table you can always reach down and tap into. In a moment of mindfulness it feels like this: "Hello, world. I'm still alive. My heart is beating, I'm breathing, and I'm aware. This, in and of itself, is incredibly remarkable and profound."

> **KEEP IN MIND**
>
> The twelfth-century Zen master Hongzhi beautifully described the experience of being simply, wholeheartedly present. "Vast and far-reaching without boundary, secluded and pure, manifesting light, this spirit is without obstruction," he writes. "You accord and respond without laboring and accomplish without hindrance. Everywhere turn around freely, not following conditions, not falling into classifications. Facing everything, let go and attain stability. Stay with that just as that. Stay with this just as this." (From *Cultivating the Empty Field: The Silent Illumination of Zen Master Hongzhi*, translated by Taigen Dan Leighton 2000)

When you're just present in this moment, it doesn't matter how significant or impactful your job is. It doesn't matter how good, responsible, fit, or creative you are compared to other people. It doesn't matter whether your life is going to have a measureable impact on the world, as if that could be judged in any objective or final way. All that matters is that you're showing up for your life. The reason why life itself is meaningful and significant can't be adequately explained; it can only be experienced directly.

Even if you think you're unfamiliar with the experience of life being inherently meaningful, you're not. There inevitably have been moments in your life when *just this* was enough—when whatever was in front of you needed no reference point to make it poignant, beautiful, or precious. You may have just been looking out a window at passersby, or noticing the moonlight shining on bare, wet tree limbs. Any kind of relative analysis would not have marked the moment as important, but you were able to see how it was. This kind of significance is absolute, not relative. It's the way things appear in and of themselves, without comparison, evaluation, judgment, or analysis.

Accessing a Deeper Sense of Meaning

The effort to find meaning through mindfulness isn't direct. You don't set out one day to view your life as significant, practice some mindful awareness, and then find a new view that allows you to operate with a deep sense of conviction. Mindfulness just doesn't work that way. Instead, you practice mindfulness diligently and patiently, as described throughout this book.

At the same time you give yourself a break if you feel lack of meaning in your life, or if your sources of meaning have recently been shaken. You don't have to panic or struggle. Hopefully, you'll be able to set aside any frantic efforts to find new, conditional sources of meaning and instead focus on mindful awareness of your life just as it is. More and more often you'll find yourself tapping into the inherent value and preciousness of this moment—which is manifested through *your* life. Your life becomes valuable not because of its worth as compared to anyone else's life, or because of how it figures in some grand scheme, but because it's a vehicle for awareness.

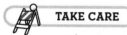 **TAKE CARE**

When trying to access an unconditional sense of meaning in your life, it's important not to just set up more concepts. It may be tempting to tell yourself a story about how you should feel about your life. Someone's told you if you're really mindful you'll feel grateful for your life. If you don't feel grateful, you figure you must not be doing mindfulness correctly, which only proves further the inadequacy of your life. This is taking mindfulness and making it into a new standard, instead of simply practicing it.

It can be disconcerting or even distressing or painful to begin contemplating the question of meaning, to face it head-on. What if you discover the sources of meaning you've been relying on don't work anymore? What if you begin to doubt your ways of making sense of the world and your place in it? These questions can be daunting, but consciously investigating them with mindfulness will always lead to greater happiness in the long run when compared to ignoring them. When examining your sense of meaning and purpose, it helps to continue cultivating the receptive attitude described in Part 3. This can give you the courage to face what's really going on in your life.

When Life Is Difficult

What about finding meaning when life gets difficult? What about when your questions about life aren't just considerations of whether you contribute enough to the world, or whether your life is significant in the grand scheme of things, but whether the pain outweighs the benefits? How do you find enough meaning and purpose to go on? It can be especially challenging when your physical, financial, or social circumstances become problematic or constrained because your ability to seek out meaningful and rewarding activities will also tend to be limited. Just when you need extra motivation and inspiration, it can be difficult to access them. Add to this that pain and stress can make it harder to do formal mindfulness practice, and things can start to seem pretty hopeless.

The Perfection of Forbearance

Finding meaning and purpose in the midst of difficulty with mindfulness involves the practice of forbearance. Forbearance, or *kshanti*, is considered one of the Buddhist "perfections," or "bases for training" toward the goal of spiritual liberation. The other perfections are generosity, morality, energy, meditation, and wisdom. All five of these other perfections are things you would probably like to either have or display. Even if they don't sound like they'll be all that much fun, at least you'll look good doing them. Not so with forbearance.

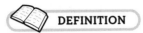 **DEFINITION**

Kshanti is one of the six Buddhist "perfections," and can be translated as forbearance, endurance, or patience.

Chances are when you conceived of taking up mindfulness practice, trying to see your life more clearly, and working toward greater happiness for self and others, forbearance was the last thing you thought of—waiting, putting up with, enduring, getting through, or surviving. This is the least glamorous aspect of mindfulness. It is quite natural to want to minimize the amount of forbearance we have to practice.

Kshanti is often translated as patience, and sometimes it does involve patience, but patience implies there is something we are looking forward to. Unfortunately, forbearance often involves enduring external or internal conditions you are afraid will never improve, and sometimes it involves acceptance of conditions that really won't change, so patience seems too limited a translation. Alternatively, kshanti can be thought of as endurance or forbearance, depending on whether you want to focus on the "doing" or the "not-doing" required.

Doing and Not-Doing

Endurance is the ability to withstand hardship or adversity, and refers to an inner quality that allows you to stand strong (the "doing"). Depending on the severity of the hardship you are facing, this can manifest as tolerance, patience, or a fierce and stubborn determination. You can strengthen your endurance through practice (that is, repetition), and by recalling your aspirations—what do you hope to achieve by enduring? In this case the achievement is not necessarily a selfish goal. For example, you might hope to obtain or create something of benefit to yourself *and* the world, or to "achieve" harmonious relationships.

If I have to pick one word to translate kshanti, however, I choose *forbearance,* which emphasizes the "not-doing" aspect of this perfection. This is because endurance can seem like an awfully tough row to hoe when things get really difficult; any aspiration can pale in comparison with what you have to put up with, and once the aspirations are gone, endurance can seem like a life sentence of drudgery. The word *forbearance,* on the other hand, evokes the moment-by-moment experience of kshanti: "to control oneself when provoked." This points to how forbearance involves refraining from all the things you would like to do when you encounter discomfort or pain: react in anger, escape the sensations by any means available, perseverate in denial, or struggle ceaselessly for a solution to your problems even when your actions don't seem to be doing any good at all.

When you practice forbearance you don't have to *do* anything besides *be*. This is, of course, extremely difficult. What does it mean to just be? Who are you when you stop obeying the dictates of your thoughts and feelings, which are telling you to react, escape, deny, or fight? If you investigate these questions deeply as you try to hold still in your forbearance, your investigation can lead to the direct experience of the inherent meaning and value of your life that was discussed earlier—even though your circumstances aren't conducive to conventional happiness.

The Benefits of Letting Go

When you're faced with ongoing hardship—which usually consumes most (or all) of your energy—you may fear that because of your hardship you can't practice mindfulness. Fortunately, this is not the case, but practice will require you to let go of any ideas whatsoever about how you want your practice to look, how you want your life to be, and all the things you wanted to do *besides* practice forbearance. Forbearance usually means your practice is fairly private; there are few opportunities to make a display of your forbearance, and often all you have to share with others is, "Yes, still putting up with the same old stuff," even though every day, perhaps every moment, is a new and unique struggle to forbear. Despite the immense effort and skill it requires, there are rarely awards, kudos, or promotions given out for forbearance. On top of everything else, you have to give up any concern about what other people think of you.

 MINDFUL EXERCISE

> Forbearance is a practice of not being provoked. Think of a few interactions, situations, or conditions that tend to provoke you into anger, despair, depression, judgment, or simply giving up your mindful awareness. The next time you encounter one of these provocations, try thinking of it as an adversary. It may cause thoughts and emotions to arise in you, but these don't have to be a problem. What if you refuse to allow the provocation to further disrupt your mindfulness or push you into prolonged negative mind states? You do this not by fighting, but by resolutely returning to mindful awareness of the moment. You might think to yourself, "This will *not* knock me off my center."

It's a problem if you expect your mindfulness practice to make you feel better but then you find the experience of forbearance is painful, or at least uncomfortable, most of the time. It's important to realize that the "better" you achieve through mindfulness can be quite subtle. In the case of kshanti practice, it might only mean your perspective on your struggle is shifted ever so slightly, such that you can see the dignity and nobility of your life and practice, and such that you can appreciate the legitimacy, depth, and value of your life. The balance of each moment will still usually be less than pleasant, but this shift in perspective can make all the difference in your ability to soldier on and appreciate being alive.

Coping with Loss

The biggest problem when trying to cope with the pain that comes with loss is facing and acknowledging your thoughts and emotions without getting overwhelmed by them. Despite the power of mindfulness to influence your mind state, it's not a way to escape real pain. At times life just deals you a terrible blow, and it takes time to heal. Mindfulness can help with this process by encouraging you to be present with your pain instead of suppressing it or distracting yourself from it. It can also help you function in the meantime by enabling you to act in the present moment, letting go—at least for a while—of thoughts about the past and future.

In Chapter 17 I discussed the true nature of your "self"—how you're actually a boundaryless flow of causes and conditions as opposed to the definable, graspable entity you usually think you are. You *do* exist—just not the way you might think. Those boundaries around self that most of us are obsessed with aren't fixed, and who you are is dependent on all the people, things, and conditions around you. This means major aspects of your life, like your job, your home, and your important relationships, aren't just important *to* you. In a sense, they *are* you—or at least a part of you.

For example, there is no hard and fast place where "you" end and a loved one begins. Perhaps there is such a boundary in a physical sense, but think about this carefully. How intimately and profoundly have you been influenced by the people around you? How many of their ideas and habits have rubbed off on you, or affected how you think and behave? When you think of yourself, can you do so without reference to the people you regularly interact with? Each person is an autonomous individual with his or her own life, but everyone you encounter affects who you are in a larger sense. This is why, when you lose a person or animal who has been a major part of your life, you experience a trauma as if some part of you has been amputated. There's a void where something living and vital used to be, and it can be extremely painful and hard to get used to.

It's traumatic to lose any major part of your life, including a job, an important material possession, your health, or a relationship. Grief is love or care in the face of loss, and as painful as grief can be, you can't just stop loving or caring. Nor should you want to! Facing and acknowledging the grief is essential to the healing process. The pain may seem insurmountable at times, but it tends to come in waves. It can help a great deal for you to simply notice with mindfulness that sometimes the pain is unbearable but other times it isn't. Then, when the pain feels unbearable, you won't be as easily overwhelmed.

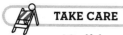 **TAKE CARE**

Mindfulness when you're coping with loss is a prime example of how the practice isn't necessarily about feeling better in the short term. Sometimes trying to be present with what's going on for you is the last thing you feel like doing. It might seem preferable to lose yourself in work, entertainment, or intoxicants. It's important to be gentle with yourself, but also firm. Give yourself a break when you need one, but stay committed to being mindful throughout your experience of loss. It helps if you recognize and work with the natural cycles of sadness and confusion followed by relative relaxation—and let yourself relax when that's what's happening.

It's possible to emerge from loss without hardening your heart, closing your mind, losing your sense of positivity, or becoming wary of placing any hope in future opportunities. With mindfulness you can maintain a strong center around which the tempest of grief and confusion can swirl—and when the storms die down, you'll find yourself stronger and wiser. That may seem like cold comfort when you're coping with a recent major loss, but it may help if you think about staying true to what you care about most. Mindfully grieving discourages you from shutting down or becoming bitter, and allows you to maintain a connection to what you love—and trying to do this can add a sense of meaning to your life even when you're experiencing great emotional pain.

Embracing Relative Purpose

The first part of this chapter was about how you can find a sense of meaning in your life without depending on conditional things. No matter how your life circumstances change, the absolute value of being alive and aware is something you can experience through mindfulness. However, this doesn't mean the practical aspects of your life don't matter. In fact, to be able to rest in mindful satisfaction regardless of conditions is only one side of the practice. The other side is letting go of whatever satisfaction you happen to find in order to step forward and function in the world.

Even when you know your ultimate happiness isn't dependent on a particular conditional source of meaning such as a job, relationship, or successful outcome, it's important to take the risk of participating in the world. It's even important to *care*—to get invested, excited, or passionate. You risk failure, disappointment, and loss, but this is preferable to hiding out in a kind of unconditional "spiritual" satisfaction. To do this is actually selfish; it's primarily about *you* staying happy, or at least safe. Ultimately, this kind of happiness is very constrained and limited, and may even lead to suffering because you don't let the world see who you are, and don't try to benefit others.

In his book *Man's Search for Meaning*, Viktor Frankl writes, "Ultimately, man should not ask what the meaning of his life is, but rather he must recognize that it is he who is asked. In a word, each man is questioned by life; and he can only answer to life by answering for his own life; to life he can only respond by being responsible."

In Chapter 17 I talked about how you're not the same as the details of your life. Instead, you're a flow of causes and conditions. However, just because your "self" can't be grasped doesn't mean your particular causal flow doesn't have something special to offer the world. You have a unique role to play, even if it's small—but be careful about the judgment "small." This kind of judgment can keep you from recognizing and embracing a purpose that can benefit the world as well as yourself.

After all, what is a "small" purpose? When someone wholeheartedly fulfills a role or devotes themselves completely to a particular thing, the outcome is always beneficial and beautiful. For example, someone may be a friendly but efficient cab driver who helps stressed people calm down, or a conscientious dentist who significantly improves the health of her patients. Someone may quietly volunteer to keep prison inmates company, or bake a batch of fresh cookies for new neighbors. When you meet someone who isn't second-guessing what they do, but who generously and carefully does his or her part, you're inevitably touched.

What's *your* part to play? Sometimes it can be easier to recognize the value of "small" contributions when it's others who are making them. Is there something in your life that you can devote yourself to wholeheartedly? If you examine your circumstances with mindfulness, you'll find at least one thing, and probably more. This mindful examination can't include judgments about relative significance or comparisons to others. It involves looking directly at your life and staying receptive. If you don't compare your life to any standards or to anyone else's life, what needs doing that you can do? Is it making a beautiful garden for people to enjoy? Is it fostering a stray dog, meeting the eyes of people who are homeless, or doing your job better than you have to?

This kind of relative purpose is conditional, but you can relate to it in an open-handed, mindful way. You can derive satisfaction from the activity without that satisfaction being contingent on outcomes. If it's simply a matter of what you enjoy doing or feel inspired to do, you can offer your efforts with generosity and joy regardless of whether or not they're noticed, or whether they make a "big" difference compared to the contributions of others. Again, this is a moment-by-moment experience of satisfaction and purpose, not something you can hold on to or list on some kind of spiritual curriculum vitae. This is about treasuring and honoring your unique life.

The Least You Need to Know

- Whether or not a sense of meaning seems important to you, it can provide a profound level of motivation and strength.

- The typical ways of finding meaning in your life are to take joy or pride in conditional things like your activities, relationships, skills, possessions, or experiences.

- Conditional sources of meaning can provide great joy, but are also subject to change and interpretation.

- It's possible to experience your life as deeply significant and precious through the practice of mindfulness, regardless of your circumstances.

- Once you can access a sense of unconditional meaning by simply being aware of the present moment, it's time to take the risk of devoting yourself wholeheartedly to a conditional purpose.

Glossary

attention   Placing your mind on a particular object and then trying to keep it there.

awareness   A receptive state of mind that involves a special effort only in that you need to let go of thoughts in order to allow it to operate.

concentration   Focusing everything you have on one thing, including your attention, will, interest, and energy. The more of yourself you can bring to the object of focus, and the smaller (or more specific) that object of focus is, the more concentrated you are. Concentration is a tool for obtaining answers to questions and solving problems.

decentering   The process of becoming less identified with your thoughts and emotions. Rather than perceiving your internal experience as being synonymous with and inseparable from who you are, you develop a sense of awareness that is no longer centered on that internal experience; it becomes *part* of your overall experience and therefore you have some choice in how to respond to it.

default mode   A highly active mental state that occurs when the mind is not otherwise occupied—such as when you are engaged in a very simple activity, or not doing anything at all. In default mode, your mind is busy with self-referential processing, including evaluating past events, anticipating future ones, imagining the outcomes of various plans of action, and guessing how other people might feel about you.

dharma   Can refer to the teachings of Buddhism, but it also refers to what is true and helpful in a larger sense.

dukkha   A Buddhist term that refers to the pervasive and sometimes subtle stress of living. It can be translated as stress, unsatisfactoriness, unease, or suffering. It results from your resistance to life being impermanent, out of your control, and ultimately impossible to grasp.

emergent   Arising out of the functioning of a complex physical system, but not from the functioning of any of the parts taken in isolation, nor from all of the parts taken together unless they are configured and functioning in a particular way.

emotions   Compared to *feelings,* emotions are more complex experiences that include a feeling-reaction but also thoughts, memories, and usually some kind of narrative.

exteroception   The awareness of the world outside your body. All of these kinds of perception can serve as objects for mindfulness practice.

feelings   Your immediate emotional responses to stimuli, including external things as well as your own thoughts and actions, usually arising before conscious thoughts. Feelings fall into three categories: like, dislike, and neutral.

ill will   A psychophysical factor that requires active maintenance of negative feelings, such as anger or aversion over time, plus a narrative that justifies them.

interoception   The awareness of sensations inside your body, such as pain or hunger.

kshanti   One of the six Buddhist "perfections," kshanti can be translated as forbearance, endurance, or patience. The other perfections are generosity, morality, energy, meditation, and wisdom.

metta   Literally "friendliness," metta is a meditation exercise for cultivating a feeling of good will toward a particular living being by calling him or her to mind and then reciting, "May you be free from fear and anxiety. May you be at ease. May you be happy."

mindfulness   Consciously maintaining awareness of your present experience with a receptive attitude, in order to perceive things more clearly and consequently increase happiness for self and other.

mirror neurons   Cells in your brain that are activated when you witness another being's experience or action. They fire in a similar area of your brain as they would if you were the one having the experience or doing the action.

natural anger   A feeling that arises in your body-mind in the present moment, in direct response to a perception that you, or something you care about, is under threat. Natural anger subsides relatively quickly. *See* ill will.

proprioception   The awareness of your body's overall position, movement, and acceleration.

psychophysical   For the purposes of this book, something experienced with both body and mind.

reaction   An impulse to think, speak, or act that arises more or less spontaneously in your body-mind after you experience something. It's likely to be habitual and highly conditioned. *See* response.

response   Conscious and deliberate thought, speech, or action that you choose as being your best way to answer or deal with the situation in front of you. *See* reaction.

tolerance for ambiguity   The ability to experience ambiguous situations or problems without finding them too uncomfortable to bear, or perceiving them as a threat. A high tolerance for ambiguity allows you to remain calm and patient when faced with things that are complex, vague, contradictory, or unresolved. A low tolerance compels you to avoid or resolve the ambiguity by any means necessary.

Resources

Articles

Barnes, Sean, Kirk Warren Brown, Elizabeth Krusemark, W. Keith Campbell, and Ronald D. Rogge. "The role of mindfulness in romantic relationship satisfaction and responses to relationship stress." *Journal of Marital and Family Therapy* 33, no. 4 (October 2007): 482–500.

Birnie, Kathryn, Michael Speca, and Linda E. Carlson. "Exploring self-compassion and empathy in the context of mindfulness-based stress reduction (MBSR)." *Stress and Health* 26, no. 5 (December 2010): 359–371.

Brewer, Judson A., Patrick D. Worhunsky, Jeremy R. Gray, Yi-Yuan Tang, Jochen Weber, and Hedy Kober. "Meditation experience is associated with differences in default mode network activity and connectivity." *Proceedings of the National Academy of Sciences* 108, no. 50 (December 2011): 20254–20259.

Hasenkamp, Wendy, and Lawrence W. Barsalou. "Effects of meditation experience on functional connectivity of distributed brain networks." *Frontiers in Human Neuroscience* 6, no. 38 (March 2012).

Hasenkamp, Wendy, Christine D. Wilson-Mendenhall, Erica Duncan, and Lawrence W. Barsalou. "Mind wandering and attention during focused meditation: A fine-grained temporal analysis of fluctuating cognitive states." *NeuroImage* 59 (2012): 750–760.

Hofmann, Stefan G., Alice T. Sawyer, Ashley A. Witt, and Diana Oh. "The Effect of Mindfulness-Based Therapy on Anxiety and Depression: A Meta-Analytic Review." *Journal of Consulting and Clinical Psychology* 78, no. 2 (2010): 169–183.

Kabat-Zinn, J., E. Wheeler, T. Light, A. Skillings, M. J. Scharf, T. G. Cropley, D. Hosmer, and J. D. Bernhard. "Influence of a mindfulness meditation-based stress reduction intervention on rates of skin clearing in patients with moderate to severe psoriasis undergoing phototherapy (UVB) and photochemotherapy (PUVA)." *Psychosomatic Medicine* 60, no. 5 (1998): 625–632.

Killingsworth, Matthew A., and Daniel T. Gilbert. "A Wandering Mind Is an Unhappy Mind." *Science* 330 (November 2010): 932.

Miller, J. J., K. Fletcher, and J. Kabat-Zinn. "Three-year follow-up and clinical implications of a mindfulness meditation-based stress reduction intervention in the treatment of anxiety disorders." *General Hospital Psychiatry* 17, no. 3 (1995): 192–200.

Pidgeon, Aileen, Klaire Lacota, and James Champion. "The Moderating Effects of Mindfulness on Psychological Distress and Emotional Eating Behaviour." *Australian Psychologist* 48, no. 4 (August 2013): 262–269.

Prazak, Michael, Joseph Critelli, Luci Martin, Vanessa Miranda, Michael Purdum, and Catherine Powers. "Mindfulness and Its Role in Physical and Psychological Health." *Applied Psychology: Health and Well-Being* 4, no. 1 (March 2012): 91–105.

Reiner, Keren, Lee Tibi, and Joshua D. Lipsitz. "Do Mindfulness-Based Interventions Reduce Pain Intensity? A Critical Review of the Literature." *Pain Medicine* 14, no. 2 (February 2013): 230–242.

Shapiro, Shauna L., Doug Oman, Carl E. Thoresen, Thomas G. Plante, and Tim Flinders. "Cultivating mindfulness: effects on well-being." *Journal of Clinical Psychology* 64, no. 7 (July 2008): 840–862.

Sheline, Yvette I., Deanna M. Barch, Joseph L. Price, Melissa M. Rundle, S. Neil Vaishnavi, Abraham Z. Snyder, Mark A. Mintun, Suzhi Wang, Rebecca S. Coalson, and Marcus E. Raichle. "The default mode network and self-referential processes in depression." *Proceedings of the National Academy of Sciences* 106, no. 6 (February 2009): 1942–1947.

Tang, Yi-Yuan, Yinghua Ma, Junhong Wang, Yaxin Fan, Shigang Feng, Qilin Lu, Qingbao Yu, Danni Sui, Mary K. Rothbart, Ming Fan, and Michael I. Posner. "Short-term meditation training improves attention and self-regulation." *Proceedings of the National Academy of Sciences* 104, no. 43 (October 2007): 17152–17156.

Books

Bays, Jan Chozen. *How to Train a Wild Elephant: And Other Adventures in Mindfulness*. Boston: Shambhala Publications, 2011.

Brach, Tara. *True Refuge: Finding Peace and Freedom in Your Own Awakened Heart*. New York: Bantam Books, 2013.

Einstein, Albert. *The World As I See It*. San Diego: The Book Tree, 2007.

Frankl, Viktor E. *Man's Search for Meaning: An Introduction to Logotherapy*. New York: Simon and Schuster, Inc., 1984.

Fronsdal, Gil, trans. *The Dhammapada: A New Translation of the Buddhist Classic with Annotations.* Boston: Shambala Publications, 2011.

Hanh, Thich Nhat. *The Miracle of Mindfulness: An Introduction to the Practice of Meditation.* Boston: Beacon Press, 1999.

———. *Present Moment Wonderful Moment: Mindfulness Verses for Daily Living.* Berkeley: Parallax Press, 1990.

———. *Transformation and Healing: Sutra on the Four Establishments of Mindfulness.* Berkeley: Parallax Press, 2006.

Leighton, Taigen Dan, trans. *Cultivating the Empty Field: The Silent Illumination of Zen Master Hongzhi.* Boston: Tuttle Publishing, 2000.

Sapolsky, Robert M. *Why Zebras Don't Get Ulcers: The Acclaimed Guide to Stress, Stress-Related Diseases, and Coping, Third Edition.* New York: St. Martin's Griffin, 2004.

Uchiyama, Kosho. *From the Zen Kitchen to Enlightenment: Refining Your Life.* Translated by Thomas Wright. New York: Weatherhill, 1983.

———. *The Zen Teachings of "Homeless" Kodo.* Translated by Shokaku Okumura. Tokyo: Kyoto Soto-Zen Center, 1990.

Wright, Dale S. *The Six Perfections: Buddhism and the Cultivation of Character.* New York: Oxford University Press, 2009.

Websites

www.afsp.org

American Foundation for Suicide Prevention.

www.thecenterformindfuleating.org

The Center for Mindful Eating. "An international not-for-profit forum for professionals across all disciplines interested in developing, deepening, and understanding the value and importance of mindful eating."

www.umassmed.edu

Center for Mindfulness in Medicine, Health Care, and Society. Located at the University of Massachusetts Medical School, this is where the eight-week mindfulness-based stress reduction course began, and where qualified teachers are trained and certified.

www.dharmanet.org

DharmaNet. Includes a directory of Buddhist centers all over the world, plus access to online courses in Buddhism and lots of articles on Buddhist topics.

www.mindful.org

Mindful: Taking Time for What Matters. This website is full of resources, including articles about applying mindfulness in everyday life, online courses, and a subscription to *Mindful* magazine.

www.mindfulschools.org

Mindful Schools: Integrating Mindfulness Into Education. The mission of Mindful Schools is to integrate mindfulness into educational settings by offering "online courses for educators, mental health professionals, and parents to use mindfulness with youth."

www.secularbuddhism.org

Secular Buddhist Association. Articles, podcasts, links, and meditation support from a non-religious point of view.

www.treeleaf.org

Treeleaf Zendo. An online Zen Buddhist group that includes meditation and retreats you can participate in virtually.

Twelve Principles
of Mindfulness

The 12 mindfulness principles are explained at length in Chapter 3.

Aspiration

1. You, and all other beings, just want to be happy.

2. The greatest happiness is that which applies in the longest term and at the largest scale—which includes the happiness of others.

3. Change occurs naturally when you see clearly what leads to greater happiness.

4. You can only take care of your life and the lives of others by clearly seeing what does and doesn't lead toward greater happiness.

Awareness

5. To see clearly, you have to drop below the level of ordinary thinking and experience things directly.

6. When your mind wanders, your perspective shrinks and your ability to see clearly is compromised.

7. You can change your mind's default mode by repeatedly turning your attention to something that is happening in the present.

8. Attention is deliberately focusing your mind, but it can lead to a more continuous, natural, receptive awareness.

Attitude

9. The first step to learning something new is admitting you don't know.

10. You are unlikely to see something clearly as long as you fear or reject it.

11. Comfort with inner and outer stillness and silence is comfort with reality.

12. Mindfulness is its own reward.

Mindful Exercises

How's Your Body?

Get started right away! As you read this book right now, what is your posture? Are you seated or standing? Don't change your posture—not yet. Just become aware of it. Is your body aligned, or are you slouching in some way? Are there any areas where your body is tense where it doesn't need to be? Don't judge, just notice. How often throughout the day do you become aware of your posture like this? If you spend most of the day unaware, you can carry around lots of tension without ever realizing it. (See Chapter 1.)

What Makes You Who You Are?

Make a list of all of the things you feel help define who you are. Be honest! Don't censor your list because you know something is impermanent or because you think it's superficial. Your gender, height, nationality, family-of-origin story, physical attractiveness, musical tastes, ability to cook, etc., are all valid characteristics to identify. Consider how long this list could get, and how almost everything on it is subject to change—if not literally, then in terms of how you think about it. Instead of letting this make you feel insecure, however, see if it can help you feel grateful for these things that compose your unique life. (See Chapter 2.)

The Experience of Deep Happiness

Get into a comfortable physical position and close your eyes. Imagine you're in a setting in which you feel completely happy and at ease. Are you sitting next to a campfire in the wilderness? Are you at home on a Friday evening with your cat on your lap? Are you at a concert listening to deeply moving music? What is present or absent in your body and mind? Is there a sense of fullness in your chest? Is your breathing deeper? Do you have a sense that, for now, nothing needs to be done? Explore the nature of the deepest kind of happiness you can call to mind. (See Chapter 3.)

Mindful Waiting

The next time you're waiting—for the bus, for the doctor, in a line—experiment with not entertaining yourself with anything. Don't listen to music or a podcast, and don't read anything (including the magazines at the checkout stand). Just stand or sit there. Go ahead and look around at your environment. Watch people, and notice things like noise levels, temperature, and your sense of impatience. Observe how strong your urge is to find something to occupy yourself! Anything but just being there. Gently hold the question, "Why do I feel this way?" (See Chapter 3.)

Noticing the Busy Mind

Either keep the body still or engage in a very simple physical task. Make an effort to keep your attention in the present, focused on what is happening right now. When you realize your mind has wandered, return your attention to your physical experience. Note how quickly your mind jumps into thinking about the past, future, or something abstract every time you bring it back to the here and now. Try to observe this without judging, and without getting frustrated. You're witnessing firsthand the habitual tendency of your mind to engage in stimulus-independent thinking, and this is the first step to being able to calm your mind when you want to. (See Chapter 4.)

Aware of All Sensations

Pick a simple, mostly physical task like cleaning, gardening, cooking, or fixing something. Set a period of time during which you want to practice mindfulness—10 minutes, 20 minutes, or as long as the task takes. During this time, as much as possible, try to keep your attention on the movements of your hands, or on the position and movement of your body. Or, if it works better for you, try to maintain such an open awareness that you notice every smell, visual texture, and touch. When your mind wanders, gently return it to the task with a minimum of fuss. Return to the present over and over, reminding yourself you want to appreciate each moment of your life. (See Chapter 4.)

Exploring a Negative Feeling

The next time you find yourself feeling an unpleasant response to something—such as irritation, aversion, impatience, or frustration—turn toward your response with mindful awareness. Simply note what you're feeling, and say to yourself silently, "I am feeling (whatever it is you're feeling)." Don't judge your response or try to change it. Then explore a little further. How strong is the feeling? Where does it manifest in your body? Ask your feeling what it's about, without worrying about whether or not the feeling is justified. Don't suppress the feeling, but notice at some future point when you realize you've forgotten all about it in the interim. (See Chapter 5.)

Staying with a Neutral Activity

The next time you're doing something you feel neutral about—like waiting for a doctor's appointment, cleaning the house, or sitting through a rather boring meeting—notice what's happening. Chances are your mind is wandering because you're not very interested in the activity, but you also aren't particularly averse to it. Notice how your mind resists maintaining awareness of the neutral activity. Holding your attention on it may actually start to make it seem unpleasant. See if you can notice something interesting about the situation, though. People watch, or take note of sights and sounds, or play some kind of game like counting how many times someone says, "Ah." Anything to keep yourself from dismissing your current experience. (See Chapter 5.)

Awareness of Your Mind State

Close your eyes and pay attention to your breathing. What happens to your mind? Does it leap away from the breath, to something you need to get done? Does it get drawn into thinking about something from the past, or drift toward something random that isn't even that important to you? Does it feel sluggish, or does it respond to your intention readily? Is it fairly easy to keep your attention on the breath, or is it a struggle? Do your senses open up to the things going on around you, or does your consciousness stay more or less focused on your own body-mind? Just note your answers to these questions, trying not to judge good or bad, like or dislike. (See Chapter 6.)

What Kind of Distracting Thought?

Try to maintain awareness of your breathing in a sustained, continuous way. Each time you find yourself thinking, try to discern the nature of the thought, and use it as information about your mind state (which might change over the course of the exercise). If the thought is a plan for how to obtain something you want or avoid something you don't, chances are you're experiencing grasping/aversion mind. A stuck mind returns to the same set of thoughts you've entertained dozens or hundreds of times but nothing seems to change about them. An anxious mind imagines what bad things might happen and thinks of ways to deal with them. A scattered or dull mind generates random or trivial thoughts and daydreams. (See Chapter 6.)

Noticing the Five Hindrances

Choose a simple mindfulness practice, such as paying attention to physical sensations while you wash the dishes, or staying present while driving. Make an effort to do this practice many times over the course of a week, and note whether the practice seems difficult or easy in any given session. If you're finding it hard to stay present or keep your attention on the mindfulness practice, see if you notice any of the hindrances: desire, ill will, lethargy, restlessness, or doubt. If the practice is relatively easy, do you sense the presence of curiosity, energy, joy, ease, concentration, or equanimity? Don't try to change your experience, just note the factor and how it affects your mindfulness. (See Chapter 7.)

Noticing the Factors of Awakening

Think of a time when you felt unusually mindful. It's often easy to recall such experiences because, at the time, you were fully present and aware instead of being caught up in your thoughts. You ended up with perceptions grounded in that moment that could serve as memories. What were you doing? Did the activity or setting inspire curiosity, energy, or joy in you? Were you involved with something or someone you care deeply about? Did the situation invite your joyous participation in some way? Recall the presence of curiosity, energy, or joy, and how they influenced your mindfulness. (See Chapter 7.)

Full Appreciation

Pick a *very* simple activity you really enjoy, such as petting your dog, drinking your morning coffee, or taking a walk on a beautiful day. Try to let go of thinking about anything other than exactly what you're doing—not because you *should,* but in order to fully appreciate this activity. Maintain mindfulness in this way for just a minute or two. How often do you naturally stop all other mental and physical activity in order to do only one thing? You'll probably find mindfulness greatly increases your ability to enjoy something. (See Chapter 8.)

Watching Life Like a Movie

Sit, stand, or lie down and keep your eyes open. Widen your gaze, including what's to the sides and above and below in your peripheral vision. (This will help keep you from getting distracted by particular things you can see.) Now watch your visual field as if it's a movie—a slow-moving movie, perhaps, but one of those quiet, visually rich, artistic ones. Just keep watching. When you stop because you have gotten caught up in thinking, note you have tuned out the "movie" because it's boring, or because you think you know what's going to happen next. Ask yourself, "When I really stop to look, is anything truly boring? Do I really know what's going to happen next?" (See Chapter 8.)

Letting Go of the Judging Mind

Take a few calming breaths and then call to mind something in your life that presents a problem. Write down all the things you've tried in order to fix the problem. Then write down all the things you can think of that you haven't tried. Now set aside all of those solutions for a while and open yourself up to the possibility that real and lasting resolution will come from somewhere else. Is there anything in your mind or heart that resists change, and why? What longings or fears might lie behind your problematic choices? Is this really a problem, or do you just think it should be? Once you set aside ordinary thinking and just look, answers can arise from anywhere. (See Chapter 9.)

Instant Equanimity

Imagine you're standing in a line at the grocery store checkout and someone pushes their cart into you from behind. How do you feel? Irritated, maybe even outraged? Are you inspired to kick back at the cart and send it crashing into its owner, or do you want to yell about how inconsiderate and careless people can be? Take a moment to imagine your physical experience of this situation. Now imagine you look back and see the person behind looks faint and is struggling to stay upright. How do your feelings and thoughts change? Is it that you've suddenly become a better person who isn't bothered by being bumped, or is it just that your perspective has changed? (See Chapter 9.)

Description for an Alien

Pick up an everyday object you tend to use but tune out of your awareness, such as a coffee mug. Imagine you have to verbally describe the appearance, use, and significance of this object to an alien from another planet, where the beings don't have anything resembling our hands. You can't assume anything in your explanation. How do you go about this? You have to communicate size without comparing the object to something the alien isn't familiar with. To explain the use, you have to explain lots of other things. What aspects of the appearance do you mention that you haven't noticed in years? Compare this level of detailed observation with the complacency with which you usually regard the object. (See Chapter 10.)

One Day Left to Live

Choose an activity you do regularly that mostly involves observation. This could be driving to work, listening to other people in a meeting, or going for a walk. Do this when you don't need to carry on a conversation, and turn off the radio or music. Now imagine as vividly as you can that you have only one day left to live. This is your *last* drive to work, *last* meeting, or *last* walk—ever. You'll never have this experience again. Don't start imagining what kind of plans you'd make if you were at the end of your life, just try to be as incredibly attentive and appreciative as you would be if you had a very short time left to live. (See Chapter 10.)

Two Minutes of Stillness

Look for a time when you're resistant to stillness. You may be excited about something, or you may believe you *have* to get something done or figured out. Despite your resistance, spend two minutes trying to be mindful of something simple like your breath or sound. (No matter how pressing your concerns, you have time for a couple of minutes of inactivity.) Observe the effects. Don't jump to conclusions about how you should or shouldn't cultivate stillness in the future, just let your experience inform you. (See Chapter 11.)

Mimic a Child or Animal

The next time you're near a small child or an animal, try doing exactly what they're doing. (Choose a time when a child isn't talking.) If possible, mimic their physical position or activity. Chances are they're just sitting or lying there, or are completely absorbed in some simple activity. See if you can momentarily experience the same inner stillness and silence they have. See if you can settle entirely into the present moment the way they can. (See Chapter 11.)

Moments of Joy

Over the course of a day, pay close attention to whenever you feel even a little bit of joy. Be on the lookout for any positive feelings, but see if you can differentiate the experience of joy from being happy or satisfied after you evaluate something and decide you like it, or decide that it's going to lead to a good outcome in the future. See when and how joy arises—a simple, buoyant feeling you have when you're just happy to be alive and aware in order to experience exactly what you are at a given moment. (See Chapter 12.)

What if It Never Happened?

Sit down in a comfortable position in a quiet place. One by one, call to mind things in your life you'd like to achieve, experience, or improve. Imagine how things might change, what an ideal scenario would look like, and how you would enjoy it. Then ask yourself, "What if this never happened?" Stay present and receptive with any feelings of resistance or disappointment, but also explore what it might feel like to be content in your life without the outcome you desire. Sometimes you'll be able to access a part of yourself that will be satisfied even if certain of your hopes and aspirations never get fulfilled. (See Chapter 12.)

Self-Discipline

Call to mind something you would really like to change about yourself. If you like, write it down, along with your responses to the following questions. Make your responses as honest as possible (what you really tend to think and do, not what you think you should). Why is this change a good idea? What weaknesses or shortcomings do you have that make this change necessary, or difficult? How would you describe yourself when you're resisting change or acting out a negative pattern? Why do you think you act like this? Now look back over your responses. What kind of self-parenting approach are you taking? Is there judgment or harshness in any of your answers? (See Chapter 13.)

Loving Kindness Meditation (Metta)

This is a traditional Buddhist exercise for cultivating compassion called *metta*, which literally means "friendliness." Call to mind a person or animal for whom you feel close to unconditional love. Silently recite each of the following statements, allowing yourself to sincerely mean what you're saying: "May you be free from fear and anxiety. May you be at ease. May you be happy." Repeat this as many times as you like. Then do the same thing for other people, and eventually for yourself. Start with beings for whom it's easy to feel metta, and gradually—perhaps over the course of months or years—work up to people toward whom you feel unpleasant emotions. Sometimes the hardest person to feel sincere metta for is yourself. (See Chapter 13.)

Urge Surfing

Next time you feel a powerful surge of afflictive emotion (anger, fear, obsessive desire, self-doubt, or jealousy), see if there's an action you feel compelled to do. Perhaps you want to yell, throw something, or say something negative. Perhaps you want to check your email for the twentieth time today for the message from that special someone. Identify the action and then *don't do it*—at all, or for the next hour. Don't fight the emotion, and go ahead and do something else. Just don't do the *one* thing you identified. Let the urge arise and pass away. (In the case of self-doubt, you might need to take a positive action that's the opposite of an urge to withdraw.) (See Chapter 14.)

Standards Behind Self-Doubt

If you ever struggle with self-doubt, take some time to vividly imagine what it would take to banish that doubt and give you plenty of boldness and confidence. You may want to write your answers down. In any case, don't censor or edit your thoughts at all. Some of them may be unreasonable (such as being able to tell ahead of time exactly what will work in a given situation) or impossible (such as wanting to be taller, or an extrovert instead of introvert). It's helpful just to become more aware of the standards and expectations you're holding for yourself. Consider whether you want to keep doubting yourself until you meet them. (See Chapter 14.)

Busy Hands

While you're going about your daily tasks, pay attention to your hands whenever you remember to do it. Notice their position and movements. Be aware of any sensations you feel in or on your hands. Pay attention to whether they're resting on a table or a steering wheel, holding a cup or toothbrush, gripping something with force, or gently and skillfully manipulating an object. You don't have to change what your hands are doing at all. Simply bringing them into your awareness will bring you back the present moment. When you do this, what else do you notice? Can you taste a moment of "just being" in the midst of your activity? (See Chapter 15.)

Worst-Case Scenario

Think of a task you *really* need to do, or else terrible things will happen. Don't pick something that might result in physically endangering someone, but short of that, let the issue be something serious that's causing you stress. Let yourself imagine all of the likely negative repercussions of *not* taking care of things in a timely manner. Be specific; it may be good to write them down. If necessary, consider the further repercussions of direct results. How would you deal with each thing on your list? Although you're going to try to avoid them, can you imagine still finding ways to appreciate your life even if they happened? (See Chapter 15.)

Honest with Yourself About Change

Mindfulness requires you to be honest with yourself. Think of something you'd really like to change about your behavior. This can be a way you think, speak, or act (or a combination of these). How long have you been trying to change? How often have you mentioned to others that you intend to change? How many different approaches have you tried? Have you spent money, time, and energy on your efforts? Has anything improved? This exercise isn't meant to make you feel inadequate or discouraged—it's meant to encourage you to be honest. Sometimes it's easy to become preoccupied with your intentions and forget to face the truth of your life as it is. (See Chapter 16.)

A Beautiful Film About You

Imagine you are a filmmaker and want to make a film about you (pretend you aren't you). As the filmmaker you intend to portray your life as being rich, well-balanced, rewarding, and elegant. What real scenes and interactions from your life would appear in the film? A good-bye kiss with your partner or children in the mornings? Laughter with a friend? Being very engrossed in your work, and gratified by the result? Picture all of the positive film clips from your life that you can. What if you saw a film that showed these, and de-emphasized the parts of your life you feel dissatisfied with? Chances are you'd feel inspired, despite yourself. (See Chapter 16.)

Connections to Your Sense of Self

When you find yourself getting agitated or upset about something, stop and observe what's going on with mindful awareness. Ask yourself why you're feeling upset, and see what answers arise without editing or censoring them. Keep following reasons deeper, asking, "Okay, well why does *that* upset me?" See if you can find the point where the issue at hand connects to your Self-Concept, and your concern for "I, Me, and Mine." Is there an apparent challenge or threat to *your* reputation, *your* significant other, *your* possessions, or *your* views? Don't judge this connection as selfish, just acknowledge where your reactions are connected to your sense of self. (See Chapter 17.)

Self as Awareness

Sit still and turn your attention to your physical sensations. Concentrate on your breathing, sound, or sense of body position, or expand your receptivity to include any sensations that come your way. When you have a moment or two when you feel completely present, look for your sense of self. Note how your aliveness and awareness at this very moment don't depend in any way on your past or future, or any of the details of your life such as your education, job, interests, or possessions. Can you settle so completely into the present that you experience yourself as being nothing more than awareness itself? (See Chapter 17.)

Relationship Without Expectation

Call to mind any relationship problems you have. Do any of these people misunderstand you? Do they seem disinterested in things you care about? Do they make unfair assumptions, or fail to take their share of responsibility? Now, without arguing in your mind about who's right or who's wrong, can you imagine giving up *any* expectations of others? What if you took care of yourself within reason by making choices about what *you* do, but not by making demands or by expressing anger or judgment? What if you looked at each act of generosity, kindness, or responsibility by others as a voluntary gift? You may want to apply this exercise in real interactions and watch how things shift. (See Chapter 18.)

Paying Attention to People

The next time you're at work or out in public, make an effort to be more aware of the people around you. Choose one person at a time. Become aware of everything you can about the person without alerting her to the fact you're paying special attention to her. Be conscious of her physical proximity, posture, and movements. Can you get a sense of her mood? Does she seem to be pre-occupied, or in the present moment? Does anything about her clothing or personal possessions give you a sense of her personality? If you speak to her, what kind of response does she give? Is there anything you can do for her? People provide fascinating subjects for mindfulness. (See Chapter 18.)

Thoughts About Appearance

The next time you're looking at yourself in the mirror, notice your thoughts about your appearance. Are you pleased? A little dissatisfied? Harshly critical? As usual, don't edit your thoughts and feelings. In fact, invite them to come out clearly by engaging in a dialogue with them, as if you were commenting on someone else's body. Then become aware of whether your evaluative thoughts about your appearance arise every time you're in front of a mirror (or a reflective surface like a window). Don't judge or try to get rid of your thoughts, just acknowledge how persistent and pervasive they are. Is there any part of you that sees the whole scenario as rather ridiculous? (See Chapter 19.)

Is This Mental Processing Useful?

The next time you find yourself preoccupied with a worry or plan, bring mindful awareness to the situation and ask yourself some questions. Are you perseverating? Perseveration is when your mind ends up in repetitive loops of thinking that don't produce any positive results. Is this a good time to be working mentally on your concern? Do you have enough time to make any progress on it right now? Take an honest look at your mental processing. If you want to keep thinking about the same issue, go ahead. However, you may feel inspired to let the thinking go for the moment when you see it's not actually going to do you much good. (See Chapter 19.)

Not Evaluating Your Practice

If someone you trusted as an authority were to tell you that you were practicing mindfulness *exactly* as it should be practiced—that you were actually quite good at it—how would you feel? Take a moment to recall your recent experiences of mindfulness and meditation, along with your general (perhaps involuntary) judgments about them. If you knew for sure you were practicing correctly, how would that make you feel? Content or disappointed? Is your mindfulness practice based in any way on a subtle hope you can perfect the method and attain the rewards you want? Can you let go even further of evaluations and expectations? If you do, what does that do to your experience of this moment? (See Chapter 20.)

Just Doing Nothing

If meditation seems like work, it can be hard to make yourself do it—especially if you have lots of other demands on your time and energy. Instead of thinking of meditation as another task, try simply sitting down and doing nothing for a little while. Don't have any agenda at all—except to do *nothing*. Just put your life on pause and try to relax completely. Don't even try to control your mind. Do this for 2 to 5 minutes, longer if you feel like it. If you find yourself eager to jump up and get busy again, or to reach for some distraction, just try to think of these few minutes as a well-deserved break. (See Chapter 20.)

Noticing When Lives Are Saved or Taken

Make a habit of paying attention whenever you have the option of taking or saving the life of a living thing, or you benefit from a life that's been taken. Capture a spider in your house and take it outside instead of killing it. When you cut flowers, take note of a life being ended. When you eat fish or meat, take a moment to acknowledge the life that was sacrificed for you. Notice when you put on something made of leather. You don't have to add a judgment about whether what you're doing is right or wrong, just let yourself be aware of the intersection of your life with another living (or formerly living) thing. (See Chapter 21.)

Studying Intoxication

If you regularly use some kind of intoxicant, try to maintain mindful awareness as you do so. An intoxicant can be any substance or activity that alters your experience of life in a way that's rewarding, but which also encourages you to continue indulging in it. In a safe and typical situation, allow yourself to imbibe or engage in your usual intoxicant, but watch carefully what it does. What are the rewards? What does the intoxicant allow you to access, let go of, or do? Is there anything about your life as experienced sober that you're avoiding, resisting, or rejecting? Just notice, without judging. (See Chapter 21.)

A Deeply Meaningful Life

Take some time to imagine you're utterly convinced your life is *deeply* significant, and that all of your actions and choices are of the utmost importance to achieving something you unequivocally believe in—something critical, or something incredibly inspiring. If you don't make your unique contribution, people will suffer, or some wonderful thing will never come about. Can you imagine feeling so motivated that you leap out of bed in the morning, work efficiently because you don't want to waste any time, and diligently practice mindfulness so you can be extra perceptive and responsive? How does this imagined state compare with how you usually feel? Can you see in what way you've decided your life is *not* very significant? (See Chapter 22.)

Forbearance

Forbearance is a practice of not being provoked. Think of a few interactions, situations, or conditions that tend to provoke you into anger, despair, depression, judgment, or simply giving up your mindful awareness. The next time you encounter one of these provocations, try thinking of it as an adversary. It may cause thoughts and emotions to arise in you, but these don't have to be a problem. What if you refuse to allow the provocation to further disrupt your mindfulness or push you into prolonged negative mind states? You do this not by fighting, but by resolutely returning to mindful awareness of the moment. You might think to yourself, "This will *not* knock me off my center." (See Chapter 22.)

Index